Tragedy and Irish Literature

Tragedy and Irish Literature

Synge, O'Casey, Beckett

Ronan McDonald

First published 2002 by
PALGRAVE
Houndmills, Basingstoke, Hampshire RG21 6XS and
175 Fifth Avenue, New York, N.Y. 10010
Companies and representatives throughout the world

PALGRAVE is the new global academic imprint of
St. Martin's Press LLC Scholarly and Reference Division and
Palgrave Publishers Ltd (formerly Macmillan Press Ltd).

ISBN 0-333-92393-6

This book is printed on paper suitable for recycling and made from fully managed and sustained forest sources.

A catalogue record for this book is available from the British Library.

Library of Congress Cataloging-in-Publication Data
McDonald, Ronan, 1970–
    Tragedy and Irish writing: Synge, O'Casey, Beckett/Ronan McDonald.
        p.cm.
    Includes bibliographical references and index.
    ISBN 0-333-92393-6
    1. English drama–Irish authors–History and criticism. 2. Synge, J.M. (John Millington), 1871-1909–Criticism and interpretation. 3. O'Casey, Sean, 1880-1964–Criticism and interpretation. 4. English drama–20th century–History and criticism. 5. English drama (Tragedy)–History and Criticism. 6. Beckett, Samuel, 1906—Dramatic works. 7. Ireland–In literature. I. Title.

PR8789 .M43 2001
822'.0512099417–dc21

2001036880

10 9 8 7 6 5 4 3 2 1
11 10 09 08 07 06 05 04 03 02

Printed and bound in Great Britain by
Antony Rowe Ltd, Chippenham, Wiltshire

To My Father and Mother

Contents

Acknowledgements

A portion of Chapter 2 appeared, in an earlier form, in *Irish Studies Review* no. 17 (winter 1996/7) and was subsequently reprinted in Sarah Briggs et al. (eds) *Reviewing Ireland: Essays and Interviews from Irish Studies Review* (Sulis Press, 1998).

I want to thank Charmian Hearne, who first commissioned this book, and all the staff at Palgrave who have brought it to fruition.

This book grew out of a doctoral thesis at Oxford University and I would like to gratefully acknowledge the support of the following institutions: the National University of Ireland for the award of a travelling studentship, the British Academy for paying my fees, Hertford College for electing me to a Senior Scholarship, and the Prendergast Bequest for financial assistance. I owe thanks to Professor Terry Eagleton for his helpful and efficient commentaries on various drafts. I would also like to warmly thank my examiners, Bernard O'Donoghue and George J. Watson for their ongoing support. John Kelly has also been a kind and encouraging mentor and friend. Many of the ideas which have germinated in these pages were planted during my BA and MA in UCD. In particular, I would like to express my deep and abiding gratitude to Professor Declan Kiberd, who first encouraged me to pursue academic work.

My colleagues at the University of Reading have been unfailingly kind and have given me a stimulating and supportive environment in which to finish this book. In particular, I want to thank John Pilling.

I have been fortunate to benefit from the 'beautiful prismatic counselling' of my friends. Many of them valiantly suffered sections of this thesis over the course of its gestation. Karen McGrath was a bulwark of support and encouragement during my D.Phil. and beyond. I am abidingly grateful to her. Carol Tell has enriched my intellectual development for many years now. I would like to thank her for our many conversations. Julie Costello has offered unwavering friendship, encouragement and scholarly guidance. Ray Ryan has long been a fount of passion, pugnacity and practical advice and probably doesn't know how much I value his friendship. I would also like to thank Gerald Lang, Ben Levitas, Gary Lyons, Marc Mulholland, Richard Michaelis, Donnacha O'Brien, Sean O'Dowd, Jim O'Hanlon and Patrick O'Sullivan. Special thanks are due to Sarah Montgomery, who has sustained me with her warmth, wit and wisdom. I hope all these friends know how much I appreciate their feedback and advice. Their sustenance, of course, goes far beyond the merely academic.

I would like to thank my family. My sisters, Marlene Finuala and Frances, and my brother, Colm. My greatest thanks go to my 'accursed progenitors', Kathleen and Patrick McDonald. This book is dedicated to them, with love and gratitude.

Abbreviations

A1 and A2   Sean O'Casey, *Autobiographies*, 2 vols (London and Basingstoke: Macmillan, 1981)

CDW   Samuel Beckett, *The Complete Dramatic Works* (London and Boston: Faber & Faber, 1986)

CWI–IV   J. M. Synge, *Collected Works*, gen. ed. Robin Skelton, 4 vols (London: Oxford University Press, 1962–8)

D   Samuel Beckett, *Disjecta: Miscellaneous Writings and a Dramatic Fragment*, ed. Ruby Cohn (London: John Calder, 1983).

P   Samuel Beckett, *Proust and Three Dialogues with Georges Duthuit* (London: John Calder, 1965).

ST   Sean O'Casey, *The Silver Tassie* (London: Macmillan – now Palgrave, 1928)

T   Samuel Beckett, *The Beckett Trilogy: Molloy, Malone Dies, The Unnamable* (London: Picador, 1959), p. 320.

TP   Sean O'Casey, *Three Plays: Juno and the Paycock, The Shadow of a Gunman,The Plough and the Stars* (London: Macmillan – now Palgrave, 1957)

1
Introduction: The Loss of Tragic Value and the Value of Tragic Loss

Tragedy is an imitation of an action that is admirable, complete and possesses magnitude; in language made pleasurable, each of its species separated in different parts; performed by actors, not through narration; effecting through pity and fear the purification of such emotions.

– Aristotle

Tragedy, as it was antiently compos'd, hath ever been held the gravest, moralest, and most profitable of all other Poems ...

– John Milton

[T]ragic experience, because of its central importance, commonly attracts the fundamental beliefs and tensions of a period, and tragic theory is interesting mainly in this sense that through it the shape and set of a particular culture is often deeply realised.

– Raymond Williams

Tragedy.
When the feeling's gone and you can't go on,
it's a Tragedy.

– The Bee Gees

Introduction

One temptation for studying ideas of tragedy in relation to Irish cultural history is the ubiquity of the concept in descriptions of the Irish past. From Yeats's 'terrible beauty' to the jacket blurbs on a plethora of modern monographs, to a thousand newspaper headlines, 'tragedy' is

1

an inescapable designation.[1] Directly or subliminally, the legacy of famine, failed rebellion, emigration and colonial persecution shapes literary and cultural production in Ireland. As Denis Donoghue claims, 'to see Ireland through its received forms is mostly to see it as a lost cause'.[2] The Irish imagination teems with images and tropes of loss and guilt. The 'catastrophic' dimension to Irish history, the litany of poverty, war, and humiliation will naturally tend to mould the representations of loss, suffering and guilt in Irish writing.[3] Even the humour and lyricism for which Irish drama and prose is also famous, and never more so than with the three authors that this book treats, typically feed off stories of the utmost poignancy and pathos.

Yet these are dangerous remarks. There are obvious perils in the construction of any literary tradition, any national canon. Identifying common elements in the diversity of Irish writing can all too easily be coercive, manipulating autonomous, incommensurate texts into bogus alignment. So much is obvious. To choose three writers as ostensibly different as J. M. Synge, Sean O'Casey and Samuel Beckett, makes this danger all the more palpable. This study does not, however, seek to overrun these differences. Obviously the three diverge widely in both dramatic practice and intellectual attitude. They are chosen for reasons of contrast as well as comparison. However, they face many similar dilemmas and, arguably, there are important common strands in their dramatic representation of suffering alongside all the diversity. Here are three exemplary Irish dramatists, from different historical periods and with very different ideas of drama, chosen both to demonstrate some characteristic aspects of Irish tragedy and to illustrate aspects of each playwright's vision and achievement unique to himself.

If there are difficulties in the construction of national traditions in literature, then the espousal of 'tragedy', as a genre or dramatic category, is even more perilous. There are few areas of literary study that have provoked so much controversy and so little consensus as the thorny and fraught area of tragic theory. Definition, as Stephen Booth claims, has long proven elusive: 'The search for a definition of tragedy has been the most persistent and widespread of all non-Religious quests for definition.'[4] Attempts to define tragedy have often prompted head-scratching as to what can be considered 'authentic', especially so far as modern plays are concerned. Like other major modern dramatists such as Ibsen, Strindberg, O'Neill and Miller, Synge, O'Casey and Beckett have all, at varying points, figured in debates within tragic theory.[5] Significantly, we have had many pronouncements on the 'death' or impossibility of true tragedy in our age.[6] These elegies are usually shrouded in a language of nostalgia and cultural recrimination, where the loss of the tragic Muse is 'the result of one of those enfeeblements of the human spirit'.[7] One of the purposes of this book is to complicate and ultimately refute such notions and, more importantly, to illustrate the intimate bond between concepts of tragedy and ideas of cultural value.

Relating ideas of tragedy to Synge, O'Casey and Beckett need not necessarily dwell on their intentional use of the word. A broader if related question to the semantics of 'tragedy' and 'tragic' is the attitude and disposition of individual artists when dealing with those features of human life, death and loss that we associate with this term. Even if a doctrine of tragedy, in the sense of an elaborate structure, is not provided, such central ideas to tragic theory as meliorism, history, heroism, the notion that aesthetic representation redeems human suffering, or the powerful artistic imperative to bear witness to monstrous events or experiences, play a decisive role in an artist's engagement with suffering, loss and death. Hence, the broader field of tragic discourse can be applied to an author's work, even if that author has no overt investment in the tradition of dramatic tragedy or its associated definitions. In this way, we can amplify the dialogue between theories and practice, between abstract definitions of tragedy and the actual production of dramas that may or may not be considered 'tragedies'.

So rather than testing the three writers against a predetermined definition of tragedy, I shall examine their philosophies and aesthetics of suffering, loss and guilt within framing ideas of tragedy. Often they contravene traditional definitions. None, for instance, would meet the Aristotelian criteria as adumbrated in his *Poetics*. However, in a broader category, certain plays of Synge – *Riders to the Sea* (1904) and *Deirdre of the Sorrows* (1910) – and O'Casey – the Dublin trilogy, *The Silver Tassie* (1928) – might well fall within a canon of modern tragedy. More significant, perhaps, than the simple question of genre is the underlying tragic vision that informs a particular play. For instance, *Playboy of the Western World* (1907), ending with Christy's triumphant exit, may not look much like a conventional tragedy, yet there is a sheer tragic quality to Pegeen Mike's belated recognition, 'Oh my grief, I've lost him surely. I've lost the only playboy of the western world' (CWIV, 173). The same goes for the other ostensibly comic plays of Synge. Within the plays of each of the three dramatists, those aspects of tragedy that are asserted and those that are resisted illuminate his attitude to art and suffering, and the significance of these beliefs and dispositions to the cultural and political context within which he writes.

Discussion of tragedy usually begins with a series of qualifications, an anticipatory rendition of the various disagreements, differing conceptions, and semantic conundrums that the term evokes, both as a literary genre and a philosophical concept. As well as setting the ground for the three author-based sections, it is also now necessary to *clear* the ground: to offset, or at least address, the confusion and ambiguity that often bedevils definition and discussion of tragedy. The voluminous writings in tragic theory, combined with the ever-spiralling uses of the term in everyday life, have added knots to the concept, rather than unravelled it. This is not necessarily regrettable, for if it is important that the term and the tradition (or traditions) are illuminated, it would be scandalous to reduce an area so rich in ambiguity and so indicative of changing attitudes, ideologies and circumstances to specious simplicity or ready-to-hand formulae. If the quest for definition has proven elusive, it is because the term is fertile in contesting meanings rather than just befuddled by inaccurate usage.

The abiding dissent and disagreement that marks investigation into the nature of tragedy signifies its urgency and centrality in the history of ideas. For many centuries concepts of tragedy have been central to Western culture. From Sophocles to Shakespeare to Racine, the pinnacles of the genre are seen as pinnacles of literature. Aspiring practitioners have been legion in every age and, more relevant to the present study, *theories* of tragedy have attracted the attentions of the most distinguished heads in the history of ideas. If tragedy represents pain and suffering, if it shows up the miseries of humankind and the vagaries of fortune, why does it give pleasure?[8] Why do we choose to watch depictions of suffering, when we could easily see depictions of happiness? To name Aristotle, Hegel, Schlegel, Schopenhauer, Nietzsche, Jaspers, Lukács, Camus is to walk the main thoroughfare of Western thought. Apart from literary studies, tragic theory has impacted on philosophy, psychoanalysis, anthropology, linguistics and cultural theory. Part of the reason for the attraction of this field is that traditionally it has licensed ringing pronouncements on the human condition, the vanity of existence, the quintessence of art. 'Tragedy' as Milton intoned, 'hath ever been held the gravest, moralest and most profitable of all other Poems.'[9] Addison called it 'the Noblest Production of Human Nature'.[10] There is often a feeling that, in Clifford Leech's phrase, 'a civilization without tragedy is dangerously lacking something'.[11] Suppose, for a ludicrous moment, that this remark refers to real-life experience, rather than a dramatic genre, and it becomes clear how strikingly canonical and esteemed literary tragedy has become over the centuries.

Not surprisingly, then, 'tragedy' has long been regarded as a mark of excellence, even a synonym for 'masterpiece'. In an intriguing way, this sense has seeped into its real-life application. As a description of or a response to a *real* disaster, the designation is shrouded in a curious reverence. More than other terms descriptive of woe – 'disaster', 'misfortune', 'catastrophe' – it seems to generate or indicate an element of esteem and tribute to the loss it addresses. This sense of eulogy or recognition in the common uses of the term derives in part from its literary intersection with canonicity and, hence, with cultural greatness. The tone is typically grave, ponderous and awash with grand human significance. When other language seems tired and inadequate, this word seems to answer the need for elegy, to provide the necessary sense of paying tribute or of registering the profound poignancy of the loss. When a newspaper leader refers to the 'tragic' loss of life in an earthquake or a war or a car crash, the word imparts a sense of gravity or moment, notwithstanding the misuse and debasement to which, some argue, the term is subjected.

Elaborate models and structures, sonorous declarations about the nature of 'Life', hotly contested debates on what constitutes 'true' tragedy have been at the crux of literary critical and philosophical discourses. That 'tragedy' has long been a byword for profundity in this way is worthy of analysis. Why do we generally conceive of tragedy as grander, more insightful, more nobly confrontational than comedy? Why are the great tragedies regarded as the jewels in the crown of Western literature? Why has the term been the site of so much contention, both in terms of its dramatic and its 'real-life' designation? Part of the answer resides in the fact that those aspects of human experience we associate with tragedy in its various forms – death, great disaster, unbearable loss or waste – are also those which push human understanding to its limits, at once querying and affirming the values by which people live. If these are the features of experience that most resist domestication into rational systems, they nonetheless remind us what is most valuable in life by destroying what we think of as precious.

However, if quarrels over 'true' tragedy are a staple of philosophical and literary critical debate, sometimes they have less to do with genuine disagreement than with the use of one word to describe a variety of experiences. After all, there is no reason in principle why 'tragedy' cannot be used to describe a car crash and a play by Sophocles without necessarily implying a connection. There is actually much less confusion about the multiple functions of this word than is often sup-posed. The context generally indicates which sense is meant. We know that tragedy can refer to a disastrous event in one situation or to a great play in another. Also, as well as being a value-laden term, tragedy *can* be just a neutrally generic one, a descriptive word indicating the drama of a particular period. We speak of Elizabethan or Attic tragedy in the same way as we might refer to Restoration comedy: just a librar-ian's tag, where no value judgement is necessarily implied; we can even speak of a 'bad' tragedy.

Yet there is another dominant sense in which to call a play a tragedy, is to pass judgement on it, to grant it the *imprimatur* of 'great' art, and this underlies the fears that the word is contaminated when too loosely applied. The word 'comedy' is used, without controversy, to generically designate the work of both Aristophanes and Woody Allen. Nobody contends that the latter usage is a debasement. We automatically rec-ognize that if they share the same designation, they are nonetheless widely different forms, with at most a distant relation. When the road death is described as a tragedy, scholars will sagely say 'Ah, but that is not tragic, that is merely sad'. Why does nobody ever protest that something is not truly comic, but merely 'funny'? We have had no threnodies for the death of comedy as we repeatedly have had in the past century for the death of tragedy, no solemn lamentations that we lack the necessary cultural lyres for the 'authentic' comic vision, no jeremiads about the barren individualism or corrosive materialism of modern-day culture that disallows the enviable achievements of Attic or Elizabethan comedy.

The reason for this is that tragedy, as a category, is a value term in itself. This is crucial, for tragedy does not only address values – insofar as it pays tribute to a disaster or suffering through recognition of the greatness of the loss – it is also a sort of meta-value: *the valued expres-sion of the loss of something valued*. This underlies the hushed, reveren-tial tones with which, as seen above, devotees refer to the literary genre. There is a major tension at the heart of tragic discourse. It both *concerns* values – or, artistically speaking, the *agon* of various values like good and evil, human debasement and human elevation – and it is valued in itself. The reasons why dramatic tragedy is so prized have been various and profoundly attuned to central beliefs and ideologies of a period or culture. It has been valued for its depiction of a mean-ingful, divinely controlled universe and for its revelation of the vani-ties of human existence, for its celebration of aesthetic delight and for its didactic inculcation of moral value, for its elevation of the hero outside the orbit of humdrum humanity and for its insights into archetypal suffering, at the core of shared human experience.

A caveat may be necessary at this point. If for most of the twentieth century the nature of tragedy was one of the mainstays of philosophical and critical enquiry, it is notable that in the past thirty years or so the debate has cooled. The torrent of commentary, particularly during the 1950s and 60s (and the shadow of the World War cannot be insignificant here) has tended to ebb in recent years. Significantly, the period that witnessed the waning of interest in the nature of tragedy is also that during which academe turned its attention away from questions of literary value and evaluation. Steven Connor puts it thus:

> the rise of literary and critical theory since the 1970s has brought about a decisive swing away from a concern with judgement and towards a concern with meaning and interpretation. It is this concern that holds together and provides an institutional identity for the otherwise striking diversity of the forms of contemporary critical theory. What hermeneutics, reader-centred criticism, semiotic analysis, discourse theory, psychoanalytic theory, new historicism, deconstruction and all the varieties of politically accented criticism which draw on the former perspectives have in common is their focus on the activities of knowing, understanding, decoding and interpreting.[12]

So, the turn from questions of literary value also marks the turn from ruminations on the nature of tragedy. There are additional reasons for the shift in interest. The *analytical* methods of modern critical practice harbour a suspicion of the integrative aspects to genre as such, not just to notions of aesthetic value. This derives in part from the anti-essentialist orientation of most modern literary theory. Genre, of its nature, seeks continuity and connection, tries to establish shared characteristics in artworks, underlying apparent differences. Not surprisingly, movements from deconstruction to cultural materialism have discerned in the notion of genre a naive belief in constants or essences, a reactionary faith in a changeless form or spirit underlying historical flux. Its very *raison d'être* is regarded as coercively synthetic, harnessing the rich plurality of expression into rigidly ordained patterns.[13] Moreover, if traditional accounts of tragedy have an investment in definitions of 'what it is to be human', then, unsurprisingly, movements such as feminism or post-colonialism are likely to bristle, perceiving in the normative notion of the 'human' a category that occludes marginal or non-male elements.[14]

There is a related, if longer-standing, hostility to tragedy – and tragic theory – in Marxist thought, which perceives a fatalism and political inertia at the heart of tragic discourse inimical to political radicalism: if tragedy is anti-revolutionary, then revolution must be anti-tragic. Yet the notion that tragedy is a fundamentally conservative genre has been much disputed, with some arguing that the disruptions of tragedy can yield a powerful radicalism.[15] Raymond Williams queries the Marxist notion that tragedy leaves no room for meliorism (and meliorism no room for tragedy), and claims that an anti-tragic bias vitiates the revolutionary spirit.[16] Materialist approaches to tragedy eschew the traditional ascription of suffering to a changeless human nature and tease out the various contradictions and tensions in human relations that are as much socially and politically mediated as metaphysically inaugurated or divinely sanctioned.[17] If tragedy gives us insight into normative ideas of humanity, if it espouses a universal 'moral order' or cosmic truth, then it typically treats the moment when social stability is ruptured and norms transgressed. How many canonical tragedies treat the violation of basic taboos such as incest, regicide, matricide and parricide? Tragedy, politically minded critics might argue, momentarily ruptures the natural order only with a view to reintroducing it in stronger form. However, if we replace universal ideas of order with communal or societal norms and values, and reposition 'flaws' of character (in terms of the inner psychic life of the hero) as disruptive eddies in the larger social formation, these ruptures seem less innately perverse. With such an outlook, we can unleash the latent subversive and emancipatory power of tragedy, both political and psychological. Traditionally, most commentators, embroiled in the honorific connotations of great tragedy, have seen any transference from metaphysical to social or temporal concerns as a devaluation. To be aware of the assumptions and ideological biases behind this sort of commentary is to reactivate the urgency of this central, time-honoured area of critical and philosophical enquiry.

We should not be content to consign tragedy to a dustbin of literary terminology, if only because of the persistence of the term as a category fraught with historical significance and ideological wrangling. Instead, it may be timely to return to this area, informed by recent methodological and theoretical debates in literary studies, to illuminate not a changeless, prescriptive classification, but a constantly mutating matrix of ideas and values. Such an approach would strive to activate synergies between venerable philosophies of tragedy and more recent methods and procedures in literary and cultural theory.

Overhauling writings *on* tragedy is a useful prelude to examining modern writing *as* tragedy. I suggested earlier that it was helpful to frame, as well as to inform, the author-based chapters and this introductory chapter operates as an autonomous investigation into many of the issues raised in tragic theory, as well as simply an anticipation of the three author-based chapters. The next section traces further the various angles of approach taken towards tragedy as a genre and as a philosophical concept, especially focusing on the dimensions of response and evaluation. The third section deploys some of these arguments to examine the culture of suffering and guilt in Synge, O'Casey and Beckett in relation to the Irish context from which they write.

Undefined tragedy: varieties of value

As the originator of tragic theory, Aristotle has often been invoked as the ultimate authority on the topic. During the neo-Classical period, his *Poetics* – with its famous call for dramatic unities, noble character, *hamartia* and so on – was held as the foundation for 'authentic' tragedy. Surely the most widely quoted passage in the history of literary criticism, his definition is not a blueprint, though often held up as one. Based on his observations of dramatic tragedy, it is more descriptive than prescriptive:

> Tragedy is an imitation of an action that is admirable, complete and possesses magnitude; in language made pleasurable, each of its species separated in different parts; performed by actors, not through narration; effecting through pity and fear the purification of such emotions.[18]

For a long time the Greek note was regarded as the truest to the tragic spirit and this tendency lingers in many modern attempts at definition. However, there are problems with the notion that original meaning should be the ultimate court of semantic authority – after all, that the etymological root of tragedy means something like 'goat song' will scarcely help us understand O'Casey's Dublin trilogy.[19] Aristotle's work, an inductive enterprise focusing largely on Sophocles' *Oedipus Rex*, is of limited use when seeking a model for modern mutations and manifestations of the genre. Arthur Miller, defending his *Death of a Salesman* (1949) against accusations that it was not really a tragedy because its hero lacked the stature that Aristotle demanded, claimed that however much he might admire Hippocrates, he would be unlikely to choose him now as a surgeon.[20] Yet, if we should be wary of totemizing Aristotle's definition, neither should we discard it too hastily. Refracted through modern frames of understanding, it is still resonant. The 'imitation of an action' that is serious and has magnitude *does* incorporate a good deal of modern tragedy, even if the Aristotelian purchase on greatness and heroism has dwindled, and if notions of representation have supplanted those of imitation in the concept mimesis.[21] Similarly, the concept of catharsis is afforded considerable leverage in twentieth-century psychological and psychoanalytic investigations of tragedy.[22] Nonetheless we should not allow Aristotle the last word: 'tragedy', even as a strictly dramatic category, has had so protean a history that to tie it too closely to the Attic model is to stifle its energies. The excessive formal and generic prescriptiveness of neo-Classical theories of tragedy amply illustrates this danger.

Continuity, be it of form or spirit, does not mean repetition. Often these days, commentators begin with Aristotle but chide him for inadequately developing his definitions.[23] In general, Aristotle is criticized either for yoking his analysis too tightly to issues of dramatic form, without sufficient engagement with the human or existential plight addressed therein, or because his model so blatantly excludes many plays which are uncontentiously considered tragedies, not just Shakespearean but even within the extant Greek tragedies themselves. Michelle Gellrich, arguing for tragedy's resistance to definition and theorization, shows how

> the essential premises about dramatic consistency, intelligibility, and unity articulated in the *Poetics* and later absorbed into the mainstream of literary study ... can be effectively secured only if obstinately unsystematic and destabilizing movements of language and action in tragedy are bypassed or somehow brought to heel.[24]

We do not need to enumerate the various differences between Shakespeare and the Greeks, or the radical variations in sensibility and structure between Aeschylus, Sophocles and Euripides,[25] to recognize that, even among the most canonical and undisputed 'tragedies' (not to mention the more contentious and debated instances of modern tragedy) there are fundamental differences of temperament and execution. It is divinely ordained that Orestes will kill his mother and he is relentlessly tormented by the Furies. Yet the *Eumenides* concludes optimistically with Orestes acquitted and the prospect of harmony. Compare this to the shocking, infanticidal conclusion of

Euripides' *Medea*, or to the *Bacchae*, where Dionysian frenzy triumphs. To move to a later comparison, the spirit of evil that pervades *Macbeth* and the overweening ambition of its protagonist flout Aristotle's principle that the hero of tragedy should be a good man with a flaw which, though fatal, is out of proportion with his ensuing downfall. Indeed all of Shakespeare's tragedies to varying degrees contravene Aristotelian requirements.[26] When we bend the genre to include canonical plays, then why not for modern plays that have yet to become venerable?

Furthermore, any survey of the *meaning* of tragedy reveals a term of profound variations from one age to the next. For instance, in accordance with the values and beliefs of the eighteenth century, dramatic tragedy of that period followed the dictates of Reason; the belief that drama had a morally instructive function and the corresponding idea of 'poetic justice', wherein the good were rewarded and the wicked punished, held sway. John Dennis's sentiments amply illustrate this conviction:

> I conceive that every Tragedy ought to be a very solemn Lecture, inculcating a particular Providence, and showing it plainly protecting the good, and chastizing the bad, or at least the violent; and that if it should be otherwise, it is either empty amusement, or a scandalous and pernicious libel upon the government of the world.[27]

Not only critical interpretations of canonical tragedy, but also – as with Nahum Tate's rewriting of *King Lear* to save Cordelia – occasionally those tragedies themselves were skewed towards the predominant value-system. Such notions are alien to the modern sensibility, where tragedy broadly tends to be seen precisely in terms of meaninglessness, in terms of desperate loss without corresponding justice or progress.

Too pure or restricted a definition is unlikely to get us far, even if we also need to be wary of flaccid or catch-all uses of the term. This is as true of modern as of classical definitions. Without an unsatisfactory level of elasticity, vagueness or relativity, no definition has yet been able to include the unwieldy corpus of canonical literature typically included in the genre. T. R. Henn's claim that 'there neither is nor can be any definition of tragedy that is sufficiently wide to cover its variant forms in the history of world literature' still rings true.[28]

Efforts are frustrated by an abiding dilemma: definitions of dramatic tragedy tend to be deductive or inductive, derivative or substantive. That is to say, theory either establishes a conceptual set of principles, of which dramatic tragedy is the expression, or else it seeks to derive a common vision based upon the analysis of particular artworks. Should we start with the concept or with the corpus? Should we start with a blueprint or idea for dramatic tragedy and use it as a yardstick, testing if particular plays fit the pre-conception? Or should we begin with the plays themselves, extricating our concept of tragedy from them and then seeing if other (later) plays replicate their structures or themes? Both approaches risk methodological infelicity. As for the deductive method, how can we construct a priori criteria for tragedy? From where do we derive our initial concept if not from actual plays? As for the inductive or substantive approach, how do we choose the plays from which we should take our model? Unless we are content for all future tragedy to be second-rate imitations, mere flickerings on a Platonic wall, we cannot absolutely fixate on a Hellenic or Elizabethan prototype.

This 'hermeneutic circle' queers the pitch for all general concepts or categories and historically it has bifurcated thinking about tragedy, an area riddled with disagreement at the best of times. How does one inductively define tragedy without choosing plays based on some a priori standard? We cannot separate the conception of tragedy from the dramatic practice, or vice versa. Nor can we arrive at some tragic worldview without some pre-conception of what it will contain. Tragedy, as befits a descriptive term that is also, partly, a value judgement, comes from disposition as much as derivation. As H. A. Mason interprets it, 'You cannot reach the tragic unless you have in some sense pre-imagined it.'[29]

The induction/deduction dilemma is further complicated and polarized by the many non-dramatic and even non-literary senses that the term has accrued in academic and common usage. As descriptive terms, 'tragedy' and the 'tragic' have long come unmoored from their dramatic origin and can have an applicability as a tone or structure in non-dramatic works of literature. Hence, we talk of a tragic novel or tragic poem. In one of the earliest occurrences of the term in English, Chaucer has his monk define tragedy as any narrative in which a person of high station is brought low:

> Tragedie is to seyn a certeyn storie,
> As olde bokes maken us memorie,
> Of him that stood in greet prosperitee
> And is y-fallen out of heigh degree
> Into miserie, and endeth wrecchedly.[30]

So the initial sense in English was a corruption of the Greek origin, with its firm basis in dramatic spectacle. We think of 'the tragic' as a spirit or attitude within literary works as well as just a dramatic genre with strict formal characteristics. It is, in other words, a mood as well as a mode. Furthermore, eschewing all references to literary works, many have drawn on what have variously been dubbed the 'tragic vision', the 'tragic sense of life' or the 'spirit of tragedy'. Influential works like Miguel de Unamuno's *The Tragic Sense of Life in Men and Peoples* attempt to delineate a 'whole conception of life itself and of the universe, a whole philosophy, more or less formulated, more or less conscious'.[31] This is a non-literary, non-narrative concept: the tragic sense of life is a way of viewing reality, an attitude of negation and pessimism, a feeling of profound alienation and dislocation in a malign and indifferent world. Therefore, as well as the idea that tragedy is a certain view of the world derived from a body of plays, the term has developed an existence independent of the corpus. The pessimistic notion of a tragic 'lifeview', such as that espoused by Unamuno and others, is only a distant cousin of a play by Sophocles.

It is, perhaps, not coincidental that this philosophical extension of the term in the past century occurs at the same time as a popular broadening, where tragedy seems to have come to refer to almost any death or deeply sad event. However, unlike the common usage, the academic respectability of the philosophical tradition has protected it from accusations of semantic flaccidity and journalistic debasement. If a general lifeview, or even life itself, is dubbed 'tragic', experts rarely complain; yet many bristle when the road accident or earthquake is so described. Curiously, too *general* an application of the term 'tragic' is regarded as more distortive than a *general* tragic worldview.

Despite the conflicting definitions and senses of tragedy, to say comprehensible or useful things about the category, it is necessary to identify a common denominator, a unity within the ambiguity, avoiding both the Scylla of relativism and the Charybdis of singular, restricted meaning. Perhaps a course can be steered between an essentialist notion of tragedy and a purely diffuse, relativist approach, through harnessing some version of Wittgensteinian 'family resemblance' – a network of overlapping but sometimes discontinuous affinities that is neither wildly heterogeneous nor coercively homogeneous.[32] However, if we are compelled to acknowledge that absolute definition is elusive, we still need to establish some shared features in order to speak about an identifiable entity. To locate a cohesive modern meaning, we may have to jettison some outmoded or eccentric definitions. Tragedy, most commentators now agree, concerns loss and suffering, though few would hold that *all* loss and suffering is tragic. The loss of pain is comic and the suffering of incarcerated torturers is a matter of justice. Moreover, the loss, all agree, must involve a certain intensity and seriousness: while a flattened hedgehog may be a matter of regret, few would call it tragic. While comedy espouses a funda-mental trust in life, a confidence in the restorative and palliative powers of human communication and social organization, in tragedy the destructive forces are not contained or controlled. Most theorists nowa-days tend to veer away from the Hegelian notion that the destruction unleashed in tragedy is ultimately in the service of some greater good, such as the revelation of *Geist* or world spirit.[33] Some even go so far as George Steiner and claim that the slightest trace of meliorism or salvation renders an artwork anti-tragic. For Steiner, various worldviews, from Judeo-Christianity to Romanticism to Marxism, are in principle anti-tragic because each contains a strain of optimism, whether it is belief in the restorative justice of an afterlife (Christianity) or faith in the power of social and political organization to alleviate human suffering (Marxism).[34]

Even if we stop short of the extreme anti-meliorism of Steiner's definition, we would have to recognize that the modern connotation of tragedy evokes a profound sense of waste, an awareness of destruc-tion without corresponding progress or redemption. This encompasses both the colloquial nuance, when the death of a child in a road acci-dent, for example, is described as 'tragic', and also the sense of a great deal of modern tragic writing, from Hardy and Ibsen onwards. The shooting of Bessie Burgess in O'Casey's *The Plough and the Stars* (1926) is of course related to social and political factors, but it is also just a horrible, senseless accident and this, in a sense, is what makes it align with a modern sense of tragedy.

So a high emphasis on accident and meaninglessness pertains to tragedy now, however antithetical this would have appeared to previ-ous generations of commentators. There is another facet that may help us see a continuity behind the vicissitudes in meaning and definition across the ages. The crucial question, perhaps, does not just concern denotation in the neutral, descriptive sense – external phenomena, generic characteristics – but also the more slippery question of *response*, central to the field (if not always foregrounded) since Aristotle's (unelaborated) assertion that the effect of tragedy is the 'catharsis' of 'pity' and 'fear'. What is important in tragedy is not just the work of art, but also the work of the work: the effect it has on the spectator. This, too, seeps into the real-life meaning of the word: 'We begin to live when we have conceived life as a tragedy', says W. B. Yeats with a sonorousness typical of discussions within the field, yet touching, significantly, on the notion that tragedy has to do with *perception* or *response* as much as on the neutral features of phenomena.[35] That tragedy has a mysterious, salutary impact on an audience has always been central to theories of dramatic tragedy, even if there have been widely divergent beliefs as to what this effect constitutes. Like other issues connected with aesthetic judgement, this emphasis on audience response, together with broader mutations in the meaning of the term, can lead to a high degree of subjectivity when it comes to definition. As Booth has it: 'It appears also, from observation of the word tragedy, that its use is determined not so much by a particular quality of what happens as by a particular quality of our response to what happens – that tragedy is in the eye of the beholder.'[36] However, despite the implication of Booth's 'eye of the beholder', allowing a subjective element to enter the search for definition will not inevitably lead the debate into some sort of affective fallacy. (But, then, save for the most sceptical aesthetician, 'Beauty' is not wholly in the eye of the beholder either.) To have any meaningful engagement with tragic theory, one must acknowledge and foreground the central importance of *evaluation*. In all the various, often contradictory theories of tragedy this is, perhaps, the closest to a common denominator. This goes for both the dramatic and the 'real-life' senses of the term. As already seen, if loss is to have any significance, and hence any tragic import, it must be the loss of something valued. This inevitably has a subjective dimension, even if it is not reducible to individual proclivity. After all, the death of a soldier on a battlefield, whilst a tragedy for his family, may be a triumph for his enemy and an heroic sacrifice for his comrades.

If it is crucial to recognize that subjective dimension, it nonetheless emperils academic enquiry. Definition cannot be constant because response is not constant, even if it is not random either. Trying to incorporate the response factor, without at some point generalizing about response, can make definition a flaccid and nebulous affair. It certainly inhibits the establishment of unchanging, absolute criteria – formal or structural elements of plays, distinctive facets of real-life loss and death – that would help to sustain a permanent definition. Hence, eager for neutral, classifiable characteristics, theorists often baulk at incorporating response into definitions of tragedy, unless it is in some way all-encompassing. In one of many attempts to tighten up sloppy misuse of the term by establishing an ur-definition, Oscar Mandel shuns 'definition by emotional effect', claiming that this must result in 'confusing subjectivity and historicity':

> If tragedy is to be defined, even in part, by a response in the reader or spectator – a response, that is, of the kind which changes like a Proteus from age to age, from person to person, from nation to nation, within one person even from period to period – then the term becomes useless as a description of a work of art.[37]

Yet, however desirous we may be for the Holy Grail of a stable, unchanging, definition of tragedy, it is demonstrably the case that its meaning *does* change, even if it is not the chameleon Mandel dreads. Only an extreme individualism, one that implicitly occludes social mores and cultural connections, would regard 'historicity' as equivalent to 'subjectivity' in this way. Mandel seems to regard both individual and social values as wholly arbitrary and divergent. Yet, while there are of course individual variations, people within one age or nation do tend to share values and assumptions. Self-evidently, social and communal connections are powerfully cohesive. More tentatively, we could also venture that despite the obvious mutations and diversity of value-systems from age to age and from culture to culture, there are also continuities. The concept that is strikingly excluded from Mandel's account is that of *tradition*; despite the shifting patterns there are threads of continuity across the ages. The *Zeitgeist* might change, epistemes might shift, but there are surely broad parameters – life, death, love, power, sexuality, society – within which evaluative changes take place. We cannot make absolutely deterministic relations between an event and a response to an event, but no response is purely random or reducible to the whim of a spectator. Perhaps the way around the dilemma of continuity and difference in tragedy is to recognize that whether or not some constants of human experience are conceived as tragic depends on the perspective of a particular culture. In other words, *historicism* is the middle ground between the strictures of a changeless tragic essence and the dissipation of sheer tragic subjectivity.

It is important to bear in mind this continuity, while still allowing for subjective and historical variations. Whilst it is true that the historicist approach sidesteps the homogenizing force of rigid genre, so disdained by recent critical proclivities, it too has its perils. Eva Figes contends that 'cosmic laws are in fact human laws, and have to do with the way society orders itself, or the way society believes itself to function, which may or may not be the same thing'.[38] Such an assertion may be an important corrective to the tradition in tragic theory of rushing headlong into the universalizing idiom of the 'human condition' and 'ultimate reality', briskly eliding socio-political and historically specific dimensions. Impatience with the historical or the social, regarded as merely contingent or accidental to a changeless human essence, is a common, ideologically-based manoeuvre in a tragic discourse eager for grand significance (as indeed it often is in the plays this theory strives to illuminate). In that respect, Figes and Williams provide a healthy demystification. However, recognition of the importance of response, subjectivity and evaluation in tragedy needs to draw back from a fragmentary relativism. If cosmic law is often human law in disguise, does that mean that there are no laws outside those that are socially invented? Are there, as Figes seems to suggest, *no* exceptions? No moral value outside that deployed to reinforce the status quo?

If there are radical and bridgeless differences between our values and those of the Ancient Greeks, does that necessarily mean that no shared experiences come from shared humanity? Is suffering in one age always incommensurate with that of all ages? Is there no sense of material, if not 'cosmic', continuity in the forces that govern human existence and human relations? If not, how is it that we still find Antigone's tragic relationship with Creon so pressingly urgent? How indeed can the literature of the past have any relevance other than as an anthropological document, giving us vaguely decipherable glimpses of intrinsically and absolutely alien cultures? To concede that we interpret and evaluate literary works according to our own cultural and ideological lights – which may include at least some of the 'lights' of the past – need not mean that no glimmer of meaning sneaks in around them. Can we allow no 'family resemblance' between the laws and values of all ages, however mediated and historically inflected they may be? In considering the tradition of tragic literature, we would do well to remember the dialectic that Raymond Williams occasionally seeks to construct: 'If we could admit that all these periods are in certain radical ways distinct, we might be able to go on to see what, nevertheless, they may have in common.'[39]

Nonetheless, if tragedy has much to do with perception, response and evaluation, and if these mutable factors are mediated by the *Geist* or milieu of an age, then a definition of tragedy based in stable, neutral phenomena is sure to wane. It is easy to discern the 'death of tragedy' when value-systems, ideologies and epistemes shift. If we say that heroism, greatness or aristocratic grandeur are essential components in tragedy, then there can be little surprise if tragedy is absent in a society to which these features are alien, aberrant, no longer valued or no longer accessible. We might be content to allow the word 'tragedy' to fall into disuse or to employ it solely as a historical term, were it not for its persistence, its centrality in literary-critical and philosophical discourse, and its status as a concept heavy with semantic and cultural baggage. Perhaps, then, the crucial question is not 'what is tragedy?', but rather what does tragedy mean to a particular period or to a particular author, not simply in subjective, but in historical and cultural terms? This approach would recognize that attitudes, definitions and, particularly, the actual usage of the word indicates those aspects of suffering and loss that cleave to the central mythologies and structures of belief of an age. As Raymond Williams has it, 'tragic experience, because of its central importance, commonly attracts the fundamental beliefs and tensions of a period, and tragic theory is interesting mainly in this sense that through it the shape and set of a particular culture is often deeply realised.'[40] Individual response can be extended to cultural or historical response. Hence, tragic theory is important because it is about much more than tragedy. The centrality of the topic to criticism and philosophy and the many, often contradictory meanings and connotations associated with it throughout the ages reveal it as a barometer of changing attitudes to suffering, loss and death. And in this distinction lies a welter of ideological and political implications. The type of suffering we value, the type we deem worthy of tragic response, in both literary and existential senses, is a highly charged indication of social significance. It resonates with the assumptions and mythologies through which a society negotiates its response to major human catastrophe. As Williams claims, 'what is in question is not only the use of "tragedy" to describe something other than a work of dramatic literature ... What is more deeply in question is a particular kind and a particular interpretation of death and suffering.'[41]

If Williams is right, then debates on the nature of tragedy are no mere pedantic or semantic exercise. If certain types of death are relegated to the ancillary and accidental, then this has important ideological significance. For instance, what is perceived as not 'really' tragic can have class and gender reverberations. (As already seen, feminists have complained that men are always tragic heroes, women tragic victims.) The sense of tragedy as a 'meta-value' examined above underpins highbrow efforts to defend it from perceived loose, debased or journalistic uses. If tragedy is to be distinguished (with the appropriate double meaning of both evaluatively exalted and empirically distinct), then it must be made distinct from lesser phenomena. Hence generations of schoolmasters, guiding credulous pupils through Thebes and Elsinore, have emphasized an aristocratic imperative. Tragedy happens to princes, not to 'you or me'. Its rarity is part of its value, though paradoxically it is also somehow 'typical', if not at all average; communally experienced but never merely common.

The denial of tragic significance to death in a road accident is the classic schoolmasterly instance of the effort to defend the word from debasement. Perhaps the most sophisticated modern member of this school is Stephen Dedalus. In *A Portrait of the Artist as a Young Man*, Stephen disputes the use of 'tragedy' to describe the accidental death of a young girl in a hansom accident: 'The reporter called it a tragic death. It is not. It is remote from pity and terror according to the terms of my definitions.'[42] But it may be that his definitions are symptomatic of the overly abstract and intellectualized Stephen, whose bloodless aesthetic theorizing detaches him from the everyday reality and suffering which ought to be the source of his art. This old commonplace about the road accident is still regularly aired. In regretting the 'depreciation of common usage', Richard H. Palmer complains that 'the journalistic jargon that labels an automobile accident tragic equates tragedy with any disaster.'[43] This sort of defensive posture emerges from the assumption that tragedy is an unchanging, descriptive word, rather than a mutating, evaluative one. It also comes from an ideological prejudice that wants to preserve for tragedy an aura of prestige and greatness, but that ends up disconnecting its power from fundamental sources of human suffering, as experienced by men and women in real social life. As Williams puts it:

> The events which are not seen as tragic are deep in the pattern of our own culture: war, famine, work, traffic, politics. To see no ethical content or human agency in such events, or to say that we cannot connect them with general meanings, is to admit a strange and particular bankruptcy, which no rhetoric can finally hide.[44]

Significantly, this defensive rhetoric can very quickly look antiquated, even bathetic. Consider Geoffrey Brereton's hairsplitting analysis of the tragic possibilities of the traffic accident. 'The death of a great man in an air crash qualifies for tragedy unequivocally; if he is killed in a sports car, the tragic quality becomes more dubious; if by falling off a bicycle, the whole conception is endangered.'[45] What we consider 'grand', like Brereton's prestigious sports car, can look flashy and cheap to future generations.

Ironically, however, everyday or journalistic usage of the term these days tends more to brush against the traditional definitions of tragedy. An event is most likely to be described as a tragedy in the newspapers when there is a high level of waste or loss that involves neither grim fatalism nor human culpability. Indeed the word is most often ushered in to describe a meaningless, profoundly unnecessary loss: the child killed in the road accident, the carnage of the earthquake, the casualties of war, as opposed to the causes or ends of the war. 'And then tragedy struck ...' is the common locution. But rather than bemoaning this meaning as an inaccurate debasement of the term, it might be wiser to try to gauge and assess why it has evolved in this direction. The sense of tragedy as random, unnecessary accident stands incongruously against the Hegelian tradition of tragic philosophy, which holds that it is precisely when death and destruction are teleological and progressive, ultimately revelatory of *Geist* or world spirit, that it can be called tragic; this shift perhaps reveals something of the different value systems of the eighteenth as against the twentieth century. Journalistic tragedy is most intense precisely when the disaster in question is *accidental*. It could be argued that this meaning is not just a woolly colloquialism but, signalling loss of faith in the humanist emphasis on individual agency, picks up on something of the classical sense that the tragic is released when one is not wholly responsible for one's downfall. The 'accidental' and the 'predestined', though they seem opposites, both exclude the power of humans to mould their own destiny. Indeed, examined closely they have much in common: once an accident has happened – once the child has fallen under the wheels of the car – it becomes part of the past, and the past has all the inexorable irremediability of the most pitiless fatalism. If the future is full of endless possibility, the past is rigidly linear: fate, the will of the gods, is just that linearity anticipated in advance. Related to the notion of accident, the modern sense of tragedy, for all its supposed journalistic flaccidity, doubles back and reactivates the profound sense of *waste* that was part of the Hellenic understanding.

As suggested already, the most important seepage from the literary genre into popular uses of 'tragedy' is the sense of esteem and power surrounding the area. The common, colloquial description of an event as a tragedy is not so much related to any determinate or determinable features of an event or episode but is rather blurred by evaluative, response-based dimensions. If the term is now brought into service to describe simple accidents, this is indicative of a reverential response in the face of the disaster that has occurred. When language cannot adequately encompass the terrible event, this word seems to provide a trace of elegy, a recognition of *significance*. This trace lies in the implied connection with a shared set of experiences and values: a communal recognition of loss, if not, as traditional definitions of tragedy have sought to stress, a recognition of communal loss. In other words, the 'accidental', in both its philosophical and its everyday sense, ceases to be simply the peripheral. This grammar of significance underlies Williams's view that the separation of the common sense of tragedy from its academic counterpart is ideologically suspect: 'The real key to the separation of tragedy from "mere suffering", is the separation of ethical control and, more critically, human agency, from our understanding of social and political life.'[46] For Williams, it seems the crucial question is not what events it is possible to connect with general meanings – ethical content or human agency – but rather what is the nature of these meanings themselves. Notwithstanding ideological construction, they are not permanent and universal, but mutable and culturally specific. The recognition of 'the tragic' as a term replete with this sort of ideological significance is central to understanding the history of the term. However, one can recognize the variability and vicissitudes of values without being wholly agnostic about their substantive reality, without thinking them entirely ephemeral.

So if it is true that tragedy is a highly valued literary genre, then the reasons for this evaluation, as with the historically conflicting definitions, are manifold and often contradictory. Like a diamond examined from various angles, different facets of tragedy shine from different perspectives. And, predictably, when a culture values the representation of one facet – be it the triumph of ultimate justice, the revelation of the vanity of human wishes, the heroism of suffering humanity or a welter of other reasons – then it becomes elevated to an 'essential' component of 'true' tragedy. In other words the definitions of tragedy that have been examined above coalesce with those aspects perceived by a culture to be 'valuable'. Space forbids an exhaustive survey, but we can illustrate some of the sheer incommensurabilty within the field. The values of tragedy have been variously sourced in psychological, metaphysical, ethical, social and political benefits. It has been prized as a source of profound insight and revelation, and also as a view of life which orbits around a core of mystery.[47] It has been lauded for its consoling depiction of meaning and divine control behind human disaster; and for its stark, unflinchingly honest depictions of meaninglessness, chaos and vanity. It has, as exemplified above by John Dennis, been valorized as a didactic inculcator of moral values and by neo-Nietzscheans as a transethical category, too great for the strictures of good and evil.[48] The notion of a morally balanced universe often goes hand in hand with the belief that tragedy has an instructive function. However, Schopenhauer's position is a direct inversion of this model. He sees the benefit of tragedy precisely in its revelation to a spectator of the vanity, injustice and futility of the phenomenal world. This insight, if harrowing, is nonetheless improving in that it leads to the proper attitude of renunciation and asceticism.[49] For those of a Romantic temperament, tragedy is esteemed for the elevation of a hero who rails articulately against cruel Fate with nobility and Promethean defiance. Strains of this approach persist: hence the battles over the tragic status of the little men, of Willy Loman and his ilk. One of the ongoing tensions in modern commentary is the insistence that the hero should be greater than run-of-the-mill humanity, but at the same time *representative* of it, always archetypal, but never merely typical.

Crucially, what all these contradictory and contesting notions of tragic value share is that they provide meaning or conceptual control or ritualized response where it is sorely needed – where chaos and confusion threaten to overwhelm all equilibrium, psychological and social. Tragedy achieves its prominence through a process of radical counterpoint: by imparting the outline of discursive meaning and order where meaning and order are under attack. This is not to say that it always explains or understands suffering. Many modern tragedies would rather seem to assert the inexplicability and randomness of suffering. But to underline meaninglessness is, in a sense, to negate it: to underline chaos one must first be outside it. Conceptually speaking, in so far as one can speak of tragedy one is a spectator, observing turmoil without partaking in it. Even a play like Beckett's *Endgame* (1957), where comfort is in as short a supply as Hamm's painkillers, communicates something – even if that something is the impossibility of communication. As we shall examine, this is a paradox with which Beckett persistently struggles, remorselessly seeking a medium to express confusion and suffering without yielding to the beguiling coherences and cognitive control inevitably imposed by language and stagecraft.

The value of tragedy rests, if not in tragic loss offset by the gain of some greater value (ethical or social resolution, for instance), then at least in its relation to some wider context. At its most basic, this is achieved simply through a process of recognition – the acknowledgement that a terrible loss has occurred. The eagerness to give loss a meaningful context, even if only in terms of an evaluative response, goes some way to explaining the compulsive reaching for the term in the newspaper headlines. Faced with needless loss of life or a terrible disaster, the category of the tragic seems to answer the need for recognition, for a sense of the significance of the loss. This is why the word begins to answer our elegiac urge. A loss or catastrophe may not make sense, but when responded to as a tragedy, it no longer seems just a 'dead' loss.

Among the most important compensatory values within literary tragedy, countering and redeeming the pain and suffering of the subject matter, are the consolations of symmetrical form and lyrical craftsmanship. Beautiful language, eloquence of expression, choreographed dramatic structure, all allegedly transform misery into aesthetic delight. There is a venerable tradition in tragic commentary that emphasizes this dialectic. Its most famous and enthusiastic modern proponent is Friedrich Nietzsche. For Nietzsche, tragic harmony issues from the symbiotic strains of Apollonian and Dionysian fusion. The Dionysian sphere pertains to the untempered nature of reality, the Apollonian to the modes of its appearance, or to its artistic re-presentation. For Nietzsche and his disciples, the Dionysian is a primal swirl of chaos which can only be tolerated by the imposition of an illusory, controlling Apollonian force:

> The more aware I become of those omnipotent art impulses in nature, and find in them an ardent longing for illusion, and for redemption by illusion, the more I feel compelled to make the metaphysical assumption that the truly existent, the Primal Oneness, eternally suffering and contradictory, also needs the delightful vision, the pleasurable illusion for its constant redemption.[50]

There is a tug-of-war between the metaphysical pull towards chaos and the aesthetic pull towards a transcending and containing order. For Nietzsche, the Apollonian order and artistic organization of form transfigures Dionysian chaos into exhilarating spectacle. This frisson generates tragic pleasure, as well as metaphysical insight. The Wisdom of Silenus is a desperate credo: 'The best of all things is something entirely outside your grasp: not to be born, not to *be*, to be *nothing*. But the second-best thing for you – is to die soon.'[51] In the Nietzschean model, the presentation of Greek tragedy on stage in choral form miraculously transforms the awful vision into a pleasurable and sublime spectacle. This is the impact of tragic form on tragic content. Catharsis becomes intrinsically associated with textual aesthetics, which distances the fear and allows the necessary counterpoint of pity. Form and language act as literary prophylactics, buffering the spectator from the horrors enacted onstage. The spectator is uplifted and purified by the transfigurative powers of the lyricism. Refracted through an aesthetic prism, the terrible vision mutates into exquisite illusion.

Yet even without the Nietzschean emphasis on aesthetic exhilaration or lyrical rapture, even without the transforming powers of poetic language, there is a sense in which the representation of tragedy always counters the object represented. In tragedy the simple act of concretization and conceptualization palliates the misery depicted. It can never be so recalcitrant to meaning, once it has been said to be so. 'The worst is not/ So long as we can say, "This is the worst"', as Edgar would have it. Hence, less aesthetically minded critics than Nietzsche have emphasized the anomaly between tragic form and tragic content. Many theorists, among them Murray Krieger, Timothy J. Reiss and Angelos Tirzakis, make a distinction between the 'tragic', as a bleak, desolate vision or view of humanity, and 'tragedy', this vision contained and transformed by its literary crystallization.[52] The representation of the tragic vision in a particular literary work becomes an attempt to redeem it by giving it a formal incarnation. By itself, the tragic, for these theorists, is inexpressible, unintelligible, and inexplicable; the representation of it – the showing of the absence of meaning – is an act that gives a meaningful context, that brings the tragic within our perceptual grasp.

Yet we can go back one step further. Even within tragic theory, the opposition, if less overt, still holds. We do not need the transformation of art or the containment of narrative to sheathe the full impact of tragedy. Simply to talk about the 'tragic' as a philosophical or real-life category is itself to distort it or remove its sting. As Stephen Booth puts it, 'theories of the nature of tragedy are more important to us than theories of the nature of other things because theories of tragedy keep us from facing tragedy itself.'[53] Even without lyrical or dramatic incarnation, to describe an event as tragic places it in conceptual patterns that make sense, which ascribe it to a meaningful context (though it may not make the event itself meaningful). It is recast by the inevitable coherence of communication, even if the subject of communication is precisely incoherence:

> If what is tragic can be *said* to be so then it has been fixed, it has become meaningful, and if that is so then one can no longer actually participate in it: the lack of knowledge has been canceled out.

As something *named*, the tragic is the creation of the discourse, tragedy. To be in a position to show the tragic presupposes an analysis which, in providing the terms in which human activity is to be deemed possible, circumscribes the domain of the meaningful. If this were not so the tragic could not be shown.[54]

This is a different point to the Nietzschean idea of lyrical transformation and can apply to non-aesthetic uses of tragedy too. For theorists like Reiss simply to name an event as a tragedy is to contain it within a controlling discursive frame and hence to contradict the meaninglessness which is asserted. It is to take one step towards containing the uncontainable.

This strange split between tragedy and its representation (or its conceptualization) generates related tensions within tragic theory, where opposing values vie for dominance. In other words, if different aspects of tragedy are prized for different, often contradictory reasons, then sometimes these aspects can clash. Historically, one instance might be the contesting notions that tragedy reveals a divinely controlled versus a divinely abandoned universe. A more revealing opposition so far as Irish drama is concerned is the clash between tragedy held up as a noble source of insight or revelation of human misery, and tragedy valorized as a source of aesthetic transformation or redemption of that misery. As we shall see, this anomaly is germane to Synge's work – and its critical reception – which veers between the imaginative or lyrical transformation of reality and the confrontation of suffering and guilt, between a gallous story and a dirty deed. If tragedy is intensely valued for its courageous revelation of human suffering, its unflinching depiction of harrowing aspects of the human condition, then the restoration of meaning in the manner described above, or the imposition of aesthetic and formal symmetries, of lyrical palliative, can rob it of this noble confrontation. In terms of tragic value, the 'mirror' and the 'lamp' are not happily coexistent. Those who prize the verities of the mirror are impatient with the lamp's beguiling transformations. Hence, in a sense, the form of tragedy denies the very possibility of what it tries to depict: 'Tragedy would enclose the inexpressible, would reduce it to an order of knowledge, at the very same time as inventing the discursive space from which that inexpressible must be excluded.'[55]

The paradoxical conflict between a chaotic vision and an ordered form is one reason why twentieth-century tragedy is often restless in its inherited forms and traditions. It must mutate and reinvent itself so

that disorder and chaos are not smothered beneath ossified conven-
tion. An ordered form can all too quickly become an ordering force:
the representative act projects its own rules and symmetries onto the
represented object. For Karl Jaspers, tragedy is too exalted a form, too
steeped in aristocratic grandeur to provide us with the immediacy of
real, mundane misery:

> A tragic philosophy lives in an aura of grandeur; it offers us personal
> fulfillment, as the fortunate result of an appropriately successful dis-
> aster, and thus lifts us high above reality. But in so doing, this phi-
> losophy narrows down our awareness. For insofar as men find
> release in an experience of this kind, they find it only at the price of
> concealing from themselves the terrifying abysses of reality.
> Misery—hopeless, meaningless, heart-rending, destitute, and help-
> less misery—cries out for help. But the reality of all this misery
> without greatness is pushed aside as unworthy of notice by minds
> that are blind with exaltation. And all the while, man presses for
> redemption from his terrible realities, which lack the glamor of
> tragedy.[56]

It is as if, in the title of Jaspers's book, 'tragedy is not enough.' The satisfactions of heroism and human grandeur, lyrical and aesthetic pleasure, catharsis – these criteria are distortive for Jaspers, as they are for a
modern playwright like Samuel Beckett, searching for the voice that
will express misery without artificial consolation. New forms must continually be sought to access suffering, because the old so quickly calcify
into attractive coherences and reassuring patterns. We can see this
dilemma very clearly in Beckett's work. Ever resistant to the artificial
solace or the metaphysical sweetener, Beckett, as we shall see, sets out
to find a new form: 'there will be new form ... this form will be of such
a type that it admits the chaos and does not try to say that the chaos is
really something else.'[57]

Form and content, language and reality, tend to have an unsteady,
largely disjunctive relationship in the Irish tradition. There is much
lyrical eloquence and poetic gesture on the Irish stage, even to the
point of self-caricature, but there is a sense that it is detached from the
ugly social reality that underlies it: a distraction rather than a redemption. Far from rapturous Apollonian transformation of chaotic suffering, far from the grandiloquent and ennobling soliloquies of
Shakespearean tragedy, the 'talk' in Synge and O'Casey often seems
peculiarly impotent, a poor compensation for the bleak and stagnant

realities that it strives to occlude. Beckett carefully crafts a similarly disjunctive relationship between form and content, language and reality. Though his meticulously precise and stringently economical dialogue reacts against the beguiling blather of some of his Abbey forebears, its carefully ordered symmetry nonetheless contradicts the confusion and desolation of his subject matter. And the subject matter contradicts it. In his drama, talk is ineluctable, but usually empty, irrelevant and impotent. Beckett continually strives to be true to his ineffable vision: an unholy combination of chaotic confusion and meagre determinism that lies beneath formal and linguistic control. That he is also an aesthete who delights in pattern and shape, be it rhythmic verbal exchange or choreographed theatrical movement, in no way lessens his distrust of distortion. Through his search for a new form, that 'does not try to say that the chaos is really something else', he does not simply ignore, but rather flouts and abuses all the conventions of tragedy, seeking to undo its traditional aesthetic consolations in order to come closer to an unmediated tragic condition. In the hierarchy of value, Beckett strives for tragic veracity, rather than tragic grandeur or tragic beauty. In Beckett, 'tragedy' is undone in order to liberate the tragic – the ineffable confusion that lurks behind the dramatic representation.

Irish tragedians? Synge, O'Casey, Beckett

To amplify and to extend the preceding considerations on tragic theory, and to anticipate further the three author-based chapters to follow, I want to conclude this introductory chapter by suggesting some ways in which we can use tragic models to consider the attitude towards suffering, loss and guilt in Synge, O'Casey and Beckett. Tragedy, as argued, should not be thought of as an immutable or neutral phenomenon, but rather as a pattern of response, a cultural structure through which profound loss is mediated and represented. When disaster is configured in these terms, the resulting narrative almost inevitably bears a relationship, more or less explicit, more or less direct, with models of tragedy. This is true for personal or immediate loss, but it is also the case for historical narrative. This chapter began by looking at the almost clichéd tendency to refer to Irish history as 'tragic'. The argument that I have advanced on the aura of 'value' that emanates from tragedy perhaps explains the faint sense of mystique that surrounds the word when applied in these terms. On one level, it might seem an appropriately reverential term for remembering the often unrecorded sufferings of past generations. But there are dangerous implications too. For instance, a certain connotation of tragedy – probably deriving from its Hellenic origins – carries an association with fate or predestination: if we see any history, personal or national, in these terms, the effect may be to rob us of agency, to hint that historical suffering is pre-ordained and irremediable.

Yet there are other systems of interpretation around which narratives of suffering can cohere, just as there are many other resonances around the word 'tragedy'. Within Irish history, how do we connect the Great Famine or the Easter Rising of 1916 or the recent Troubles to wider structures of belief? All these events have been called 'tragedies', often with very different connotations. So, for instance, when the Great Famine is described as a tragedy, it may be in the same sense that an earthquake is so described: as an awful catastrophe. As we have seen, the modern popular associations of the term would accord with this nuance. To call the Famine a tragedy in this sense would accord with an ethic of commemoration: it would draw attention to the waste of precious life, abstracting the reality of human loss from the causes or consequences of that loss. Yet if a more teleological or Hegelian version of tragic discourse is adopted, then the Famine might be explicable in terms of a necessary, if temporary Evil. 'Supreme Wisdom has educed permanent good out of transient evil', as Charles Trevelyan would have it.[58] Those contemporary Malthusian economists who regarded the Famine as the awful but necessary shedding of surplus population and unviable economic structures were unwittingly employing this model of tragedy. The point, again, is about how we relate a perceived evil to a wider system of meaning or meaninglessness. Convictions of a divinely orchestrated universe means that tragedy will be absorbed into a mode in which suffering is explicable and justifiable; and this mode, as with the changing of the end of *King Lear*, will be brought into tragedy.

Another recognizable association of tragedy stresses heroism, especially the heroism of dignity, nobility, and courage in defeat. Though prevalent in the Irish historical imagination, all three dramatists will react against this tendency, albeit in different ways. Oliver MacDonagh sees a pattern of ritualistic failure embedded in the Irish historical sense:

> a past seen in terms of subjection and struggle, seen as a pageant or tournament of heroic defeat, is one of the roads towards a fundamental distrust of or even disbelief in achievement ... the characteristic Irish time-frame inclines Irishmen to a repetitive view of

history and that such a view inclines them – perhaps in defensive wariness and from fear of failure – to prize the moral as against the actual, and the bearing of witness as against success. The *locus classicus* of this cast of mind is the Proclamation of the Republic on Easter Monday 1916.[59]

One way to render cyclical loss meaningful is to transform it into ritualistic sacrifice. This was one of the impulses underlying the Rising. When history is so recalcitrant to progress or coherence, it can only be rendered meaningful as myth. In cases where the sacrifice or its underlying mythology is not available, then ritualistic failure cannot be seen as redemptive and dwindles to empty repetition, such as we sometimes find on the Beckettian stage. Just as they react against the mythic values of the literary revival, all three of the dramatists under consideration here react against the sort of ritualistic mythology that transmutes failure into success.

The most visible in the specific terms of the Easter Rising is, of course, Sean O'Casey. The Easter Rising has been the site of much controversy amongst historians and cultural critics in Ireland.[60] Investigation of how attitudes towards the Rising – both of adulation and of condemnation – cleave to particular ideas of tragedy can help illuminate the structures of thought which underlie the event and the responses to it. When Michael Collins complained of the Rising that it had an 'air of a Greek tragedy', he was identifying the fetish for ceremonial failure, the self-conscious attempt to find redemption through gestural sacrifice, rather than through pragmatic military strategy.[61] With the Proclamation's reference to six rebellions over the previous three hundred years, the Rising sought to cleave to a ritualistic motif, just as it self-consciously strove for martyrdom and Christ-like sacrifice. Indeed, the bold march towards military failure in the interests of spiritual victory resonates with a strong Romantic tradition of tragedy, which elevates its protagonists above the merely material and commonplace. Maud Gonne's reported response – 'tragic dignity has returned to Ireland' – keys into this mythology.[62] This redemptive idea of tragedy constructs the event as ultimately positive, characterized by dignity, nobility and self-sacrifice. The self-consciously theatrical elements of the Rising buttress the notion of heroism and grandeur. As Declan Kiberd says, 'The Rising when it came was seen by many as a foredoomed classical tragedy, whose *dénouement* was both inevitable and unpredictable, prophesied and yet surprising.'[63]

Yet, so polysemic is the term that one could also describe the Rising as a 'tragedy' and impart the exact opposite evaluative connotation. As we have seen, in general, when it is not being used as a tag for literary-historical genres, the modern import of the term underplays redemptive or meaningful models, emphasizing, rather, waste, loss and intense, undeserved suffering. Just as one could say that the Rising was a 'great' or 'heroic' tragedy, it is common enough in recent Irish historiography and journalism to retrospectively depict it as a 'terrible tragedy'. In effect the judgement is reversed: it is no longer a display of heroic nobility but is rather an unnecessary, ill-conceived waste of human life, which incarnated a vicious cult of violence and blood sacrifice. The two types of tragedy are powerfully encapsulated in Yeats's 'Easter 1916', where the mythic and the actual, the beauty and the terror, are pitted in dialectical encounter. This poem is not just about how tragedy supplants the 'casual comedy', how green replaces motley; it also puts in conflict classical and modern ideas of tragedy, myths of heroic sacrifice pitted against notions of wasted lives. On one level this famous poem pays tribute to the heroism of the Rising, the tragic sacrifice based on 'excess of love'; on another it decries the fanaticism that can 'make a stone of the heart'.[64]

The Plough and the Stars (1926) is one of the first and most notable dramatic attempts to usurp the heroic with the 'wasteful' view of the Rising. Ostensibly, this play privileges the domestic over the historical, the family over the nation, and shows how the Rising is based on a delusory rhetoric, destructive of family life. The play incarnated this sense of the tragedy of a tragedy – the idea that it was precisely the dramatic, mythological overlay that made the episode most cruelly and abjectly wasteful. Along with the rhetoric of idealism and bombastic heroism, tragedy in its classical or dramatic sense is seen as dangerous and delusory when erupting into real social life. O'Casey is famously concerned with a supposed 'deflation' of the metanarratives of Irish nationalist history, and is often regarded as a sort of 'revisionist' *avant la lettre*. He has also been acclaimed for espousing that 'common-sense' humanity supposedly lost in the heady nationalist rhetoric that beguiled the revolutionary generation, lauded for deflating the official reading of the events leading up to the foundation of the Irish State – as an epic or heroic tragedy – and re-conceiving them in terms of personal and familial tragedy. Yet I shall argue that there are other eddies and forces at work in the Dublin trilogy that disturb this reading, qualifying a 'social' view of tragedy in which the suffering in Dublin is based upon unnecessary foolishness, with a far more pessimistic undertow. In O'Casey, the melioristic outlook of the socialist often hides the political disillusionment of the fatalist. This pessimism derives in no small part from the traumatic disenchantments brought on by the culmination of the revolutionary movement in a bloody Civil War.

MacDonagh notices the prevalence of cyclical views of the Irish past, but the opposite sense of a single cataclysm or decisive, devastating intervention of some kind is no less pervasive. Perhaps the most common tragic model in conceptions of Irish history is the idea of a lost Eden. The Eden myth is central to conceptions of tragedy in the Judeo-Christian tradition. The 'memory' of a lost paradise, whether it be the ancient bardic traditions that Ó Rathaille mourned in the early eighteenth century or the Ascendancy heyday/Ancient Celtic aristocracy that Yeats elegized in the twentieth, is recurrent in Irish writing. Similarly, the erasures of indigenous language and culture that colonialism effects lend themselves to the idea of a Fall of some kind. It is not surprising in the many losses of Irish history that an attitude of nostalgia would be adopted, whether directed at a utopian idyll before colonial contamination – 'the stranger in the house' – or before modernity more generally.

If the Gael was given to conceptions of the Irish past as a Fall from Eden, then the tendency is even more predominant in the Anglo-Irish imagination, especially where loss of Ascendancy hegemony and political power was coincidental with cultural and literary creativity. W. J. Mc Cormack stresses how intrinsic an Edenic motif is in the Anglo-Irish reading of the past:

> the Golden Age always existed before some moveable disaster, before the Union, before the Famine, before the Encumbered Estates Court, the Land War, Parnell, the Rising, the Troubles, an accelerating succession of unfortunate falls each one briefly inaugurating some (retrospectively acknowledged) idyll which is itself soon dissolved by the next disaster. Ascendancy is the principle medium by which this fleeting vision of a stable, pre-lapsarian order is imposed on the insolence of fact and circumstance.[65]

If the Ascendancy mind often cleaved to a Fall narrative, then we can also, if less overtly, discern that Edenic counterpoint: tragic guilt. Writers from an Anglo-Irish tradition frequently display an elegiac mood for the decline of Ascendancy, yet this feeling is often interwoven with the culpability of a privileged culture whose great achievements were historically enabled by conquest. Irish Gothic – with the haunting of the Big House because of some ancestral wrongdoing – is the most frequently identified literary manifestation of this caste guilt.[66] Of course, the material independence and freedom from labour that artists need is often based on exploitative power-relations. The most valuable artefacts of civilization carry this 'Original Sin.' 'There is no document of civilization', as Walter Benjamin famously put it, 'that is not at the same time a document of barbarism.'[67] In this respect, it is striking how often in Anglo-Irish drama the characters' social position, however benevolent or desirable, is contingent on an aboriginal transgression, often committed before the action proper of the play. A short list of plays which raise this moral issue might include G. B. Shaw's *Major Barbara* (1905), Oscar Wilde's *An Ideal Husband* (1895), J. M. Synge's *The Playboy of the Western World* (1907) and W. B. Yeats's *Purgatory* (1939). It is tempting to speculate on a linkage between the preponderance of this narrative structure and the barbarous history of the Ascendancy's rise to power in Ireland. Cultural riches, art and civilization grow from these roots, just as the social position of Vivian Warren and Sir Robert and Lady Chiltern is dependent on a violation of the codes by which they pretend to live. The tragedy is that however desirable and good the cultural flowering, it often springs from political and social ordure. And, not coincidentally, Synge gives a comparable juxtaposition for his aesthetic project: 'there is no timber that has not strong roots among the clay and worms.'[68]

Chapter 2 argues that an acute, uneasy awareness of this tragic imbrication of culture with barbarism – from a man so infatuated with the native Irish culture and people – deeply imbues Synge's work. Despite the fact that he is the more 'authentic' member of the Ascendancy, he does not elegize the Big House as much as Yeats, tending to refract his elegiac mood into a threnody for Irish peasant and rural life, under threat by encroaching modernity. There are exceptions, however, most notably his prose piece 'A Landlord's Garden in County Wicklow', written for the *Manchester Guardian* in 1903:

> Everyone is used in Ireland to the tragedy that is bound up with the lives of farmers and fishing people; but in this garden one seemed to feel the tragedy of the landlord class also, and of the innumerable old families that are quickly dwindling away. These owners of the land are not much pitied at the present day, or much deserving of pity ... (CWII, 231).

The final caveat here suggests that Synge does not fetishize Ascendancy cultivation and seems aware that its privilege was bought at a high price. His instinctive impulse to mourn his own people is contradicted by a sense of their historical culpability. As befits Synge's strongly Protestant upbringing, Edenic loss is counterpointed by Edenic guilt. I shall argue that, unlike Pegeen Mike, Synge is poignantly aware that there is no great gap between the gallous story and the dirty deed which enabled its composition; in his drama's fusion of poetry and ugliness, he subliminally asserts the parasitic connection. As we shall see, it is most overtly expressed in his early, unperformed play *When the Moon has Set*. Yet the relation is continually encrypted in the dialectic between poetry and violence in Synge's work. It is not only manifest in the notorious brutality of his poetic imagery but, in a wider sense, in his aesthetic project more generally, continually veering as it does between confrontation with the squalor of peasant life and a lyrical evasion of it. As already noted, it is characteristic of Irish drama to refuse a Nietzschean redemption of ugly reality by lyrical alchemy but to leave, instead, heightened language and degraded reality in uneasy counterpoint. Yet there is a deeper tragic veracity in Synge's work. He confronts his own impulse to evade, indicting himself, in the figures of his poetically gifted tramps and vagrants, of attempting to sidestep reality by way of imaginative and lyrical virtuosity. Reality remains painfully recalcitrant nevertheless. Nora Burke, like the spectator, knows that she leaves her home with the tramp to a life of homeless squalor and degradation. Similarly, for all the comic trappings of resolution at the end of *The Well of the Saints* (1905), the two heroes depart not for superannuated bliss in the south, but to probable death by drowning along the way.

Politicizing Syngean tragedy, analysing his work in terms of the tensions and contradictions engendered by the social space he occupies, opens up fertile areas for investigation neglected by conventional criticism. Of the three dramatists Synge arguably approximates the classical tragic form most closely. Even Daniel Corkery praises *Riders to the Sea* as 'one of the few modern plays written, and successfully written in the Greek *genre*'.[69] The tightly controlled structure where the action hinges on an inexorable sense of doom, which the characters are agents in hastening, seems to many to resonate with the 'true' tragic spirit. Moreover, the cult of Synge as a dreamy, melancholic figure – the sensuous passion for the world of experience coupled with a sensitivity to decay and an urge for oblivion – seems to cast him as the quintessential, if not stereotypical, Keatsian figure.[70] Yet the analysis of *Riders* in accordance with some putative formula for 'authentic tragedy', coupled with the related assumption that Synge's artistic attitude must be of perpetually 'universal' significance, has skewed attention from political and historical elements of his attitude and disposition. Synge's aesthetic, though often congruent with many conventional paradigms of tragedy, is also rooted in a specific historical moment, for all the 'timeless' resonance of Maurya's cry. A particular discourse of tragedy has contributed to these omissions in Synge criticism. W. B. Yeats praised Synge as a man 'incapable of a political thought', and this effort to 'raise' Synge to universal significance has lingered.[71] It is not always a token of praise. Picked up by Seamus Deane, Synge's putative apoliticism becomes a badge of evasiveness.[72] But Synge's work is acutely attuned to its cultural and historical context and, if he is guilty of evasiveness, it is a charge which he often lays at his own door, just as he depicts the imaginative virtuosity of the Douls in *The Well of the Saints* as self-delusion, not only at odds with reality but also, ultimately, self-destructive.

The theme of guilt and the incorporation of Edenic imagery is also, if in different ways, a central concern of the chapter on Samuel Beckett. After all, in his early monograph on Proust, Beckett, borrowing from Schopenhauer, defined tragedy as 'the expiation of the original sin ... the sin of having been born' (P, 49) one of the principal allusions of the tree in *Waiting for Godot* (1953) is to the tree of knowledge. In that play, Pozzo answers to both Cain and Abel and Estragon at one point thinks his name is Adam. Discernible in such wry allusions, the theme of guilt is one of Beckett's most obsessive concerns, from his earliest writings to his later, purgatorial images. The keynote is usually some variation on original sin:

> *Vladimir*: Suppose we repented.
> *Estragon*: Repented what?
> *Vladimir*: Oh ... [*He reflects*] We wouldn't have to go into the details.
> *Estragon*: Our being born? (CDW, 13)

Estragon's answer, far from the imperious, self-assured tone of *Proust*, is no longer adequate. The mature Beckett moves away from the pessimistic language of his early, Schopenhauerian phase, opting instead for a voice of advanced bewilderment and confusion, albeit expressed in a prose of scrupulous exactitude. Philosophy is cast off like an outworn shoe, too remote and cumbersome to be of any greater consolation than Lucky's 'think'. This anti-philosophical turn has many implications for Beckett's art, as we shall see, but it is especially relevant for his treatment of suffering and guilt. Paul Ricoeur's claim that 'Nothing is less amenable to a direct confrontation with philosophy that the concept of original sin, for nothing is more deceptive than its appearance of rationality ...' could have been written with Beckett specifically in mind.[73] Like Kafka, in Beckett's world the crime and the punishment seem perversely intertwined. The punishment is there but the crime is elusive. Macmann in *Malone Dies* ponders these issues:

> The idea of punishment came into his mind ... And without knowing exactly what his sin was he felt full well that living was not a sufficient atonement for it or that this atonement was itself a sin, calling for more atonement, and so on, as if there could be anything but life for the living ... And truth to tell the ideas of guilt and punishment were confused together in his mind, as those of cause and effect so often are in the minds of those who continue to think. (T, 249)

It seems that life is both original sin and original punishment, coiled desperately together. In general, clear origin, like a recognizable relationship between cause and effect, is refused in Beckett's radically uncertain world, just as he seemed to spurn his Irish provenance for a cosmopolitan transcendence of nationality. Yet many of the concerns of his Anglo-Irish dramatic forebears, including those of loss and guilt, persist in his work, if in a radically disorientated way. There is no shortage of loss in Beckett's world – we continually have the sense that something is wrong, that there is an ineffable lack at the heart of his characters' lives – yet it seems, paradoxically, that the loss was there from the beginning. Memory, like the narrative itself, is splintered and uncertain and if, like Nagg and Nell, the characters sometimes indulge in nostalgia, there is little hearkening back to a pre-lapsarian past. The past, like the subjectivity or selfhood that it would cohere, is too indefinite. The same is true of the guilt. If we consider a play like Yeats's *Purgatory*, often considered proleptically Beckettian, this point is forcefully made. The depleted setting (with lone tree) and the emphasis on endless cycle and repetition evoke a Beckettian world, yet in Yeats's version the guilt is massively centred, originating in a violation of the Yeatsian eugenic ideal through the coupling of a Big House heiress with a stablehand. *Waiting for Godot* is entirely shorn of any such primordial transgression, though, as noted, it is permeated by the sense of a Fall. The motif is now shattered and dispersed, like the other tragic myths and canonical tragic plays to which Beckett's drama alludes but never amalgamates into a stable narrative sequence.

The removal of the 'origin' of original sin has political overtones. The configuration of the 'Law' – all the trappings of persecution and paranoia that permeates Beckett's mature writing – is characterized by the arbitrary and inscrutable handing down of punishment for elusive crime. Why does Godot beat one boy but not his brother? Why, as Pozzo himself wonders, is he the master and Lucky the slave? An uncertain aetiology may make the relation of guilt to punishment less definite, but it also renders it less self-contained, and the patterns and shapes of obscured, exploitative power structures, begin to appear. Hence so much of the suffering in Beckett's world is haunted by echoes of authoritarian and fascist persecution, for all its apparent deracinated and unspecific nature. The uncertainty, the disruption of cause and effect, is of a piece with the wider formal and epistemological subversions of Beckett's aesthetic which, as Theodor Adorno well knew, subliminally critique prevailing orthodoxy through resisting the well-worn grooves of conventional systems of thought and representation.

Ostensibly, the political import of Sean O'Casey's drama is far less oblique than Beckett's formal innovations. With their didactic political (or anti-political) lessons, the 'value' to which O'Casey's tragedies subscribe is, in a sense, an updated version of the neo-classical ideal, where tragedy's 'purpose' is to inculcate moral principles. On the surface, the Dublin trilogy teaches us to avoid the dangers of political idealism through a demonstration of the terrible destruction these ideals cause to family life, to the hearth and home humanity represented by the women. This, at any rate, has been the usual humanist interpretation of the trilogy. *The Plough and the Stars* does not just replace princes with slum-dwellers – a common enough manoeuvre in modern tragedies. As already seen, what makes this play intriguing from the point of view of tragic theory is that its target is precisely the mythology and evaluative structures that Romantic tragedy draws upon, a system of codes that the Easter Rising sought to emulate. In other words, it is not just that O'Casey replaces the aristocratic, public and heroic with the domestic, private, and intimate, but rather that he makes a virtue of the latter through actively denigrating the former. O'Casey spurns any celebration of heroism, *hubris* or grand sacrifice; in this respect – so far as the heroic ideals of conventional tragedy go – we could claim that he is an anti-tragic writer.[74] Certainly, what we see in this play is not just tragic conflict, but a conflict of different tragic values, the modern and domestic pitted against the mythic and heroic.

However, there are problems and inconsistencies in O'Casey's approach. Many critics have condemned him for a simplistic or coarse opposition between human compassion and abstract politics. Speaking of *Juno and the Paycock* (1924), G. J. Watson complains: 'we are asked to feel the irrelevance of nationalist politics and their centrality, at the same moment. These politics focus and embody the tragedy, yet O'Casey does not begin to try to explore the forces behind the tragedy, so that we feel a hollowness at the play's core.'[75] However, the opposition between empty rhetoric and pragmatic realism, between deluded men and compassionate women – whether the opposition is vaunted by O'Casey's admirers or derided by his detractors – fails to recognize the various elements of these plays which resist and subvert such neat polarities. The subterranean inconsistencies of the Dublin trilogy are far more dramatically interesting, I shall argue, than the surface anti-political polemic. That these inconsistencies and countervailing thematic eddies have been largely overlooked – or simply mocked – is partly ascribable to the predominance of naturalist and realist productions of the trilogy, which order the skirmish of stylistic registers into a straitened narrative and thematic coherence. It is quite possible to read – or produce – O'Casey's early drama against itself and to save it from the didacticism that diminishes so much of his later drama. Much in the *Plough*, as in his other two Dublin tragedies, brushes against the grain of the ostensible anti-mythical, anti-heroic polemic.

The arena where the different ideologies in O'Casey's work contest can be located in the thorny question of meliorism – a contentious notion in tragic theory, since it was debarred by George Steiner and others from the 'authentic' tragic vision. Can 'truly' tragic problems be solved, or are they irremediable conditions of human experience? O'Casey, like Ibsen or Brecht, ostensibly embraces a model of tragedy in which suffering is avoidable. For this reason alone, O'Casey would not gain admittance to George Steiner's canon of Great Tragedy. In relation to Ibsen's *Ghosts* (1881), Steiner drily claims that true tragedy cannot be avoided with the installation of proper plumbing; nor will Lear's plight be solved by provision of adequate homes for the aged.[76] Mindful of the theoretical debates, particularly between Steiner and Raymond Williams, the question of whether the suffering that O'Casey depicts is avoidable or reparable will be the thematic key of Chapter 3. The socialist O'Casey's belief in the possibility of social reparability, combined with the strong sense in his work that the plight of his characters is avoidable, is strikingly at odds with the unnuanced indictment of political ideology in the Dublin trilogy. This anomaly itself merits scrutiny. Nor, as is sometimes suggested, is the indictment of political ideas in the trilogy simply aimed at nationalism, not international socialism. The portrayal of Jerry Devine and the Covey show the Marxists to be as self-deluded and bombastic as the nationalists. Furthermore, the entire domestic construction and realist method of the plays are designed to brook no intrusion of political ideology, be it of the green or the red variety. After all, if the Easter Rising had been a class war rather than a nationalist uprising, it would have been scant solace for the widowed Nora Clitheroe; if Johnny Boyle had been fighting for the working classes rather than for Ireland, Juno would still think that he lost his best principle when he lost his arm. In the trilogy, and in contrast to some of his later leftist plays like *The Star Turns Red* (1940) or *Red Roses for Me* (1942), O'Casey is led into the paradoxical conclusion that politics as a whole is anti-social. Why, given his staunch radicalism in life, does he strive in the trilogy for this withdrawal from social critique in favour of a simple adulation of the 'apolitical' family?

As might be expected given the trauma of Ireland's revolutionary period – especially the Civil War, a far less glorious enterprise than the Rising by any standards – historical events were responsible for undermining O'Casey's rooted beliefs in political reform and revolution. Ever a strident battler and with a deeply held faith in the social reparability of human suffering, O'Casey was distraught by the failure of politics to remove the appalling conditions in which he was brought up. He sublimates the pessimism and extreme disillusionment of the Civil War into another 'cause': the dramatic castigation of dangerous myths and rhetoric, the celebration of human kindness in the face of adversity. In other words, he finds another way of indicting a suffering that is *avoidable*. Behind O'Casey's depiction of political rhetoric as dangerous delusion is his own profound disillusionment with politics. There is an undertow of pessimism, a sense of an absurd or chaotic world, underneath his indictment of deluded ideologues. The drama of the plays lies in the conflict between the two attitudes, between Captain Boyle's view that the world is in 'a terrible state o' chassis' and his wife's more humanistic query: 'What can God do agen the stupidity o' men' (TP, 74, 70). At its most poignant, then, the tragedy of his Dublin trilogy is not just a criticism of his supposedly self-deluding characters, nor is it principally an attack on changeable political and social conditions – Mollser's suffering could be avoided with minimal medical care, but her story remains a subplot. For all the attempts to personalize the suffering – to demythologize the national tragedy – the domestic story chronicled in these plays is also the tragedy of Ireland in the nineteen-twenties, the story of the degeneration of O'Casey's own faith in political amelioration.

If O'Casey wrote a sort of 'anti-tragedy' – insofar as he inverted or disputed the values of the classical model – then we could claim that Beckett wrote a sort of 'sub-tragedy', a tragedy that deliberately falls beneath the conventions and procedures of previous versions. We saw above how Beckett's work often tries to liberate the unmediated quiddity of tragic suffering by unstitching the conventional formal structures and the conventional formal consolations. *Waiting for Godot* and *Endgame* in many ways resemble the shell or outline of a tragedy. They include shards of soliloquy, the remnants of action – 'something is taking its course' – glimmers of feeling and companionship, a hint of dignity within loss. Yet, the pervasive sense is that we have moved to some realm beyond tragedy; values are profoundly disorientated, subjectivity diffuse. Bennett Simon concludes of *Endgame*: 'there is no opportunity to feel for, to sympathize, to pity. No catharsis of pity and terror, for there is no pity – it has been choked in the cradle.'[77] Beckett's characters are not just denied the eloquence to lyricize their condition, in the manner of Lear or Hamlet. Because Beckett's work queries the whole structure of meaning and value from which tragedy takes its coherence, the loss is so great, so ultimate, that even the very capacity to recognize that loss is threatened. In other words, there is no site of perception that can transcend the 'confusion' on stage, no controlling objectivity from which the diagnosis – 'this is a tragedy' – can confidently be made. Continually in Beckett's critical writings, from *Proust* on, he insists that the lines of communication have been ruptured, that representation is always distortive and doomed to failure. As we saw above, his mature plays and novels move away from his early philosophical discourse and strive to embody this belief, rather than just asserting it. One feature of Beckett's work that has been under studied by critics is the radical *confusion* underlying and fuelling the palpable torment of the characters. To demonstrate the confusion dramatically or artistically helps avoid the danger of self-contradiction involved in asserting it philosophically. After all, how can one assert as an absolute certainty the unavailability of absolute certainty? How, like the Beckett of *Proust*, can one communicate the impossibility of communication? Beckett comes to this realization after the war when he becomes aware of his 'own folly.'[78]

Beckett's work seems sub-tragic or beyond the tragic because it strains the seams of the articulable. As seen above, he is mightily distrustful of the Apollonian dimension, of the tendency of lyrical representation to transform the chaotic object represented. Yet at the same time he is a highly aesthetic novelist and playwright, drawn to shapes and patterns of scrupulous exactitude and beauty. As we saw above, this leads to a certain distancing between form and content, especially as his work progresses. One occasionally feels that the form strains to free itself of the object represented, as if it could get on perfectly well without being shackled to the distortive, and futile business of representation. Hence Beckett is perpetually led into creative dilemmas: 'to be an artist is to fail' (P, 125). Beckett's world is so confused and ineffable, that it seems to have lost the sense of containment necessary for even the most ecumenical notion of tragedy. Yet, as I shall argue in Chapter 4, the tragic paradox is such that even the loss of tragedy can itself be considered tragic. As a discourse which, in varying ways, extracts gain from loss, it can double back on itself and regain a sense of tragic urgency. This is particularly the case given the contesting ideologies of loss and the mutating meanings gravitating to the term. As argued earlier, if a chronicle of loss is, by implication, redeemed by being called a tragedy, this can be both a blessing and a curse. It can artificially sweeten or provide a seductive coherence to an event that cries out to be apprehended, interpreted and responded to in all its brutal immediacy. Cutting back on the redemptive or transformative aspect of tragedy strengthens its competing role as a testament, as a source of unflinching recognition. This impulse to bear witness without the blasphemy of aesthetic consolation manifests itself in the need to excise any trace of tragic portentousness from the act of representation. If tragedy takes its meaning from a process of loss, then it can readily turn back upon itself and, in destroying its own value (or at least those aspects which have traditionally been valued), it can magically rejuvenate its tragic aspect. Responding to cultural forces, the literary text is replicated in the social context. If, as George Steiner nostalgically contends, tragedy is dead in our times, its death has itself been a tragic loss – how tragic that our society is incapable of tragedy.

If those consoling residual structures of character, shape, emplotment and so on impose coherence, then these overly formulaic features may need to be debunked in order to access the immediacy and the poignancy of the suffering which the author is trying to transmit. It must also remould the form so that the meaningful context within which suffering occurs can be deciphered. The shift in form is also an index of how a new context for perceiving suffering invades the old mythology. Hence, it is often said that the predominant dramatic form of the twentieth century is tragi-comedy.[79] If 'comic relief' is sometimes designed as a respite from tragic bleakness, it can also ironically serve to sharpen its impact.[80] In an age where traditional tragic consolations – Fortune, aristocratic heroism, a more tightly communal society, a divinely ordered universe – have atrophied, the poetic eloquence and clearly ordained dramatic unities will predictably be undercut by comic deflation. But the need to excise any trace of tragic portentousness is a symptom of a deeper need to return dramatic tragedy to the realities of suffering of our time or, more importantly to the evaluative framework, and context of meaning, we have for responding to those sufferings. So, cutting out the classical elements can render the drama more attuned to the spirit of the times and hence, in a sense, more tragic. We are reminded of Jaspers's complaint that tragedy, as it is conventionally formulated, is not enough. The cruelly anti-heroic characters who loiter on the Beckettian stage, denied stature or the comforting, cathartic sense of closure characteristic of conventional tragedy, recapture the sense of poignant struggle expressed in the tragic precisely because of this privation. How tragic that there is no certain subjectivity, no narrative closure, no lofty soliloquizing. In losing its soul, sub-tragedy paradoxically regains it. Modern tragedy is most acute when, under the pall of Auschwitz, it is most stripped bare of consolation. The most loudly expressive Beckettian voice is mute. A feeling of tragedy is often most intense during the pauses and the silences just as the most tragic moments in *King Lear* occur over the dead body of Cordelia, when the traditional language of tragic soliloquy breaks down – Lear's terrible 'Never, never, never, never, never.'

2
A Gallous Story or a Dirty Deed?: J. M. Synge and the Tragedy of Evasion

Et ton heritage? Mes têtes de mort te saluent. My compliments to the little Irish pigs that eat filth all their lives that you may prosper.
— *When the Moon Has Set*

Introduction: The evasion of confrontation and the confrontation of evasion

On a short visit to Paris in March 1903, John Synge made the mistake of soliciting the young James Joyce's opinion on a manuscript of *Riders to the Sea*. As Richard Ellmann notes, 'No manuscript was ever read with less sympathy.'[1] In a penurious period for both men, material scarcity does not seem to have engendered professional magnanimity. The previous January Joyce had felt piqued by Yeats's praise of Greek echoes in the play, territory over which he kept a jealous watch.[2] It was with some relish, then, that Joyce stripped the play of any lofty Hellenic pretensions: 'I am glad to say', he wrote to his brother Stanislaus, 'that ever since I read it I have been riddling it mentally till it has [not] a sound spot. It is tragic about all the men that are drowned in the islands: but thanks be to God Synge is not an Aristotelian.'[3] Citing Aristotle's *Poetics*, Joyce insisted that the play, with its one-act brevity and emphasis on natural disaster, was just a tragic poem, not a tragedy. It was, he claimed, merely a 'dwarf drama'.[4] Richard Ellmann records that a disgruntled and unconvinced Synge found Joyce a stickler for rules and definitions.[5] The same might be said of the Stephen Dedalus in the fifth chapter of *A Portrait of the Artist as a Young Man*,

42

where, in the celebrated exchange with Lynch, he denies tragic stature to the girl killed in the hansom accident: 'The reporter called it a tragic death. It is not. It is remote from terror and pity according to the terms of my definitions.'[6] This scene has been interpreted as an example of the overly abstract and intellectualized Stephen, whose bloodless aesthetic theorization denies him the everyday reality and suffering which his nascent creativity so desperately needs.[7]

It seems that Joyce later revised his opinion of Synge's play: he learnt several passages by heart and translated it into Italian in 1908.[8] The younger Joyce, searching for a reason to criticize *Riders*, found one in Aristotelian criteria for tragedy. If the play could be proven to lack classical tragic qualities then this was a convenient way for Joyce to decry an artwork that, owing to sibling rivalry, he wanted to dislike. In many ways, this manoeuvre was a portent for future Synge criticism. Sketching the critical history of *Riders to the Sea* offers a useful case study of how definitions of tragedy intermingle with notions of literary merit, an imbrication considered at length in the Introduction above. From the earliest reviews to recent scholarly essays, commentary has ruminated on this generic question and rather than just a matter of neutral designation, the debate is usually a coded value-judgement on the play.[9] Association with the august tradition of literary tragedy is high praise indeed. David R. Clarke hails it as 'one of the great modern tragedies', while Ernest Boyd claims that 'Maurya takes on the profound significance of an Aeschylean figure, in her vain protest against Fate, and her ultimate resignation.'[10] A tightly controlled structure where the action hinges on an inexorable sense of doom, which the characters are nonetheless agents in hastening, prompted even Arthur Griffith, in an otherwise hostile review, to praise its 'tragic beauty'.[11]

Conversely, like the young Joyce, detractors over the years have indicted *Riders* by questioning whether it is 'truly' a tragedy – it is, allegedly, too passive or too short, lacking in *anagnorisis* or lacking in moral complexity to merit the designation. Where is the heroism, the great action, the *hamartia* and the *hubris*? Accusations of formal infelicity and deviation from a blueprint are deployed in arguments about the play's genre, which are also arguments about its literary merit and expressive profundity.[12] Apart from the Aristotelian issue, Synge criticism resonates with wider strains of tragic theory. We saw in the Introduction that tragic theory has often prized the notion of 'confrontation' and 'revelation'. Georg Lukács in his essay 'The Metaphysics of Tragedy', typifies this tendency when he claims that tragedy is 'the becoming real of the concrete essential nature of man'.[13]

If Maurya achieves some heroism, it is the heroism of endurance, the elevation that comes from facing reality without flinching. Yet, apart from the objections of the *Playboy* rioters or Gaelic League disgruntlement at the all too gritty depictions of Irish peasantry, the most common criticism of Synge has, ironically, tended to be the opposite offence of evasiveness, of tending towards the poetic flourish rather than the emboldened confrontation. This makes him a non-tragic writer. Though Daniel Corkery praises *Riders* as 'one of the few modern plays written, and successfully written, in the Greek *genre*',[14] he criticizes much of Synge's other work through unfavourable comparison with the great tragedies – *King Lear* and *Oedipus the King*. Unlike the creators of these masterpieces, Synge indulges in a misleading prettification, a weakness for the exotic or Romantic gesture that prevents him from truly seeing 'into the life of things'.[15] The impulse to evasiveness was always, Corkery claims, 'immanent in the depths of his being. That cause was his own reaction to the greyness of the world. The instant's escape from that sense of greyness was his moment of exaltation.'[16] Astutely, Corkery's complaint is not of a smug indifference or blindness. He recognizes that the playwright is so sensitive to the spectacle of a transient, destructive world, that he must flee from it; this is a reactive impulse, not just coy exoticism. Synge was so in thrall to the wonders of the imagination that he allegedly yielded to a distortive escapism from the greyness and dullness of the environment.[17] This is the cause of his supposed 'monological vision'. For Corkery, Synge's inflation of one faculty, the imagination, above all others is really a shirking of the fullness of aesthetic experience unlocked in the great tragedies and other serious drama. In other words, it is anti-tragic because epistemologically enfeebled. Great tragic art is founded, for Corkery as for countless other theorists, on a principle of revelation or ontological insight – seeing into 'the life of things'.[18] In Corkery's view, Synge can only witness reality through the distracting prism of 'aesthetic pleasure', hence his work prettifies the unsavoury, the grey and the dull. Synge shies away from the universal, if harrowing, spectacle revealed by the great tragedians because he cheats in the artistic game; like Christy Mahon, he tries to snatch the prize prematurely. Buffering reality by a vision of beauty, rather than finding the beauty within reality, he slips into an easy evasion. Corkery rhetorically poses the question: 'Is aesthetic pleasure preliminary to seeing into the life of things or is seeing into the life of things preliminary to aesthetic pleasure?'[19]

The critical habit of indicting Synge for evasion, for being merely a romantic Ascendency eavesdropper, has endured, though it has subtly transmuted. Critics such as Seamus Deane have complained that he remains oblivious to the political issues, such as the land movement and emigration, that played so large a role in the West of Ireland at the time.[20] Yeats famously praised Synge for being 'by nature unfitted to think a political thought'.[21] What Yeats regards as an artistic virtue, Deane interprets as an Ascendency vice. Whereas Yeats sees Synge's supposed apoliticism as a badge of authenticity, a mark of an artist motivated by a more profound and enduring vision than the transient, ephemeral world of politics, Deane sees it as the mark of the self-serving primitivist, wilfully eschewing ugly material realities for exotic self-indulgence. Synge is taken to task for luxuriating in fine language for its own sake, 'in which the political and the social are surrendered for the 'lonely impulse of delight'.[22] Just as Corkery explicitly indicts Synge for not being tragic enough, for not seeing into the 'life of things', so Deane indicts him for not seeing into the tragic life of Ireland, with its traumatic tale of emigration, famine and exploitation.

Before defending Synge against the complaints of Deane and others, one must concede that they – no less than the *Playboy* rioters – are bolstered by Synge's persistent claims that his drama stood not just for mythic verity but also for verisimilitude. In other words Synge aims, or claims to aim, for literal as well as symbolic truth.[23] In the prefaces to his major plays he boasts of strict fidelity to the real experience and spoken language of the peasantry.[24] Furthermore Synge was obsessed about the accuracy of his portrayal of Irish customs in his productions. Much to Lady Gregory's bemusement, he notoriously insisted that genuine pampooties be shipped from Aran for the first staging of *Riders*, and searched Dublin until he found an old woman originally from Aran who could rehearse the actors in the genuine funeral keen.[25] It is well to remember these attempts at authentic and literal representation before we too harshly condemn the 'philistinism' of Synge's early nationalist detractors, who complained about his violent and profane depictions of the Irish peasantry. Stripped of their more pious rhetorical flourishes and sensitivity to Ascendency condescension, these complaints are simply against perceived inaccuracies in Synge's depiction of rural Irish life, complaints which Synge's own avowed naturalism invites. Yet we can defend Synge by *not* taking him at his word. To be sure, his plays are energized by the particular – by the sounds, tastes, smells and textures of rural Ireland – but they are far more elliptical, abstract, modernist pieces than is often allowed.[26] The sensuous immediacy of their setting and the colloquial veracity of the Hiberno-English idiom suggest a literal or realist drama, but the plays brim with fertile tensions and multifaceted contradictions. Synge's work at once luxuriates in the everyday *and* holds it at arm's length.[27] The language foregrounds the unusual, the exotic and the gorgeous, even as it treats the mundane, the squalid and the violent.

This chapter seeks to explore the politico-cultural undertow to these tensions and contradictions in order to defend Synge against the charges of escapism and apoliticism. If the *Playboy* riotors and significant elements of contemporary Catholic nationalist opinion were infuriated at Synge's depictions of the Irish as profane and violent, then Deane is suspicious of his underestimation of brutality, his patrician portrayals of the impoverished peasantry as colourful and twee. There is also something appropriate in this critical shift: it accords with the celebrated interplay in Synge's work between fancy and fact, romance and reality. Christopher Innes sums up Synge's 'major themes' as 'illusory fantasy versus squalid reality, and the transmuting power of language'.[28] Synge famously declares in the Preface to *Playboy*, 'On the stage one must have reality, and one must have joy'(CWIV, 53–4). His repeatedly avowed mission was to create art of joy mingled with realism: 'what is highest in poetry', he writes,

> is always reached where the dreamer is leaning out to reality, or where the man of real life is lifted out of it, and in all the poets the greatest have both these elements, that is they are supremely engrossed with life, and yet with the wildness of their fancy they are always passing out of what is simple and plain. (CWII, 347)

Synge's language here is suggestive. The 'real life' is not to be countered by an alternative reality but by a 'dreamer' lifted out of life by the wildness of his 'fancy'. Real life is still there, however, and the dream, if admirable, is still but a dream. In Synge's dramatic practice we often find a tragic incompatibility behind this 'real life'/dream opposition that critics have tended to occlude, a disjunction between the fondness for exuberant language and the pained sensitivity to dismal reality.

Often this uneasy combination is taken at face value and, in general, the positive or comic aspects to Synge have been stressed. The standard reading sees him as a late Romantic and, in particular, a powerful advocate of the transformative powers of language and the imagination.

Robin Skelton's declaration that Synge's work heralds 'a triumph of spirit over reality' is typical.[29] Repeatedly, the orthodoxy goes, characters who embody this 'spirit' – Christy Mahon, Nora Burke, Martin and Mary Doul – forge a path of liberation from a repressive, mundane and emotionally impoverished society into a fantastical world of poetry and possibility. Similarly, more recent politically charged interpretations of Synge have tended to regard him as comic and imaginatively liberating. He has been lauded for constructing models of post-colonial liberation and for offering visionary alternatives to mundanity and oppression.[30] Christopher Murray claims that his 'whole artistic project was the celebration of energy directed towards forms of freedom', and speaks of 'a declaration of independence' in Synge's writing.[31] Even with *Riders* and *Deirdre*, the tendency has been to yoke them to the 'positive', 'joyful' message imputed to *The Playboy*: Murray claims that 'In Synge's tragedies, underpinned by Nietzsche's dialectic of Apollo and Dionysus from *The Birth of Tragedy* (1872), the song of liberation has a deeper, more sombre melody, but it is still as in the comedies, a song of deliverance.'[32] That song, this chapter argues, goes to a much more cracked tune than Murray allows and, in both comedies and tragedies, deliverance is fraught with an abiding unease. As often as not, it is a rejection as much as a celebration of human life.

The path towards imaginative liberation that Synge dramatizes is shot through with a fundamental *precariousness*. This valorization of language and poetry is typically layered with qualifications and ambivalence. We should remember that if Synge is on the side of the poets – Christy, Nora, Martin Doul, et al. – he also has a guilty eye on the ordinary villagers, and their materially squalid, imaginatively impoverished life. Like Pegeen Mike, he is a lover of stories but mistrusts actions. The characters occasionally take strength and solace from the power of poetry: Christy is notably transformed by the awakening of his own imaginative prowess. Yet both society and the natural world are more often presented as intractable, unredeemed by the lyrical and imaginative virtuosity that is preferred as an alternative. The scruple he feels at the 'imaginative alternative' he supposedly offers to mundane reality is evinced in a certain menace underlying the choices that Synge's heroes make. As Nora Burke knows well, her life with the Tramp on the open hills will be far from the idyll he has promised. The Douls head off triumphantly, but Timmy the Smith predicts that they will be drowned on the road south. Though presented as heroic, their choice of the imaginative alternative offered by blindness is still based in denial; it is not just poetic self-creation but also self-delusion, ignorance as much as exalted innocence. For all his enthusiasm about the autonomous imagination, part of Synge's sensibility continues to fret about the obstinacy of the external world, the brutal unavoidability of old-age and decay. This may, in part, derive from his early fascination with natural science. We certainly see it in certain parts of *Aran* (and in *Riders*) where the powers of nature seem irresistible, by language or anything else. Yeats occasionally finds solace in the notion that the 'external' world is formed by the power of the human imagination, that 'Death and life were not / Till man made up the whole, / Made lock, stock and barrel / Out of his bitter soul.'[33] For Synge, by contrast, the external world – with all its ugliness, death and decay – is never less than materially there, independent of the perceiver.

Synge's supposed valorization of imaginative escape is most undermined by the form of the theatrical medium itself. Christopher Innes rightly points out that 'In reading it is all too easy to take such "brave" words for reality, but the stage relentlessly exposes this mythologising as an illusion.'[34] After all, we never glimpse the world in which the Playboy or Nora or the Douls find triumphant refuge. Christopher Murray notes that 'Synge always leaves the audience in possession of the stage, while suggesting that the world off-stage (existing only in the imagination), exile or the unacceptable road, may have a lot more to be said for it, fictional though it be.'[35] Murray underestimates how this can cut both ways. If the unseen imaginative alternative rebukes the world left onstage, then the unredeemed stagnant society we are left with rebukes the efficacy of the imaginative alternative. The audience is always left with the emotionally and spiritually penurious society which is being rejected. We, like Pegeen Mike, lose the playboy of the western world once he leaves the stage, and have but the meagre consolation of Michael James: 'By the will of God, we'll have peace now for our drinks' (CWIV, 173). We have no more chance of following Christy or Nora into imaginative freedom than of following Deirdre and Naisi into the grave. That their liberation, apart from the beguiling poetic flourishes, always seems to happen off-stage suggests that, for Synge, imaginative redemption is a shakily held credo. It cannot be visualized, let alone dramatized. Just as the penurious social conditions in which the characters live give the lie to their elevated, intricately wrought language, so the recalcitrant materiality of the stage undercuts the poetic never-never land to which the heroes are bound. There is a metacommentary here. The dramatic form contradicts the dramatic action: the materiality of the stage rebutting the exuberance of language, Christy's physical smallness querying his heroic status, the immovable squalor of the shebeen and its denizens at odds with all the 'poetry talk'. It is in this knowing opposition that Synge's achievement as a dramatist lies, and it takes a production alert to the deflationary powers of the stage, its capacity to contradict the imaginative extravagance of the characters, to realize properly these creative tensions.

Synge's plays are characterized by a broken aesthetic or imaginative promise. The breach between fact and fancy, reality and illusion cannot be healed; this feature is of decisive significance in the light of tragic theory. If tragedy has been prized for its ennobling confrontation of desolation, there is, as we saw in the Introduction, an opposing tendency to laud it for various transformative or redemptive powers, in which suffering and loss are somehow incorporated into a meaningful context. One way in which this transformation is seen to occur is through the aesthetic alchemy of language and representation. Nietzsche's opposition between the Dionysian and the Apollonian forces is perhaps the most famous manifestation of these contesting poles, embracing as it does a tragedy which confronts abysmal, chaotic reality but at the same time transmutes it into rapturously coherent lyricism. Synge's work, with its own uneasy oscillations between 'reality' and 'joy' instructively replicates that polarity and, as is bluntly evident in his early, rejected play, *When the Moon has Set*, Synge was much influenced by Nietzsche's writings. Yet the two poles are always restless and uneasy bedfellows in Synge's work. We sometimes have the impression that, as in his successor and urban imitator Sean O'Casey, the language of his characters, though carefully crafted and lyrically enhanced, seems to counterpoint and heighten, rather than sweeten or redeem, the squalor of their material conditions. Like Pegeen Mike, Synge yearns for a route out of oppressive, dismal reality but the alternative preferred, like the promises of Martin Doul or the Tramp, turn out to be chimerical. What distinguishes his work and prevents him from sliding into mere confusion and inconsistency is his anxious interrogation of his own tendency to seek poetic transformation: the undertow of guilt that queries and undermines the temptations of imaginative escape.

Reality or romance?

Gloom came early to Synge. Friends and contemporaries remember him as a stereotypically Keatsian personality: sickly, ponderous, aloof and melancholy, yet with an explosive sensuous passion for the phenomenal world.[36] Yeats, in all his eulogizing, repeatedly uses the terms 'morbid' and 'melancholy' in describing the younger man.[37] However, for Yeats, this sensibility distinguishes rather than demeans him: 'All minds that have a wisdom come of tragic reality seem morbid to those that are accustomed to writers who have not faced reality at all.'[38] Throughout Synge's work there is an obsessive dread of death and decay. Yeats recognized this feature, but felt that the fresh winds of Aran purged him of unhealthy melancholia.[39] Though not so overt as his earliest pieces, there is plenty of blackness interwoven with the primitivist joys of *Aran*, emerging at the two funerals he attends or when, alone in a squall, his mind settles on destruction and the transience of the natural world. So far as the drama is concerned, we need not go to the 'tragedies' and Deirdre's macabre obsessions with old age, the loss of beauty and the loss of love to find the sombre, sometimes desperate tone.[40] It is a thematic bulwark of the comedies as well, providing the incentive, along with the imaginative and emotional impoverishment that governs social relations, to reject stagnant society and embrace a sensuous world of poetic intensity:

> It's a pitiful thing to be getting old, but it's a queer thing surely ... It's a queer thing to see an old man sitting up there in his bed, with no teeth in him, and a rough word in his mouth, and his chin the way it would take the bark from the edge of an oak board you'd have building a door ... God forgive me, Michael Dara, we'll all be getting old but it's a queer thing surely.
>
> Nora Burke, *The Shadow of the Glen* (CWIII, 53)

> It's as good a right you have, surely, Sarah Casey, but what good will it do? Is it putting that ring on your finger will keep you from getting an aged woman and losing the fine face you have, or be easing your pains ...
>
> Mary Byrne, *The Tinkers Wedding* (CWIV, 37)

Decay, the fear of decay, is always beneath the surface, raising its head at expected and unexpected moments. In all Synge's plays, there are repeated allusions to loss – of freedom, of imagination, of beauty, of life. A glance at his early work makes this unsurprising. The overwrought, autobiographical *Vita Vecchia* and *Étude Morbide* are riddled with contemplations on the passing of beauty and his own mortality.

However, and despite Synge's early convictions of scientific atheism, the former contains several Job-like moments of enraged resistance, poignantly inflected with the sense of sin and guilt imbued by Synge's evangelical upbringing:

> Thrice cruel fell my fate,
> Did I, death tormented, see,
> A God, inhuman, great,
> Sit weaving woes for me.
>
> So hung as Hell the world,
> Death's light with venom stung,
> Toward God high taunts I hurled,
> With cursing parched my tongue. (II, 22)

The parallel with Job is made explicit in *Études Morbide* when, in his atheism, Synge feels bereft of Job's clear target for misfortune: 'I feel a lack in my scepticism which leaves no name for malediction, and envy Job who had his choice to curse God and die' (CWII, 30). The loss of his faith was a momentous formative experience for Synge. The notion of the absent God is a staple of much twentieth-century tragic theory: exemplary of his time, Synge felt the absence acutely.[41] Synge's creative life was fuelled by the search to replace the absent God, to find a surrogate faith following the harrowing loss of childhood certainty. The Job-like impulse to curse God, coupled with the distressed intimation that there was no God to curse, finds its expression in Synge's later fascination with the funeral keen, a custom which, though in his mind a pagan impulse, also seemed to carry a cathartic and ennobling sense of raillery against Providence. As a counterbalance to this impulse towards impassioned protest, Synge is later to favour the stoic yet nonetheless heroic passivity of Maurya: 'No man at all can be living for ever, and we must be satisfied' (CWIII, 27).[42] Yet this attitude of stoicism or stasis is not just the alternative to Jobean resistance, but a mean between it and an impulse towards withdrawal or oblivion. Significantly, Synge said to Yeats that he sought to create a drama which synthesized asceticism, stoicism and ecstasy, and we find these conflicting impulses throughout his work.[43] More than occasionally, the Beckettian urge for annihilation slips overtly into Synge's contemplations: 'Yet bliss our credence new / That sleeping soothes the strife, / annihilation due / To pall the pang of life' (*Vita Vecchia*, CWII, 23). This siren call of oblivion occurs particularly in the early work, but a strain of the sensibility remains throughout the drama, just as on Aran the sea sometimes exerts an alluring pull towards amnesia.

Yet it would be a mistake to think of Synge as simply gloomy. Overwhelmingly, his melancholy humour and his constant contemplations on death and decay serve an opposite impulse, vitalizing a keen, exuberant sensibility made animate by its own threatened extinction:

> I am haunted by the briefness of my world. It brings me at times a passionate thirst for the fulfilment of every passive or active capacity of my person. It seems a crime that I should go home and sleep in trite sheets while heaven and earth slip away from me for ever... . (CWII, 20)

This, too, is very Keatsian: the more intense the sensation, the more overshadowed it is by inevitable loss. It is the counterpoint that is often transmitted in the autobiographical writings, usually when Synge is speaking of nature. He devours the glories of the living world around him. Yet the opposing temptations of withdrawal and oblivion hover around as a subtextual principle. The strange identification between the two opposites, always subtly evident in Synge's work, is made explicit in the affirmation/renunciation of Synge's last play, *Deirdre of the Sorrows*. Here, the two conflicting urges – to live, yet to escape the transience of life – reach a climactic nexus when Naisi and Deirdre settle on the grave, not as a rejection of life, but as a triumphant and hubristic assertion of youth and sensual experience against its decay and temporal waning. If it is true that comedies end in marriage and tragedies in death, then the grave forming the centrepiece of the third act is both tomb and marital bed: 'it's that grave when it's closed will make us one forever, and we two lovers have had great space without weariness or growing old or any sadness of the mind' (CWIV, 251).[44] Here, the affirmation of life seems indistinguishable from its renunciation.

Synge's arrival at a vista where the private world of imagination, passion and autonomy was in conflict with the objective world – with both the 'natural' world of decay and death and the 'artificial' world of poverty and stilted social relations – is traceable from his early development. Spurning his family background and religion gave him autonomy as an artist, but it also made him lonely and led to a dissonance in sensibility that he never fully overcame. He never managed to reconcile the religious, scientific and romantic impulses that underran his work. Yet it was precisely this failure that led to the constructive tensions and ambivalences of his best plays.

Throughout his life, he was haunted by an awareness of himself as betrayer. The religious sensibility instilled by his mother was strongly evangelical and puritanical, encouraging an image of a base, fallen human race, bestial and sinful apart from the intervening promise of divine salvation. As W. J. Mc Cormack's biography demonstrates, Synge's imaginative formation is inextricably meshed with his Protestant upbringing.[45] When Synge cast off his earlier religion, this Protestant sensibility was to mutate, not disappear. Like Joyce he kept the *form* of religious devotion even as he threw off its doctrinal content.[46] Though he considers the forces which encouraged the abandonment of his religion to have done him 'an important service' (CWII, 10), it was nonetheless a traumatic renunciation. The process was set in motion by the fascination with natural history he felt in his youth. He spent many hours rambling with his cousin Florence Ross around the Wicklow hills, birdwatching and collecting specimens of flowers and plants. Reading Darwin's theory of evolution, he comes across a passage which emphasizes the similarity between a man's hand and a bird's wing. The fourteen-year-old Synge has a violent reaction:

> I flung the book aside and rushed out into the open air – it was summer and we were in the country – the sky seemed to have lost its blue and the grass its green. I lay down and winced in an agony of doubt. My studies showed me the force of what I read, [and] the more I put it from me the more it rushed back with new instances and power (CWII, 10–11).[47]

However, even as he threw off the yoke of his religious upbringing Synge was afflicted by its systems. Ceasing to believe in religion is configured as a specifically religious betrayal: 'It seemed that I was become the playfellow of Judas. Incest and parricide were but a consequence of the idea that possessed me' (CWII, 11). The feelings of guilt attended by membership of his privileged class were buttressed rather than alleviated by those engendered by the betrayal of his class and religion. The further removed from his origins he became, the more guilty he felt for this abnegation. Curiously, a guilty religious sensibility merges with a new scientism. Another passage from his autobiography illustrates this alliance (or misalliance). Musing on his ill-health, he experiences an ominous sensation:

> This ill health led to a curious resolution which has explained in some measure all my subsequent evolution. Without knowing, or,

as far as I can remember, hearing anything about doctrines of hered-
ity I surmised that unhealthy parents should have unhealthy children – my rabbit breeding may have put the idea into my head.
Therefore, I said, I am unhealthy, and if I marry I will have
unhealthy children. But I will never create beings to suffer as I am
suffering, so I will never marry. I do not know how old I was when I
came to this decision, but I was between thirteen and fifteen and it
caused me horrible misery. (CWII, 9)

That Synge asserts the importance of this intimation in such strong
terms, stressing that it explains 'all my subsequent evolution', is telling.
It is probable that, having heard 'nothing about the doctrines of hered-
ity', the young Synge, saturated in the Fall doctrine, transmuted the doctrine of poisoned inheritance from religion to genetics. (As we shall see
later, guilt, particularly familial guilt, is a strong force in his work.) That
he sees himself as in some way 'contaminated', affording the memory
such importance in his development, is richly significant. The drift from
the theological to the physical and corporeal was to have continued
importance for him throughout his development.

Synge's early encounters with science and nature were formative.
Ever eager to energize his drama with the immediacy of live experience, he disdained the mythic and occult extravagance of his fellow
Irish revivalists. It is probable that Synge's insistence on the priority of
'reality' – of the smells, tastes, textures and sounds of the living world –
is an enabling residue from his earlier pull towards natural science. His
fascination with the natural world, which was also the source of
trauma since it seemed to confirm the unbending, inexorable forces of
Nature, was redeemed by a sensuous, artistic appropriation of its phenomena, and yielded in maturity a coupling of the spiritual with the
physically natural. If natural science ousted religion's supremacy in
Synge's worldview, then a sublimated religious or spiritual impulse
replied by transmuting his scientific naturalism into an aesthetic
system. Synge scintillated his science with an overlay of romanticism.
Yet, not surprisingly, the impulses often conflicted: Synge was at different times an objective journalist/ethnographer and a subjective
artist. Musical training was also an important formative influence and
fed into his romanticism, most overtly in *When the Moon has Set* and
certain passages of *The Aran Islands*. Synge records the divided sensibility of his late teenage years with a revealing triumvirate: 'I wished to be
at once Shakespeare, Beethoven and Darwin; my ambition was bound-
less and mounted to real torture in my life' (CWII, 12).

The torture must have come not just from vaunting ambition, but from the conflicting directions in which it pulled him.

Synge's hostility to ephemerality and over-abstraction, inculcated by his convictions in natural science, may be the root of a crucial facet of his poetic technique. Synge, as one critic astutely observed,[48] indulges in a plenitude of extravagant simile to the virtual exclusion of metaphor or symbol: 'CHRISTY [*with rapture*]. If the mitred bishops seen you that time, they'd be the like of the holy prophets, I'm thinking, do be straining the bars of Paradise to lay eyes on the Lady Helen of Troy' (CWIV, 149); 'MARY DOUL [*defiantly*]. When the skin shrinks on your chin, Molly Byrne, there won't be the like of you for a shrunk hag in the four corners of Ireland' (CWIII, 121). The preponderance of 'like', 'as' and 'the way' indicates an empirical reluctance to undermine the autonomy and particularity of observed phenomena – an unwillingness to bring objects any further than comparison. He pulls short of metaphor, with its power to pass through mere comparison into contiguity, and is far from the polysemanticism of a Yeatsian symbol. For all Synge's espousal of imaginative virtuosity, things stay the same. Imagination and poetry can change the perceiver, the way they change Christy, but their powers are severely circumscribed in the face of intractable reality. Despite the accusations of prettification, Synge tacitly admits the recalcitrance of the external world. The mirror of representation and the lamp of imagination operate together, but they are also tragically incommensurate.

Synge's early infatuation with natural science – apart from the suffering imposed by his atheistic conclusions – was the largely positive, or at least innocuous, interest of a specimen-collector. During his apprenticeship in Aran, however, his attitude substantially mutated as he developed the public voice of his drama. Science and the external world no longer cleave seamlessly to a luxuriant aesthetic, but gradually start to prove resistant to imaginative appropriation. In Aran, the passage from religion to science, to an aestheticized construction of nature, yields to a disruptive and distressful intrusion of a historical and political consciousness. Commentators are right to emphasize the transformative impact of Aran on Synge.[49] We can discern a maturing sensibility over the course of his visits. Initially Synge has the values of a primitivist (though, significantly, a primitivism steeled with far more scientific credentials than that of his fellow revivalists[50]): 'The absence of the heavy boot of Europe has preserved to these people the agile walk of the wild animal, while the general simplicity of their lives has given them many other points of physical perfection' (CWII, 66). He endorses the Yeatsian 'noble and beggarman' ideology, contrasting both the aristocratic thoroughbred and the wild stallion with the unfavourable middle-class carthorse (CWII, 66). The islanders are admired and envied for their proximity to natural reality, a conjunction denied the modern, cosmopolitan, urban dweller.

But Synge's attitude to nature as authority becomes ambivalent. The progression of his Aran trips has generally been seen as one in which he matures from a subjectivist romanticism to a more objective stance of genuine sympathy for the life of the islanders. This shift in perspective corresponds with his dualistic natural vision. Initially nature is an alluring prospect, an imprimatur of origin, authenticity and verity which fills an acute gap in Synge's fissured, alienated identity.[51] Nature is equated with the Good, the original, Wordsworth championed as his personal laureate. But even on his earliest visit to Aran he encounters another Nature, one which is cruel and destructive. Nowhere is this impression stronger than in the powerful relentless sea. Curragh-bound in a tempest or gazing out on the inexorable swell, Synge's thoughts seem to instinctively return to familiar obsessions of mortality and decay. These themes, so well rehearsed in *Vita Vecchia* and *Étude Morbide*, and in the philosophical passages of *When the Moon has Set*, occur here in a more public environment. A tension develops. If it is natural to die, it is best to die in a natural way. On his first visit to Aran, in a particularly threatening squall, Synge decides that 'if we were dropped into the blue chasms of the waves, this death, with the fresh saltiness of the sea in one's teeth, would be better than most deaths one is likely to meet' (CWII, 97). Though this is an observation that Synge would be unlikely to make on later visits, even now his own vision of the tragic is being unravelled in these confessional passages, where he discovers two sides to 'nature' – intrinsic, authentic and true on the one hand, yet wildly destructive and cruelly transient on the other. The celebrated description of the funeral in Aran I is exemplary of this construction – death is seen as terrible and inevitable, yet the natives' communal response is admired for its authenticity and deep, organic connection with nature. An old woman has died, but the attitude of the people extends beyond individual mourning to find some putatively universal resonance. During the funeral, thunder starts to rumble and hailstones fall, for in Inishmaan, 'one is forced to believe in a sympathy between man and nature, and at this moment when the thunder sounded a death-peal of extraordinary grandeur above the voices of the women, I could see faces near me stiff and drawn with emotion' (CWII, 75). This mysterious sympathy is a prelude for a moment of sheer *anagnorisis* which is more communal than individual. The passage is reminiscent of Yeats's Nietzschean definition of tragedy as 'the breaking down of dykes that separate man from man'[52]:

> The grief of the keen is no personal complaint for the death of one woman over eighty years, but seems to contain the whole passionate rage that lurks somewhere in every native of the island. In this cry of pain the inner consciousness of the people seems to lay itself bare for an instant, and to reveal the mood of beings who feel their isolation in the face of a universe that wars on them with winds and seas. They are usually silent, but in the presence of death all outward show of indifference or patience is forgotten, and they shriek with pitiable despair before the horror of the fate to which they all are doomed. (CWII, 75)

The communion with nature which the people enjoy is valued and envied – Synge can witness, but not share it. The theatre generates a similar arena of communal experience from which the author is absent. One can almost feel the strain this scene exerts on its medium, and sense Synge's urge to give the *caoine* dramatic incarnation, as he was to do in *Riders to the Sea*. Just as the keen 'contains' the communal rage, so theatre is needed to contain the communal catharsis of the keen. Speaking of this episode, Synge declares that 'the supreme interest of this island lies in the strange concord that exists between the people and the impersonal limited but powerful impulses of the nature that is round them' (CWII, 75n). For Synge, proximity to 'Nature' transforms the islanders into a conduit for the tragedy of loss, decay and death. They are ennobled by this proximity, by their mediatory role, and by the heroic raillery with which they meet the piercingly vivid insights that this organic connection imparts. The way Synge bears witness, and the symbolic mould in which he casts his experiences, are telling indications of his developing aesthetic. He goes on to construct the tragic insight of the islanders at the funeral in the explicitly revelatory terms of Nietzsche or Schopenhauer, and even speaks of the 'veil' in a manner strikingly similar to the latter's 'veil of Maya.' After the funeral the women are still sobbing, but already the protective layers of habit are reforming: 'They were still sobbing and shaken with grief, yet they were beginning to talk again of the daily trifles that veil from them the terror of the world' (CWII, 75).

A few pages after the above funeral scene, following some evictions on the island, the idiom of tragic revelation slides into a highly political setting.[53] The last policeman has embarked onto the steamer, and an old woman comes forward 'pointing at the bailiff and waving her withered arms with extraordinary rage.' She identifies the man as her own son and proceeds to vilify him with such fury that Synge fears her son will be stoned before he gets back to his cottage.

> On these islands the women live only for their children, and it is hard to estimate the power of the impulse that made this old woman stand out and curse her son.
>   In the fury of her speech I seem to look *again* into the strangely reticent temperament of the islanders, and to feel the passionate spirit that expresses itself, at odd moments only, with magnificent words and gestures [Emphasis mine]. (CWII, 92)

Again, the veil breaks away and Synge bears reverent witness to the islanders' rebellious spirit. Here, though, the event cannot be generalized in terms of a communal response to cosmic inevitability – 'the fate to which they are all doomed'. The tragic moment in this instance comes from too specific and political a source. The evictions occur on the island because a man called Patrick has 'sold his honour' and will identify cattle for the bailiff. Initially, 'the mechanical police' call on homesteads where pretexts – money from relatives, an intervening doctor – are found to forestall the evictions but, finally, they arrive at a house where an old women has no relatives to intercede for her:

> She belonged to one of the most primitive families on the island and she shook with uncontrollable fury as she saw the strange armed men who spoke a language she did not understand driving her from the hearth she had brooded on for thirty years. For these people the outrage to the hearth is the supreme catastrophe ... the outrage to a tomb in China probably gives no greater shock to the Chinese than the outrage to a hearth in Inishmaan gives to the people. (CWII, 89)

The language of 'the supreme catastrophe' is intoned of this highly social and political tragic occurrence in a manner remarkably similar to the universalism of the funeral scene.

Daniel Corkery wonders suspiciously why Synge chose to dramatize the drowning, but not this eviction scene.[54] He regards Synge's *Aran* as depicting the islanders' sufferings – in response to a funeral or sea-tempest – in grandiloquent gesture, eliding the bleak, quotidian miseries and triumphs of their everyday life. It is true that references to famine, typhus and emigration are rare and often stated in a deadpan, factual way, but it would be a mistake to regard this tone as simply indifferent. On later trips to Aran an interesting pattern emerges in which mention of the plight of the people oscillates uninterruptedly with recounting of supernatural tales Synge has been told on the island. One can simply place the emphasis on Synge as a folklorist, and indict him for evading or prettifying the harsh material realities around him; alternatively, one can decipher within these asides a potent register of a silent yet ever-present subtext to the chronicle. Mary C. King provides a fascinating reading of the fairy tales in the text as allegories of the various suffering of the islanders: emigration, famine, cholera. 'This tight but non-linear structuring of the thematic pattern', claims King, 'suggests that Synge was very well aware of the symbolic interactions between the tales the people told, the way they told them, and the social and historical forces at work in their daily lives.'[55] This allows for ambivalent, contradictory elements in Synge: an urge to repress the suffering around him to be sure, but also a deep sense of guilt as passive witness, which cannot find its catharsis in an easy representation, but must sublimate its burden from the natural to the supernatural.

Book IV, which is pervaded by an atmosphere of suffering and desolation, sees both the storytelling and its repressed underside reach their highest intensity. In one extended episode Synge recounts in eerily deadpan succession how a young woman he knows well is dying of typhus; how her brothers and father have risked their lives in a rough sea to find help on the north island; and how that morning a young man's drowned body was washed ashore. '[S]huddering with cold and misery', he returns to his cottage to find that the woman will likely be dead in the morning – if the men make it back from the north island at all, it will be too late; there are no boards to make a coffin for the woman and there are two other women and an infant also afflicted by the fever. In a howling hurricane (in the islands, where the people are so deeply connected with their environment, Nature spontaneously follows the rules of pathetic fallacy), Synge makes his way home past the cottage stricken by typhus and the house of the drowned man. That evening he sits up with an old man talking of the 'sorrows of the people' (CWII, 158–9). This dense interlude of the people's suffering punctuates the folklore. Immediately after recounting these island tragedies, Synge relays a story told him by the old man. This story, of a woman taken by the fairies, has an obvious thematic linkage to the actuality of the woman dying of typhus, but also seems to bear a relation to *Riders to the Sea*. There is a wish-fulfillment element to the tale: its heroine, apparently dead and buried, has really only been stolen by the fairies. She comes back nightly to feed her child and to take milk and potatoes from the dresser. She tells the men that she is hungry, for the fairies give her no food. Happily though, she can be freed from captivity if the men of the house follow her instructions. She and the fairies 'would all be leaving that part of the country on the Oidhche Shamhna, and there would be four or five hundred of them riding on horses, and herself would be on a grey horse, riding behind a young man' (CWII, 159). She instructs the men to throw something on her and on the young man, so that they would fall over on the ground and be saved. The symbolic parallels of this tale, with its elements of death, disappearance and hunger, are resonant not only with the woman who, afflicted with typhus, cannot be rescued, but also with other repressed communal memories of famine and emigration. The tale provides a surrogate, if subtextual, re-enactment of these tragedies, here granted a happy outcome. Interestingly, in *Riders*, Synge reverses the palliative aspect of the folklore: Maurya is unable to give bread to her son on the grey horse, and cannot or will not save him. Synge preserves the mythic structure gleaned from the islanders, yet expunges the wishful mythic solace. In this case, then, far from being an anthropologist interested only in the quaint habits and customs of the natives, Synge unleashes the latent tragic potential of their tale, hitherto hidden by a traumatic amnesia, and derived from socially based sufferings, not from an irremediable universal conflict.

Following the story, he directly returns to the unalleviated natural world and the funeral of the drowned man. This he finds more harrowing than the funeral of Aran I:

> the grief of the people was of a different kind, as they had come to bury a young man who had died in his first manhood, instead of an old woman of eighty. For this reason the keen lost a part of its formal nature, and was recited as the expression of intense personal grief by the young men and women of the man's own family. (CWII, 160–1)

The formalized, orchestrated aspects of the keen are thinner here than before, the veil of which he spoke then flimsier and more violently stripped away; the grief of the mourners is exposed with less ritualistic mediation, less formalized protection. As theatre it is more exposed and immediate; the communal edifice cracks and the conventions of the keen, designed to contain abandonment, are themselves abandoned. However, as we saw in the Introduction, when the conventional formal elements of tragedy are pared back, tragic content can emerge more intensely. Murray Krieger diagnoses a specifically modern tragedy in these terms:

> [P]icture a world into which Dionysus cannot be reabsorbed by way of the Apollonian with its final assertion of Greek 'cheerfulness' and aesthetic form ... Our modern tragic vision is the Dionysian vision still, except that the visionary is now utterly lost, since there is no cosmic order to allow a return to the world for him who has dared stray beyond.[56]

Synge's Godless eyes – bracketing for a moment his wilful elision of the islanders' own devout Catholicism – are here moving towards that desolate vision. The mother of the household picks up a skull from the open grave – that of her own mother – and 'began keening and shrieking over it with the wildest lamentation' (CWII, 161). Synge's earlier admiration of the islanders' enviable connection with Nature coexisting with the pain of their loss, is here replaced by the recognition of a highly anguished torment, too traumatic for ritualized containment. However, as before, Synge sees a generalized significance in this atmosphere of death. After the funeral, he walks down to the shore to watch some men drag-net fishing. Speaking to them, he feels that all are 'under a judgment of death': 'I knew that every one of them would be drowned in the sea in a few years and battered naked on the rocks, or would die in his own cottage and be buried with another fearful scene in the graveyard I had come from' (CWII, 162). Synge vastly overestimates the number of drownings likely to occur;[57] the casual way in which he inserts the far more likely place of death – the man's own home – indicates a scarcely concealed impulse to distance himself from a mortality which he shares. Even when he is being at his most confrontational, there is still an element of evasion. He is assiduous throughout in using the third rather than first person, speaking of the mortality of the islanders rather than contemplating his own mortality, which he obsessed over in his pre-Aran writings. In a poignant irony, Martin McDonough and many of Synge's other friends from the islands were destined to spend their old age reminiscing to literary researchers on the long-dead John Synge.

Synge began writing his serious drama in 1902, following his fifth and last visit to Aran and following the abortive escapism of *When the Moon has Set* (written 1900–1, between his third and fourth visits). His understanding of the hostility and recalcitrance of the external world as a daily struggle, not just a cosmic conflict, will generate the power and immediacy of this theatrical art. Had Synge not taken these trips, Yeats probably could not have claimed of him that 'He loves all that has edge, all that is salt in the mouth, all that is rough to the hand, all that heightens the emotions by contest, all that stings into life the sense of tragedy.'[58] The suffering he saw in Aran complicated his early tendency towards moroseness in important ways. Synge's sensibility refuses that strain in twentieth-century writing which finds integrative or archetypal patterns behind historical change. Not for Synge the Yeatsian consolations of the gyres, or the construction of some historically governing mythic structure. As many commentators have stressed, such an escape was particularly alluring to the Anglo-Irish psyche of the time which, faced with the prospect of its own demise, sought a backdoor to Byzantium. But despite the enticements of this evasion, Synge's philosophical attitude doesn't permit it. In his world, things pass away and are not built again.

One might suppose that this resistance to ahistoricism renders his aesthetic especially sensitive to the particularities of the culture and politics of his time; that bereft of modernist guile, Synge's work will be less prone to political evasion or easy platitude, and will more honestly incorporate its surrounding historical forcefields. However, such an apologia, founded on Synge's acute sensitivity to the bleak reality of loss, might be countered with the contention that the idea of 'loss' can itself be hypostasized as a transcendent constant, gaining therein the status of a universal, metaphysical category. A 'disengagement from history', as Seamus Deane puts it, is 'achieved by the constant relocation of the specific sequence of incidents in the frame of the universal, human condition'.[59] Hence, the critical orthodoxy runs, the setting of *Riders to the Sea* off the west coast of Ireland is simply the pretext for the expression of fundamental, irremediable features of the human condition. However, one need not view Synge in these terms. The concept of universal loss is a risky business, which carries the germ of its own undoing. The permanent denial of all permanence is a shaky philosophical structure, for by its definition transience is hostile to the process of transcendence. Based in temporal flow, it is difficult to make timeless. When the 'form' of loss is emptied of historical content, it ceases to have any meaning: to be capable of passing away, things must have some material existence. The idea of inevitable loss must be deduced a posteriori and arrived at through a derivative process. To be constructed and maintained, it must originate and rejuvenate in the phenomenal world, where loss is often found as *dispossession* – with its connotations of human agency, not natural inevitability. In other words, time may change everything, but only in *context*, and this context includes the web of human relations. This is not to claim that all loss is politically derived, but a great deal, conceived of as inevitable and irremediable, has been derived from socially determined factors and *is* reparable. The common metaphysical abstraction of 'Time' as a privileged category, with the events of history merely accidental accoutrements caught in its barbs, is in danger of being exposed by the idea of loss. (Similarly, the idea of a cosmic, generalized tragedy privileged above the 'mere' catastrophes of everyday life is endangered by the former's ultimate parasitism on the latter.) So the craving for some essence prior to phenomenal reality is undermined by the inevitably phenomenological, grounded nature of change and loss. The generalization 'We all must die' necessarily begins in observation and experience. Despite the ideological construction of loss as a transcendent constant, it must, in truth, have an ultimate immanence, always open to the actuality of historical process.

If this is so, then, for all its putative universality, traces of history and immanent social concerns may inflect Synge's personal reflections, like the 'thousand militia', or the 'loosed khaki cutthroats' that drift around *The Playboy of the Western World*. Nonetheless, as already seen, the impulse towards evasion – as well as evasion itself – has its register in his work. If the obstinately realist dimension of Synge's aesthetic makes it potentially difficult for him to avoid the nightmare of history – with its burden of Ascendancy guilt and prospect of Ascendancy demise – escape into some primitivist Eden has, nonetheless, a seductive allure. However, Synge not only negotiates this impulse to evade, he also inscribes the temptation in his work. Coexisting with his veneration of the imagination is an anguished consciousness of a tendency to evasive exoticization. The Douls sidestep the bleak, discomfiting world they momentarily experience by choosing to return to a soothing darkness which also spells their destruction. Interestingly, one of the original enticements proffered by Timmy the Smith is both brutal, and political:

MARY DOUL [*persuasively, to* TIMMY]. Maybe they're hanging a thief, above at the bit of a tree? I'm told its a great sight to see a man hanging by his neck, but what joy would that be to ourselves, and we not seeing at all?

TIMMY [*More pleasantly*]. They're hanging no one this day, Mary Doul, and yet with the help of God, you'll see a power hanged before you die. (CWIII, 78–9)

Like Pegeen Mike, the Douls discover a great distance between the idea of brutality and its actual enactment. When they find themselves entrapped and alienated in an imaginatively impoverished society, where self-worth and identity are undermined by the drudgery of material labour, they choose an evasion of the stubborn reality principle. Martin Doul is forced into the world of labour and exchange but opts to return to the untainted realm of imaginative freedom and self-identity, unbeholden to the obligations of material survival. This play stands in interesting opposition to *Riders to the Sea*: Maurya's resolution is achieved through an endurance of social reality, by passing through and surviving all the torments of the world; the Douls achieve theirs through the aestheticization of an ugly reality, a manoeuvre that is irremediably based in delusion. If Maurya heroically confronts, then the Douls comically evade.[60] Yet as the Douls stumble offstage to their deaths, we might ponder which play is really the more tragic.

For all Synge's advocacy of the powers of the imagination and evident approval of the spry lyricism of Martin Doul, there is a discomfiting ambivalence between this espousal and an acknowledgement of the recalcitrance of social imperatives and factual reality. The rhetorical prowess and imaginative verve of the Douls may give them succour after the return of their blindness, but there is a poignancy in the audience's realization that, while they may succeed in changing the world of their perceptions, they are helpless in the face of a brutally real environment. At the end of the play, when Martin declares that they will go to the South, where 'the people will have kind voices maybe', there is a deliberate duplicity in his hopeful prediction: 'we *won't know* their bad looks or their villainy at all' [my emphasis] (CWIII, 149). Yeats praises Synge for his 'dream of the impossibly noble life' and regards the Douls in a heroic light:

> these two blind people of *The Well of the Saints* are so transformed by the dream that they choose blindness rather than reality. He tells us of realities, but he knows that art has never taken more

than its symbols from anything that the eye can see or the hand measure.[61]

This aesthetic sounds far more like that of Yeats himself. Synge, on the other hand, is painfully aware of a far less biddable external world than suggested here.[62] In an unpublished manuscript, he reveals his ambivalence about poetic symbolism, yearning for a way to validate it with the science which he trusts much more:

> Blake taught me that true imagination was a view of the eternal symbols of Being, but who may know in his own mind or that of others these symbols from mere hallucinations. I am driven back on science – of all names the most abused. If science is a learning of the truth, nature and imagination being a less immediate knowledge of the same, the two when perfect will coincide.[63]

Regarding science as the source of a more 'immediate' knowledge of truth than nature and the imagination puts Synge in the opposite camp to Yeats. He never found that magical cooperation between art and nature that he sought. The scientist in Synge refuses the idea that the imagination can wholly redeem and transform reality. It can, as in *Playboy*, transform people's perceptions of themselves, and this can unleash repressed aspects of their personality, but perceptions of the external world are far less liberating. Rather, in the teeth of unbending reality, the powers of imagination and poetry are tragically limited. The scene where Martin Doul woos Molly Byrne, though the comic incongruity can be emphasized in performance, is a profoundly poignant encounter. He manages to sway her, but she resists and, though critics have castigated her cowardice, there is something preordained about her resistance. After all, the audience see an old withered man, sensitive and poetically gifted though he may be, endeavour to turn the head of a young beautiful woman and lure her to a life of majestic penury. We might upbraid Molly for choosing the bourgeois safety of Timmy the smith, but ultimately Martin's lyrical temptations are not enough. In a comparable scene from *The Shadow of the Glen*, Nora follows the tramp away from her home comforts and, though she does so defiantly, she has no choice and is not taken in by his promises of splendid squalor.[64] Against the brutal ever-encroaching vagaries of material survival, suffering, transience and decay, Synge's protagonists can heroically pitch their measure of poetry, but, momentarily assuaged, reality will return. Hence Timmy the Smith's prediction that 'the two of them will be drowned together in a short while, surely' (CWIII, 151).

The image of the Douls walking off-stage to their deaths is, perhaps, the moment when Synge's self-critique is at its sharpest: here, he accuses himself of the evasiveness that Seamus Deane later lays at his door. For the Douls, like the Playboy, like the Tinkers, like Nora Burke and the tramp, manifest the imaginative principle within the play. Synge famously espoused proximity to the 'real world', to the foul rag and bone shop of lived experience, as a means of vitalizing art. Yet if he held that reality transforms the imagination, he could not (despite the optimistic reading of many critics) muster the reciprocal confidence that imagination transforms reality. Again, there are many reasons for this lack of faith, not least of which, as already seen, is his early and deeply affecting encounter with the writings of Darwin. Part of Synge's sensibility, nurtured by his botanical forays around Wicklow during his teenage years, is that of the natural scientist. (This ethos of the specimen collector no doubt influenced the anthropological tone of his early visits to Aran.) This element of his development, along with his own physical illness, made it impossible for him to forget the body, and the natural shocks that flesh is heir to. It gives him a sense of the intractibility of external reality, with its prospect of old age, death, loss and the pressing needs for material survival. For all his manifestos on the necessity for imaginative art to root itself in the real world, Synge feels an acute incongruity and guilt for aestheticizing the world around him, for blacking out (or painting over) harrowing pictures of reality.

The art of guilt

The tendency to occlude unpalatable facts is evident early in Synge's career when, as already noted, a strong pull towards amnesia is at its most explicit. For all the seductive charms of escape, it proves a fraught, highly ambiguous temptation. In *Aran*, there is an eerie dream episode where the siren-call is only checked at the last moment, and we feel the return from an abyss. It begins with a 'rhythm of music beginning far away on some stringed instrument. When it was quite near the sound began to move in my nerves and blood, and to urge me to dance with them.' There is a profound danger in this alluring dance:

I knew that if I yielded I would be carried away to some moment of terrible agony... In a moment I was swept away in a whirlwind of notes. My breath and my thoughts and every impulse of my body, became a form of the dance, till I could not distinguish between the instruments and the rhythm and my own person or consciousness.

For a while it seemed an excitement that was filled with joy, then it grew into ecstasy where all existence was lost in a vortex of movement. I could not think there had ever been a life beyond the whirling of the dance.

Then with a shock the ecstasy turned to agony and rage. I struggled to free myself, but seemed only to increase the passion of the steps I moved to. When I shrieked I could only echo the notes of the rhythm.

At last with a moment of uncontrollable frenzy I broke back to consciousness and awoke. (CWII, 99–100)

The music is a Dionysian force where ecstasy comes with an inebriate forgetfulness. But this proves a poisoned chalice, for with the loss of memory, of history, there is a concomitant threat to identity; if it offers the ecstasy of momentary liberation – 'where all existence was lost in a vortex of movement' – it also threatens the very fundamentals of selfhood. There is a seductive pull away from the nightmare of history, but Synge is canny enough to realise that without history there is no identity, no possibility.

Music also proves an ambivalently attractive escape route elsewhere in Synge's early writings. Rejected by the Abbey directors, Synge's first full-length play *When the Moon has Set*, bears a Nietzschean influence.[65] The play, showing strong remnants of Synge's Parisian flirtations with the literature of decadence, is set in the library of a big house. It principally concerns the relationship between Sister Eileen, a young nun, and Columb Sweeny, her distant cousin. Widely regarded as Synge's most autobiographical play – with Cherrie Matheson, who refused to marry Synge on religious grounds, cast as the nun – it is marred by some undigested lumps of philosophy that further belie the Yeatsian image of Synge as the anti-intellectual, 'pure' artist.[66] The play opens with Sister Eileen, in mourning for the master of the house, Columb's uncle. From the manuscript of a philosophical treatise written by her cousin, she reads aloud:

'Every life is a symphony and the translation of this sequence into music and from music again, for those who are musicians, into literature, or painting or sculpture, is the real effort of the artist. The emotions which pass through us have neither end nor beginning, are a part of eternal sensations, and it is this almost cosmic element in the person which gives all personal art a share in the dignity of the world ...'[67]

When Ascendancy culture is under threat, the spectacle of cosmic permanence, here found in the eternal symphony, proves a wistful solace. The governing theme of the play is the escape into a blissful musical recurrence with 'neither beginning nor end', away from the spectre of death – including the death of the way of life of which the Big House setting is a trope – and the restrictive repression of a religion which Columb considers unnatural. The impulse is towards an evasion of history. At the close, Sister Eileen, seduced by the young man's philosophies, gives up her nun's habit for a green dress and follows him away from the decaying house into the 'symphony of natural life.' The play, though registering historical process through the Big House, seeks to impose on it a timeless aesthetic order. In an inversion of the Yeatsian play, the emerald-clad Cathleen ní Houlihan is enchanted, for a change, by the young idealist.

Yet as we have seen, Synge is ultimately uncomfortable with an aesthetic of transcendence and, for all its apparent ahistoricism here (and irritating philosophical preachiness), we can discern an underlying unease at odds with the surface meaning. Behind the lofty dialogue, we witness the death throes of the Big House and the life it represents – a feeling of loss openly expressed in Synge's essay 'A Landlord's Garden in County Wicklow' (CWII, 230–3).[68] An air of decadence, morbidity and madness pervades the play, a sense of a culture in its dotage. But coexistent with the urge to evade the harrowing spectacle of loss and decay, we can discern a parallel impulse to escape from the burden of Ascendancy guilt.[69] In an early draft, Columb says of his uncle, 'What a life he has had. I suppose it is a good thing that this <Anglo-Irish> aristocracy is dying out. They were neither human nor divine' (CWIII, 162). During the action, it is revealed to us that the dead uncle had a liaison with a local woman, Mary Costello.[70] At the crux of the action her brother, fulfilling an earlier vow he has made to kill the heir to the house, wounds Columb by shooting at him through a window. Like the return of a repressed memory, a wronged peasantry ruptures the integrity of the Ascendancy world and, by extension, unsettles the aesthetic edifice that Columb constructs as an escape route. The challenge to the guilt-ridden problems of inheritance and generation, which are masked in the main plot by musical terminology, comes from the peasant-aristocratic Costello family, descendants of 'old Costillian' stock now fallen on hard times. Stephen Costello figuratively violates – and absolves – the House of Sweeny by his murderous attempt to shoot Columb, who is thereby enabled to prolong his relationship with Sister Eileen (representative of Cathleen ní Houlihan). Once the crime has been expiated in this way, Columb's ancestral obligations are exonerated.[71]

The guilt pangs of this fading life pervade the play. Mary C. King sees a significance in the fact that the patriarch is an uncle rather than a father: 'By displacing the father figure to the position of uncle, by giving this uncle an agonistic, radical past and by denying him marriage/potency, Synge is striking, like Christy Mahon in *The Playboy*, a triple blow against a guilty past of exploitation and expropriation.'[72] However, the most striking fragment occurs in a letter from Columb's friend O'Neil in Paris in which, as a parting salutation, he offers: 'My compliments to the little Irish pigs that eat filth all their lives that you may prosper.'[73] This statement gives us a passing glimpse into a crucial aspect of the consciousness of Revivalist Ireland. The effort to escape from history is not just to avoid facing up to the fate of a dying Ascendancy, however much this did motivate the later Yeats. History is not just a narrative of loss, but also contains that Edenic concomitant, guilt. A reading of Synge's *The Aran Islands* is illuminated by O'Neil's remark. In Part III, the narrator witnesses a scene at Kilronan port, where twenty pigs are being shipped for the English market. As the steamer approaches, each beast is thrown on its side and a knot tied round its hindlegs:

> Probably the pain inflicted was not great, yet the animals shut their eyes and shrieked with almost human intonations, till the suggestion of the noise became so intense that the men and women who were looking on became quite wild with excitement ... Then the screaming began again while the pigs were carried out and laid in their places, with a waistcoat tied round their feet to keep them from damaging the canvas. They seemed to know where they were going, and looked up at me over the gunnel with an ignoble expression that made me shudder to think that I had eaten of this whimpering flesh. When the last curragh went out I was left on the slip with a band of women and children, and one old boar who sat looking out over the sea. (CWII, 137–8)

At the turn of the century in Ireland, through economic necessity, pigs often lived under the same roof as their owners.[74] The notorious cartoons of *Punch* testify to the fact that, along with the more familiar car-

icature of the simian Paddy, the Irish were depicted either accompa-
nied by pigs or given piglike features themselves.[75] In the above
extract, the pigs are radically humanized and the narrator feels a shud-
dering anguish and guilt under their accusatory gaze. King interprets
the passage as an

> expression of Synge's imaginative awareness of Ascendancy
> dependence upon and exploitation of the Irish peasant. As they are
> carried off by the English ship, the Irish pigs' gaze becomes a mirror
> which reflects in the artist scion of landlords the centuries of guilt
> he feels for the cannibalistic exploitation of Ireland by his class.[76]

The sense of allegory and anthropomorphism imparted by the episode
is reinforced by the inscription Synge leaves in the notebook where he
drafted this sketch. In terms almost identical to those in O'Neil's letter
to Columb, he writes: 'To the little Irish pigs that have eaten filth all
their lives to enable me to wander in Paris these leaves are dedicated
with respect and sympathy' (CWII, 138 n). Significantly, Synge seems
aware of having lived his artistic life literally on the pigs' back.

Guilt, particularly inherited guilt, has been a staple of tragedy since the
House of Atreus. Significantly, the tragic paradigm of the Judeo-
Christian tradition – the Fall from Eden – also dwells on the idea that
guilt is passed through the generations in the form of Original Sin.
Freud's theory on the origins of tragedy, as laid out in *Totem and
Taboo*, is intimately tied up with the idea of an inherited, communal
guilt in society – for him, parricide – to be purged by theatrical ritual.[77]
In *Civilization and its Discontents*, he goes further, ascribing a measure
of guilt to *all* civilization, assuming that society, the very act of living
with others, necessitates repressive mechanisms, and hence guilt. For
Freud, civilization is directly proportionate to levels of guilt in society:

> If civilization is a necessary course of development from the family
> to humanity as a whole, then – as a result of the inborn conflict
> arising from ambivalence, of the external struggle between the
> trends of love and death – there is inextricably bound up with it an
> increase of the sense of guilt, which will perhaps reach heights that
> the individual finds hard to tolerate.[78]

Others have annotated this connection between culture and guilt with
a more overtly political emphasis. It is often noted that, regardless of

the ethical sensibilities a society develops, 'civilization' and all the celebrated triumphs of culture and the arts, have been enabled by repressed narratives of dominance and brutality; the material independence of the ruling classes is facilitated through exploitation of the underclasses; the most prized flowerings in the arts and sciences are nurtured by an economic system which generates surplus income and resources through their labours. From this point of view, the triumphs and treasures of art and culture have a dark underside. 'They owe their existence', as Walter Benjamin famously puts it, 'not only to the efforts of the great minds and talents who have created them, but also to the anonymous toil of their contemporaries. There is no document of civilization which is not at the same time a document of barbarism.'[79] That is to say, even those documents which indict unjust hierarchy are not only indebted to but created by it. Ironically, the system turns back on itself. From the art, culture and philosophical and ethical postulates generated by institutional privilege and material injustice, emerges a critique of these same institutions. There is often an Oedipal trace in the impulse towards political reform: it is aimed precisely at the conditions which enabled its own creation.

We are familiar with commentary discerning traces of Ascendancy guilt behind the flourishing of Protestant Gothic in nineteenth-century Irish literature.[80] Less often observed is a related phenomenon in Anglo-Irish drama. It is striking how often in Anglo-Irish literature the characters' social position, however benevolent or desirable, is contingent on an aboriginal transgression, often committed before the action proper of the play.[81] It is tempting to speculate on a linkage between the preponderance of this dramatic narrative and the oppressive history of Ascendancy hegemony in Ireland. Refinement, culture, aesthetic sensibility and, most ironically, ethical scruple spring from these roots, just as the social position of Vivian Warren and Sir Robert and Lady Chiltern is dependent on a violation of the codes by which they pretend to live. Yeats obliquely brushes against this imbrication of culture with atrocity in an essay on Synge: 'I think that all noble things are the result of warfare; great nations and classes, of warfare in the visible world, great poetry and philosophy, of invisible warfare, the division of a mind within itself, a victory, the sacrifice of man to himself.'[82] The significance of this remark lies in Yeats's failure to complete his syllogism, to connect the first part of his sentence with the second. Rather than linking the visible and invisible conflicts, he internalizes Synge's 'warfare', projecting it into a safe psychological realm and eschewing the linkage between this internal turbulence and an

external root, between poetry and politics. For the primitivists, civilization leads to corruption. One could equally claim that corruption – in
the form of political violence – leads to civilization.

Synge came from landed gentry, though his family had lost much of
its holdings. His familial connection with, and dependence on, coercive and brutal power relations was immediate, not ancestral. The
name of Synge in Wicklow did not always conjure up the genial
Gaeilgeoir with a penchant for listening to conversations through key-
holes. In 1885 Synge's brother, Edward, acting as land agent for the
family estates, 'was busily evicting tenants in Cavan, Mayo and
Wicklow'. When the young Synge confronted his mother with the
injustice of his brother's action, he may have been forgiven for discerning a chink in her stoutly religious armour. Greene and Stephens
record that 'her answer was, "What would become of us if our tenants
in Galway stopped paying their rents?" To this he could find no answer
and was forced to hold his tongue.'[83] It is questionable whether even in
later years Synge would have been able to find a satisfactory answer to
his mother's question. His background, education and means were provided for by the family estate. He always benefited from his allowance.
His artistic achievements are in that sense parasitic on the behaviour of
his family and class. In Synge's case – to adopt Pegeen Mike's famous
phrase – there was an uncomfortably small distance between the
gallous stories he created and the dirty deeds which had enabled this
creation. That which cultivated the sensibility which grew to revere the
oppressed and impoverished Irish peasantry, was created by material
gain made from their labours and subjugation. All this is not to say
that we should be charging Synge with the sins of his fathers. But it is
to argue that his provenance must have played a constitutive role in
the formation of his later perspectives, even if subliminally.[84] It would
be difficult to understand how these childhood memories could have
stayed from Synge when he witnessed the 'wild imprecations' of the
evicted woman on Inishmaan. 'The outrage to a tomb in China', Synge
declares, 'probably gives no greater shock to the Chinese than the
outrage to a hearth in Inishmaan gives to the people' (CWII, 89). In
this biographical light, the fragments in *When the Moon Has Set* and *The
Aran Islands*, about the little pigs who suffer that he may prosper, come
to seem a far more central concern than we might previously have sus-
pected. His family background made it difficult for him to follow
Edmund Burke's appeal that Privilege should forget its own murky
origins in the interest of societal stability. For Terry Eagleton, Burke's
resistance to radicalism stems from its insistence on historical memory:

Society springs from an illicit source or aboriginal crime, which in the case of Freud is parricide and in the case of Burke those acts of forcible expropriation from which all of our current titles and estates descend. The impiety of the radicals is that they would snatch the veil from these decently cloaked transgressions, tempered and obscured as they now are by the merciful passage of time, and drag scandalously to light that which must at all costs remain concealed. They would reopen the primal scene, uncover the father's shame; and Burke himself is never more gripped by Oedipal revulsion [than] in his insistence that the sources of society are a subject better left alone.[85]

But Synge did not have a temporal buffer. This may be why he described himself as a radical.[86] And this may be another explanation for the earlier proposition that his aesthetic does not permit the mythic transcendence of history sought by other modernist and revivalist writers.

So those features of Synge's tragic art that we have examined – the impulse to evade coupled with the impulse to confront, to indict himself for evasion – are also comprehensible in the context of the underlying guilt that accompanies his sensitivity to loss and decay. Synge's cultural background is also germane to another celebrated dialectic in his work: the often troubling juxtaposition between poetry and violence.[87] This relationship can be read as a metaphor for Ascendancy culture's own brutal genesis. But it may also be symptomatic of an urge for purgation and resolution of this guilty legacy. In the Preface to his *Poems*, Synge claims that 'there is no timber that has not strong roots among the clay and worms. ... It may almost be said that before verse can be human again it must learn to be brutal' (CWI, xxxvi). This call for brutality in verse is not just an espousal of naturalistic verisimilitude – art energized by the bruising urgency of the everyday – there is also a self-reflexive critique, a silent acknowledgement of 'poetic' civilization's own roots in violence and inhumanity. In other words, Synge may find that poetry and violence go well together because he intuits a deeper linkage between culture and barbarism. Following the first production of *The Well of the Saints*, George Moore praised the playwright for a sort of alchemical prowess: 'Mr Synge has discovered great literature in barbarous idiom as gold is discovered in quartz.'[88] If this is so – and it is a commonplace in praise of Synge – then the polarity can easily be reversed. If Synge finds beauty at the heart of barbarity, then he also discovers the grossness at the heart of beauty; in finding gold at the heart of quartz, Synge also registers poetry's inseparability from violence. Examples of the juxtaposition are legion in his work, where the capacity for violence is often entwined with powers of imagination and story-telling: 'Where now will you meet the like of Daneen Sullivan knocked the eye from a peeler, or Marcus Quinn, God rest him, got six months for maiming ewes, and he a great warrant to tell stories of holy Ireland till he'd have the old women shedding down tears about their feet.' (IV, 59). But he does not just provide us with a passive *analysis* of the imbrication: his drama also actively engages with it, and more specifically tries to overcome, resolve and expiate it. As Declan Kiberd remarks, '[i]f Synge's art were simply an analysis of the *relation* between barbarism and culture in Ireland, it would merit our respect: but it gains an added depth by serving also as an example of that relation.'[89]

The logic of Edenic culpability finds its answer in the atonement of Calvary, and if Synge inherits an Adamic liability of familial guilt, he instinctively reaches for a surrogate model of Christian expiation. Enter the playboy, Christy Mahon. Christy's poetry, like the cultural flowering of the Ascendancy, is based on a dirty deed that is aestheticized as a gallous story. In the course of the action, it is exposed and then transcended. Christy comes to the Mayoites carrying a mark of culpability which, in the course of the play, he is privileged to purge. Culture confronts and expiates its violent origins in the controlled laboratory of the stage. The play comically, but unnervingly, explores the process by which violence is glorified and aestheticized. Yet it also, by a theatrical sleight of hand, reveals the violence as chimerical, and allows Christy to pass through and survive the implications of his supposed atrocity. Momentarily revered by the community he enters, they turn against him when the rhetoric surrounding his deed is exposed by its actual re-enactment in the third act. Pegeen Mike prizes violence – or, more accurately, the *idea* of violence – because, for her, it is subsumed by an enchanting aura of poetry: 'I've heard all times it's the poets are your like – fine, fiery fellows with great rages when their temper's roused' (CWIV, 81). She finally becomes disabused through the realization that the axis is easily inverted: violence does not emanate from the excitement of poetry, rather the poetry of Christy gorges on violence, just as culture, *à la* Benjamin, is inextricably linked to its barbarous origins. Attempting to root out this corruption, she also, to her deep dismay, loses its contingent, desperately needed imaginative boon. By contrast, at the end of the play, Christy's ebullient lyricism is no longer simply an antidote to his actual impotence: rather poetry and action have become complementary. In the second Act, his inflated egotism had been artificial, enabled only by the tactical repression of memories of weakness and degradation. The self-inflating delusions of the Christy of Act II are uncomfortably dependent on the double principle of an aboriginal crime and the elision or prettification of his true personal history. However, when his father publicly forces him to confront his past, Christy endures and is energized by the experience, earning a *rapprochement* within his previously troubled sense of self. His victory over his father is also a victory over origin as the source of a straitening, inherited identity. Now identity becomes a future possibility rather than a predetermined burden, just as imagination ceases to be the source of illusion in the present, becoming, instead, the generator of future reality. In an act of flagrant wish-fulfilment, Synge has those crimes of parricide which enable Christy's poetic flourish twice turn out to be illusory. Suddenly free of the mark of Cain, Christy takes the next step towards a psychic integration poignantly denied to Synge's own sensibility, with its ineradicable provenance in Ascendancy exploitation. Culture is freed from the shackles of its origins and Christy can go now with impunity 'romancing through a romping lifetime' (CWIV, 173). To his great fortune, the 'crime' that enabled his poetic apprenticeship turns out to be no crime at all.

Yet, on a deeper level, this dénouement leaves the community in irremediable stagnancy, and is thus a guilty meditation on the role of artist, who leaches material from the community without giving anything back in return. After all, if Christy is the artist-figure who the villagers idolize, he is by the same token the parasite who discovers his poetic voice in their emotional cravings. That he comes out on top is Synge's wry comment on the revivalist artist. As C. L. Innes puts it, 'although the play does deal with the power of the poetic word to transform, it also deals in its tragicomic ending with the failure of poetry, a failure which relates to the narcissistic and exploitative nature of art and the artist.'[90] This ambivalent dialectic may be one reason why Synge's talent flowers most fully on the stage, rather than in poetry. The flamboyant make-believe of stagecraft provides a site in which these tensions – the powers and limitations of the imagination – can be acted out and worked through publicly, rather than just expressed privately through the intimacy of lyric. Drama provides a forum for cathartic enactment, as well as an idiom for passive expression. The drama, then, is not just a projection, it is also an arena in which the tensions and complexities of the cultural moment in which Synge writes, and his ambivalent position therein, are enacted and embodied.

Much is made in *Playboy* of the powers of poetry to distract from loneliness or emotional penury. The clothing motif – Christy adorned in the sportsgear – is a visual repetition of this distraction.[91] There is lots of toying with Christy's clothing in the early drafts of the play (see CWIV, 82). When Pegeen is first left alone with Christy, having bustled the intrusive Shawn Keogh out the door, she hangs her apron over the window as a blind. This blocking out of reality by a physical object – symbolizing the ultimately delusory powers of language – is a common device of Synge's. We see it also in the use of the tapestry in the first act of *Deirdre of the Sorrows*. However, Christy remains a small man; the revolution in his self-image is based on the misperception of the villagers. Innes claims that

> Christy is given the clothes which are 'real' and substantial by the Mayo peasants, but he has only insubstantial words to give back. Moreover, the transformation of the real world, the joining together of reality and joy, takes place only *within* the realm of art, which by that very transformation becomes alienated from the 'reality' on which it is based.[92]

Yet there is another, specifically theatrical, dimension to this alienation. For if reality and joy harmoniously cohabit in the realm of language, then not only is the reality outside the stage distanced, but a schism develops within the stage setting itself. As we have seen, the very materiality of the stage is a rebuke to the imaginative excesses of the characters' rich poetry. The filth and muck of the shebeen, the stink of poteen and the sting of poverty, are perceivable by a spectator, who thereby experiences the creative tension between the imaginative promises of Christy and their contradiction in lived experience (or between gallous stories and dirty deeds). The fundamental dramatic irony, so obvious in *The Well of the Saints*, also applies to Synge's other drama. The audience sees small men with big talk, poor hovels and rich poetry, ugly bodies and beautiful language. From this incongruity and conflict emerge both the comic and tragic energies of these plays.

Identity and economics

Importantly, then, Synge provides us not only with an analysis of the relation between imagination and reality, culture and barbarism, but also with an example of it, which is a coded self-critique. Just as the characters in the plays seek to eschew an unbearable reality through imagination, poetry and self-delusion, so the plays can bear to cast only a sidelong glance at surrounding political circumstances. This is not, as Seamus Deane alleges, a 'disengagement from history' but rather a subliminal engagement with it, for the putative evasion is itself inscribed in the dramatic substance of the text.[93] Therefore Synge has already self-directed the complaints later levelled at him by critics. The charge is insinuated by the offence. If he is evasive or escapist, he also makes evasion and escapism his central themes. There may be an absence of overt historical reference in his drama in terms of social realism, yet there is nonetheless a silent political commentary encoded in the action. One important facet wherein we can observe this repressed concern is the obsession in his plays with the drudgery of economics. All the plays (except, interestingly, *Deirdre of the Sorrows*) are riddled with references to money, property, and the basic mechanics of material wellbeing. Synge chooses to make *Riders to the Sea* hinge not on a fishing expedition, but on Bartley's trading mission to Galway. To be sure, this adds a thematic layer of modernity's impact on tradition – urban life undermining the traditional subsistence lifestyle of the islanders – yet it also buttresses a wider motif of economic exchange in the play. In line with the intrusion of modernity into tradition, a related opposition is constructed in the play between exchange and identity. It is as if identity – subjective formation – is circumscribed and curtailed by external pressures, by the omnipresent sea and by the compromises required for material survival. In *Riders,* as much as any other of Synge's plays, the emphasis on money and material wellbeing is as dominant a concern as all the metaphysical musings which have drawn the attention of critics. In a sense, this makes it a 'modern' tragedy from the same stable as *Death of a Salesman.* Though often overlooked, a crucial part of the dramatic effect is achieved by the easy oscillation between these disparate discourses. Emotional grief and material loss are eerily interwoven in Maurya's speech. For all the talk of Synge's 'poignant awareness of beauty, amid the immanence and inevitability of death' and of 'the conflict of *Man* v. *Necessity*',[94] the islanders' *economic* dependence on the sea is the play's most glaringly obvious aspect. That critics emphasize the 'tragic' aspects of Synge's work by eschewing consideration of these material considerations indicates the ideological prejudice which conceives tragedy as confined to 'universal' or 'timeless' truths.

The reason that commentators have praised the pithiness, economy and control of *Riders to the Sea* lies not only in Synge's mastery of the one-act play, but also in that, in a sense, we join the play in the fifth act. In Beckettian style, this play is a sort of endgame: most of the action – that is most of the loss – has already taken place. The audience quickly realizes that they join the drama in mid-action by the references to Michael's absence, but they do not know the full tragic prehistory of the family until Maurya's final soliloquy. As has often been remarked, the stageprops play a crucial part in the play, yet fit seamlessly into the dramatic tapestry. The spinning wheel is prominent from the start and carries its Fortuna association lightly; the planks, stepladder, bread, and so on fit neatly and unobtrusively into the whole action. The paucity of props resonates with a wider penury. The single halter, and prized, hard-bought boards, indicate not only the general material scarcity and economic hardship in which the islanders live, but also the single remaining son. Furthermore, despite the widely held belief that, in Synge's world, linguistic wealth compensates for economic poverty, the material dearth here is, on one level, reflected in the information withheld from the audience. Indeed, until Maurya's final eloquence, we see evidence of an arrested, spasmodic language: 'who would listen to an old woman with one thing and she saying it over?' (CWIII, 11).

Yet Cathleen is unfair to her mother here, for though it is true that, fearing his death, Maurya is motivated by an overriding concern to keep Bartley away from the sea, she adopts a number of tactics to this end. Inventive in her pretexts, she tells him to leave the rope in case it is needed for Michael's funeral; she urges him to stay to make the coffin if needed, 'and I after giving a big price for the finest white boards you'd find in Connemara' (CWIII, 9); finally, when he dismisses the possibility that the body has been washed ashore, she reveals her real fears, but couched in the rationalized idiom of exchange-value that pervades the play: 'If it was a hundred horses, or a thousand horses you had itself, what is the price of a thousand horses against a son where there is one son only?' (CWIII, 9). Bartley can only ignore this question, so pointedly phrased in the language he has been forced to make his own; finding more comfort in formulating the language of economics than in being its object, he instructs Cathleen to watch out for the sheep in his absence and to try and get a good price for the pig with the black feet. This heralds a breakdown in communication between Bartley and Maurya. From this point on, he ignores her questioning and pleading, committing a secular equivalent of the breach she is later to make in refusing him her blessing. The pressure of economics has supplanted the luxury of communication.

The priest fails to discern the difference between the two realms, and regards all communication, even prayer, as part of a rationalized system of exchange. He believes that an investment of prayers will yield a return. Hence his ill-judged prediction, relayed by Nora: '"I won't stop him" says he; "but let you not be afraid. Herself does be saying prayers half through the night, and the Almighty God won't leave her destitute," says he, "with no son living."' (CWIII, 5). We are reminded of Yeats's sardonic pun in 'September 1913': 'For men were born to pray and save.'[95] This idea of investment and return pervades the play but is not complementary to language, as the priest seems to suggest; rather, it is at the root of the breakdown in communication between Bartley and Maurya. This breakdown reflects a deep tragic conflict between the incompatible imperatives imposed by body and soul, by the pressing demands of corporeal existence and the conflicting need for autonomous, imaginative self-realization. The characters strive to preserve their identity against encroaching external forces. This is not just a universal conflict, as has often been assumed; it also concerns individual and familial integrity in radical opposition to artificial, social organization. The battle is not just with Death but also with reification. Bartley dilutes his identity, just as he borrows Michael's clothes and, finally, is buried in his coffin. Death signifies the ultimate loss of identity: as Maurya says, giving eerie literalism to the cliché, 'when a man is nine days in the sea, and the wind blowing, it's hard set his own mother would be to say what man was in it' (CWIII, 23).

In the final, climactic moments of the play, Maurya is freed from the suffocating system of exchange. She no longer has to pay her dues:

> I'll have no call now to be up crying and praying when the wind breaks from the south, and you can hear the surf is in the east, and the surf is in the west, making a great stir with the two noises and they hitting one on the other. I'll have no call now to be going down and getting Holy Water in the dark nights after Samhain, and I won't care what way the sea is when the other women will be keening. (CWIII, 23–6)

Like the clash of surf from east and west, the conflict is resolved for Maurya. Following a sort of stoic epiphany, language, memory and history return. She is now able to recount the litany of her loss: 'I've had a husband, and a husband's father, and six sons in this house – six fine men, though it was a hard birth I had with every one of them and they coming into the world – and some of them were found and some of them were not found, but they're gone now the lot of them ...' (CWIII, 21). Like Yeats's 'Easter 1916', the final listing of the dead has the quality of cathartic resolution. She is freed from the imperatives of the text, she has no call to cry and keen any more, no reason to perform.

In line with the common, universalist reading of the play, this ending is sometimes regarded as an escape from history, a transcendence of the event. As Nicholas Grene puts it, 'the image of death is seen in all its timeless power against the normal sequence of events, in which Maurya through a life-time's suffering is brought to an absolute vision standing free of the individual event.'[96] However, her resolution could also be seen from the opposite perspective. Far from a detachment from history, Maurya liberates the trauma of the past into the here and now, exemplifying Walter Benjamin's *Jetztzeit* or 'time filled by the presence of the now'.[97] Through a heroic *absorption* of history, she is brought to an absolute vision *of* the individual event (not 'standing free' from it). Too traumatic to be confronted, the text represses the horrors of Maurya's past until the final, cathartic moment. Through her retrieval of language and of history, she rehabilitates her own subjectivity, enervated by years of struggle and hardship. She relives the past and relieves the present. Like Benjamin's Angel of History, her back is towards the future, but the past seeps into the present. As Maurya recounts her sorrowful history, it is re-enacted by the men and women carrying Bartley's corpse on-stage. In this manner, the past becomes synchronous with the present and Maurya manages to escape from the contingencies and reductive aetiology that has suffocated the community. Through her suffering, she gains the stature to confront the nightmare of history and *repossesses* it by suffusing it through the present.

The same set of conflicting forces and impulses evident in *Riders* is also discernible in the rest of his work. Repeatedly, a disjunction is engendered between autonomy and actuality, between the efforts of the characters to realize their human potential and the restrictions imposed by a reality that includes both the prospect of old age and decay, and the immediate social-based necessity for material survival. Synge often treats marriage as a motif which, veering between the economic and the emotional, encapsulates the competing imperatives. They are vividly brought into focus in *The Shadow of the Glen*: 'NORA: What way would I live, and I an old woman if I didn't marry a man with a bit of a farm, and cows on it, and sheep on the back hills?' (CWIII, 49). But Nora is lured away from the stasis of an economically rich but emotionally and spiritually impoverished life. If material comfort in her old age was her motive in marrying Dan Burke in the first place, thoughts of the toothless Peggy Cavanagh and her own looming degeneration now provoke her to seek an alternative to the stagnant, lonely life she lives in the glen.

Yet the conversation between Nora Burke and Michael Dara – when the dramatic tension is at its highest – is conducted over a counting out of money, which is witnessed by the audience in contrast with, and as a silent commentary on, the artistry of the dialogue. Their relationship cannot escape the economic necessities which drove Nora into her marriage in the first place, despite the fact that it is precisely an urge to escape that motivates her. Notwithstanding her self-serving attitude, Nora earns the sympathy of the audience through her imaginative vision of a life fuller than that permitted by the irksome society where her emotions are degraded into the currency of economic exchange. By contrast, the rapacious priest in *The Tinker's Wedding* is lightened by no redemptive feature. Sarah Casey learns, as her prospective mother-in-law has always known, that the priest's anaemic conventionality is organized around a straitening, anti-imaginative economy. *The Playboy of the Western World* starts, significantly, with Pegeen Mike drawing up a shopping list and this motif endures. The Widow Quinn, by no means an unsympathetic character, stands as a foil to the poetic ebullience and emotional idealism of Christy. Ever on the outlook for a 'right of way', or 'mountainy ram', marriage is a contract for her, as it would have been for Pegeen Mike had she followed through her temptation to 'marry a Jew-man, with ten kegs of gold,and I not knowing at all there was the like of you drawing nearer like the stars of God' (CWIV, 151). Christy lures Pegeen from the degrading world of exchange to an autonomous, 'celestial' sphere. With his fine words and talk of love, he offers her an alternative to the system of sexuality as material barter in which she finds herself. Shawn Keogh is incapable of appreciating the seductive privacies of the imaginary order; his store of passion is indistinguishable from the material possessions that he conceives as the measure of his worth: 'And have you no mind of my weight of passion, and the holy dispensation, and the drift of heifers I'm giving, and the golden ring?' (CWIV, 155). Representing the dull social world, Shawn is incapable of perceiving the opposition between property and passion, economics and identity. The greyness of this world is of a piece with the 'greyness' of the natural world that, for Corkery, Synge disingenuously strives to evade. The instrumental language of economics – of society – clashes discordantly with the poetic language of individualism. In this respect, what we see dramatized on Synge's stage is not only a vocabulary of conflict but also a conflict of vocabularies.

It is, then, quite astonishing that Yeats could claim that Synge's people are 'moved by no practical ambition'.[98] Most of them, and not only the villains, are moved by little else. Dan Burke and Michael Dara, like the Widow Quinn and Shawn Keogh, are not prone to the tragic dilemmas faced by those Syngean heroes capable of imaginative and poetic expression. The former are motivated solely by economic determinants and face no conflicting imperatives. The latter, however, are ennobled and elevated by their efforts to grasp a selfhood outside the penurious and imaginatively arid societies in which they find themselves. Usually however, the characters fail in these efforts. For all the lyricism and poetry of the tramp, Nora knows that their future together will be one of material drudgery. For all the gratifying mutual flattery of Martin and Mary Doul, the audience knows that their alternative, imaginatively based existence is a dreamworld, and that they leave the stage not to a happy superannuation in the south, but to death by drowning along the way.

In *Deirdre of the Sorrows*, social and familial obligation replaces economic survival as the opposite of imaginative self-realization. Lost in her dreams, Deirdre is desperately keen to evade external society and the self-compromise it demands, and is dismissive of her obligations to Conchubor. The central prop at this stage of the action is the half-finished tapestry, which, in an uncanny literalism, stands by the window, signifying the artistic and imaginative efforts employed by Deirdre to block out an intrusive reality. After Conchubor has ordered her to join him in Emain the following day, she counters her terror 'at the reality that is before her' by a prodigal display of all the opulent decoration in the house, dressing up in queenly clothes and ordering – in a concentration of the trope – the mats and tapestries to be hung by the window (CWIV, 197–9). At this stage, as in *The Well of the Saints*, imagination can hide but never erase a repellent objective world. However, by the third act, the freshly dug grave has replaced the tapestry at the epicentre of the dramatic action. This grave is ominously, brutally real but, ironically, also imaginatively chosen: 'it's that grave when it's closed will make us one forever, and we two lovers have had great space without weariness or growing old or any sadness of the mind' (CWIV, 251). Only in the grave does Deirdre find a way to avoid the impending years, the loss of beauty and, most unconscionable of all, the waning of Naisi's love for her. This is the only contract that can be drawn between reality and her uncompromising intensity:

It's this hour we're between the daytime and a night where there is sleep forever, and isn't it a better thing to be following on to a near death, than to be bending the head down, and dragging with the feet, and seeing one day, a blight showing upon love where it is sweet and tender? (CWIV, 221–3)

In *Deirdre*, unlike *Playboy*, no evasion of the inherited obligation incurred before the commencement of the action is possible. Ultimately, Deirdre must either pay her dues to Conchubor or die. *Deirdre of the Sorrows* expresses a degree of finality and resolution found in none of Synge's previous plays. If Maurya's reconciliation with the external world leads her to a stoic attitude, and Christy's to a life of romping romance, then Deirdre achieves a fusion of acceptance and resistance. She hastens her foretold destruction, not through resignation or acceptance of her fate, but through deliberately chosen action which, if it is prompted by a rejection of impending old age and decay, is also a profound affirmation of the passionate, imaginative, autonomous life she has enjoyed with Naisi – a life so prized by her that she is unwilling to see it wane: 'It is not a small thing to be rid of grey hairs, and the loosening of teeth. [*with a sort of triumph*] ... It was the choice of lives we had in the clear woods, and in the grave we're safe surely ... .' (CWIV, 267–9). Whether or not one agrees with Yeats's judgement that it would have been his finest artistic achievement, one can scarcely help feeling a sense of regret that Synge never lived to complete his final play. It is difficult and perhaps fruitless to conjecture what future direction his work might have taken, for the supreme effort to confront loss and mortality gives *Deirdre* all the airs of a swan-song. Interestingly, he returns to the identification/opposition between desire and death, imagination and oblivion, that pervaded his very earliest work. The doom that is foretold for Deirdre and the Sons of Usna proves to be more than just a disaster incurred through hubristic over-exertion. It chimes with their will.

Whatever the dramatic flaws of *Deirdre of the Sorrows*,[99] it is entirely appropriate that, approaching death, Synge should reach a conclusion that embraces both poles. It is also indicative of why he was most successful in incarnating that synthetic vision dramatically. While his pre-Aran prose and poetry often seems artificial and showy, the dramatic medium embodies his dualities and contradictions with less strain. The rollicking poetry seems both less bombastic and less ephemeral in the grounded, material context of the stage. And, as already noted, the stage highlights the *limits* of the imagination at the same time as embodying its potential. The practical impossibility of staging death in *Deirdre* – giving it to the spectators as a recognizable experience, rather than just presenting it to them as a spectacle – associates it more closely with the sensuous, imaginative, poetic world that is Synge's continually elusive Grail. There are limits to the theatrical representation of death. Except for the opera singer, who hits the most expressive notes at the moment of expiration, characters dying on stage, like people dying in the real world, can only take the audience so far on the journey. This is why so much death in the theatre occurs off-stage. The same is true for Synge's world of poetic freedom and self-realization which can be spoken *about* but not spoken, can be dramatically pointed at, but not dramatically incarnated. In this way, the consummation of *Deirdre* – an identification of imaginative liberation with death – is prefigured in the theatrical form itself. Just like Synge's early fascination with the siren-call of the sea, poetic ebullience has always been a thinly veiled version of amnesia and death.

3
Delusion and Disillusionment: The Tragedy of Meliorism in Sean O'Casey's Early Drama

> Where the causes of disaster are temporal, where the conflict can be resolved through technical or social means, we may have serious drama, but not tragedy.
>
> – George Steiner

> JUNO: What can God do agen' the stupidity o'men?
>
> – *Juno and the Paycock*

Introduction: O'Casey and meliorism

On 30 March 1960, in honour of his eightieth birthday, the *Irish Times* published an encomium to Sean O'Casey, to which many distinguished authors and personages were asked to contribute. Samuel Beckett was approached for an article and offered a characteristically brief tribute: 'To my great compatriot, Sean O'Casey, from France where he is honoured, I send my enduring gratitude and homage.'[1] He refused the invitation to expand. From an author so different in outlook and execution to O'Casey, this accolade – and gratitude – is intriguing. Though frequently approached by editors compiling *Festschrifts*, Beckett was fastidious with his homage. He was, for instance, markedly selective in choosing his Irish antecedents when, only four years earlier, he had turned down an invitation to contribute to a celebratory tribute for the birth-centenary of O'Casey's great hero and mentor, George Bernard Shaw:

> This is too tall an order for me...
> I wouldn't suggest that G.B.S. is not a great playwright, whatever that is when it's at home.

What I would do is give the whole unupsettable apple-cart for a sup of the Hawk's Well, or the Saints', or a whiff of Juno, to go no further.[2]

Beckett's lukewarm regard for Shaw in comparison with his other Irish forebears – of whose influence he seems significantly conscious – is not surprising. The two writers could hardly have more different attitudes to life and art: the austerely pessimistic, stylistically anti-naturalist Beckett found scant solace in Shaw's evolutionary Life-Force; a practitioner of scrupulous reticence, one can hardly be startled by Beckett's lack of enthusiasm for Shaw's eighty-page preface. Given O'Casey's Shavian leanings, his polemical loquacity, and headstrong, often bumptious style, one might have expected Beckett to display a similar impatience with the younger writer. Early in his life, however, he seems to have been lured by the 'whiff of Juno'. In 'The Essential and the Incidental', a 1934 review of O'Casey's *Windfalls*, Beckett claims that the author 'discerns the principle of disintegration in even the most complacent of solidities, and activates it to their explosion'.[3] The art of disintegration and the disintegration of art were soon to become characteristic Beckettian territory. The heroes of the one-act farce in question, Darry Berrill and Barry Derril, are named with a distinctly Beckettian ring, while their hopelessly self-defeating antics are reminiscent of the vaudeville, knockabout comic tradition that both dramatists drew upon. The virtue of 'knockabout in this very serious and honourable sense' that Beckett praises so fulsomely in 'The End of the Beginning', originates in the earlier *Juno and the Paycock* – lauded as O'Casey's best play because 'it communicates most fully this dramatic dehiscence, mind and world come asunder in irreparable dissociation – chassis'.[4]

The feeling was not mutual. O'Casey, it seems, had little time for his exiled compatriot, avowedly disliking what he regarded as Beckett's morose, fatalistic disposition. A short piece published in a student magazine in 1956 reveals a strong aversion to Beckett's pessimism and an explicit denial of any shared tradition or any connection with his own artistic project:

Beckett? I have nothing to do with Beckett. He isn't in me; nor am I in him. I am not waiting for Godot to bring me life; I am out after life myself, even at the age I've reached. What have any of you to do with Godot? There is more life than Godot can give in the least of us. That Beckett is a clever writer, and that he has written a rotten and remarkable play, there is no doubt; but his philosophy isn't my philosophy, for within him there is no hazard of hope; no desire for it; nothing in it but a lust for despair, and a crying of woe, not in a wilderness, but in a garden.[5]

In one sense, O'Casey's antipathy is less surprising than Beckett's admiration. Apart from the overt differences in dramatic style – O'Casey's garrulousness and polemicism contrasting with Beckett's austerity and reticence – an initial comparison might distinguish their attitudes to political art. Beckett, having signed his share of modernist manifestos, insists on the radical autonomy of the aesthetic artefact, an autonomy that refuses any overt social or political imperatives. By contrast, O'Casey, whether in his realist or expressionist incarnation, sought to write a moralistic drama of direct social and political applicability, for all his excessively self-delighting language. Aesthetically, they would seem to differ in respect to art's relation to realism and politics; philosophically, they would seem to differ in their attitudes to the fundamental basis of human suffering: extreme meliorist versus extreme anti-meliorist. O'Casey emerges as the political activist, writing a socialist drama propagating the necessity for change, Beckett as an apolitical, pessimistic artist, disdaining overt political reference and writing a drama that seems to affirm the desperate helplessness of the human situation. There is no lack of human suffering in Beckett's work, but it is always a condition which admits of no cure – as Hamm shouts: 'you're on earth, there's no cure for that!' (CDW, 118). He perpetually eschews the idea of reparability or remediability as a false consolation, a Godot who never arrives.

By contrast, O'Casey once remarked: 'There are terrible things in life, but I do not think life itself is terrible.'[6] For O'Casey, like Brecht, the horror of human suffering is based primarily in its avoidability, and theatre has an imaginative role to play in demonstrating possibilities for social emancipation. The briefest glance at the *Autobiographies* reinforces O'Casey's self-created image as a fierce battler. He styles himself as an anti-authoritarian maverick, displaying an indignant resistance to the acts of injustice he encounters at every stage of his life. While the *Autobiographies* should be mistrusted, and 'Sean' may have been less of a firebrand than he remembers, there is no doubt that he showed an early rebelliousness, which grew into a keen sensitivity to social injustice in adulthood.[7] Not surprisingly, his dramatic work is continually grounded in a satirical depiction of actual political events and social circumstances. His most famous and enduring drama, the

Dublin trilogy (consisting of *The Shadow of a Gunman* (1923), *Juno and the Paycock* (1924) and *The Plough and the Stars* (1926)) and *The Silver Tassie* (1928), concerns the War of Independence, the Civil War, the Easter Rising of 1916 and the Great War. Formed by these events, O'Casey's tragic vision is also manifest in his dramatic representation of them. From these bitter parodies to the blistering depiction of the sanctimonious, priest-ridden Irish state in *The Bishop's Bonfire* (1955) and *The Drums of Father Ned* (1958), O'Casey indulges in a drama of socio-political protest of one sort or another, even if his visions of socialist liberation occasionally coarsen into agitprop.

In his prose works and in many of his plays O'Casey celebrates the life-force of joyous freedom and uninhibited sexuality pitted against the repressive forces of church and state. He continually asserts the great potential of the human spirit, lamentably compromised and debased by poverty and authoritarianism. For the most part, then, his disposition is avowedly optimistic and melioristic. To be sure, things are not as they *should* be, but the potential for amelioration is always there. O'Casey's admirers extol his 'affirmative vision' and 'unshake-able faith in man'. Robert Lowery stresses his 'great sense of history and of man's date with destiny. He was confident that the innate good-ness of people would dominate the future and that Time would put everything into perspective'.[8] From this angle O'Casey's attitude to the world uplifts and cheers. His horror at injustice and oppression comes not from despair but from outrage that the human spirit is denied and debased. And, crucially, for him, it need not be so.

Yet there are other aspects. For all the talk of O'Casey's faith in humanity, one critic can anomalously declare:

> The most striking, indeed the almost unique characteristic of his plays is the fact that they are one long unresolved dissonance. He offers no solution; he proposes no remedy; he suggests no hope. Artistically, as well as intellectually, there is only the clash between the preposterous and the terrible. Like Captain Boyle, he finds nothing to say except that 'everything is in a state of chassis'.[9]

O'Casey's meliorism, his faith in human goodness and his belief in utopian solutions to social problems, is not so secure and steadfast as is sometimes supposed. Part of the dramatic conflict of his best work emerges from the complexity, tension and irresolution in his social outlook. One discovers an underbelly of fatalism, even nihilism, beneath O'Casey's melioristic zeal, which strongly colours his trilogy and *The Silver Tassie*. This may explain Beckett's affinity with the older playwright and it certainly is part of the reason why these early plays achieve a level of complexity and dramatic power lost to many of O'Casey's later, Utopian plays. There is here an unresolved but productive conflict between O'Casey's dogged, embattled credo of meliorism and the profound disillusionment brought on by his experiences of Ireland's revolutionary period, especially the Civil War. The cracks are discernible in the Dublin trilogy, which thematically oscillates from a secular to a fatalistic viewpoint, from Juno's plea 'what can God do agen the stupidity of men' to Boyle's dissolute recognition that 'th' whole worl's ... in a terr ... ible state o' ... chassis' (TP, 70, 73). It is precisely this conflict which makes these plays dramatically interesting, saving them from the didacticism that often mars his *Autobiographies* and his later drama.

Given this equivocation between optimism and pessimism, O'Casey has an especially angular relationship to tragic theory. As we saw in the Introduction such theorists as George Steiner would see any trace of a melioristic view as anathema to 'true' or 'authentic' tragedy: 'Where a tragic conception of life is in force, moreover, there can be no recourse to secular or material remedies. The destiny of Lear cannot be resolved by the establishment of adequate homes for the aged.'[10] Steiner is seeking to bar Ibsen and Strindberg from inclusion in a tradition august enough to include Sophocles, Shakespeare and Racine. Any hint of a secular solution – such as that found in various melioristic philosophies from Romanticism to Marxism – would erode the essential fatalism, the irremediable bleakness that, for Steiner, counterpoints human dignity and heroism in dramatic tragedy. The tragic strain within O'Casey's outwardly melioristic position, the eddies of nihilism which act against his overt beliefs, are an implicit rebuttal to Steiner's strictures. O'Casey is an instance of a writer who, while ostensibly anti-tragic in Steiner's terms, nonetheless disturbs the notion of redemptive narratives as integral and self-contained.

What is interesting about O'Casey's tragedies is their heterogeneity. 'Aristotle', he told his friend Gabriel Fallon, 'is all balls.'[11] O'Casey's work is not notable for generic obedience or loyalty to pre-given forms. His drama is typically a *mélange* of different, often conflicting modes and tones, shifting promiscuously from naturalism to expressionism, from farce and vaudeville to melodrama, from colloquial banter to ritualistic incantation. While Arthur Miller famously fought his corner against the generic purists, insisting that *Death of a Salesman* was a 'Tragedy' despite its naturalistic, proletarian setting, O'Casey, for all his pugnacity, never felt the need to battle over the niceties of Aristotelian definition. He nonetheless subtitled his three Dublin plays as 'tragedies' and *The Silver Tassie* – paradoxically the blackest of any play he wrote – as a 'tragi-comedy'. O'Casey, like Synge and Beckett, is famous for entwining tragic and comic moods. Stylistically heterogeneous, resolutely domestic, riotously hilarious, as well as unbearably poignant, it will come as little surprise that O'Casey's version of tragedy bears little resemblance to the prescriptions of the *Poetics*. 'It is of course the case', Christopher Murray concludes, 'that O'Casey is not writing tragedy in the classical or neo-classical sense. There is hardly any need to argue this point further.'[12] Indeed there is no need to hammer O'Casey into a classical tradition of tragedy to which he has no allegiance, but examining his attitude to suffering and loss, and the way he incarnates it dramatically, yields many insights into his artistic achievement and the historical context which moulded it. Moreover when we interpet O'Casey in terms of the dissonance between his outward meliorism and the undertow of pessimism and fatalism, it complicates many of the critical commonplaces within current debates about his political vision. For the success of O'Casey's dramatization of politics has come in for serious questioning in recent years.

O'Casey and politics

Since his arrival on the Dublin stage, and his great commercial success, O'Casey has been the 'darling man' of the Abbey theatre. Over the past three decades in particular his Dublin trilogy has resonated strongly in Ireland, offering, it seemed, a renewed relevance in the light of political events. There were a number of major revivals during the 1970s and 80s and the centenary of his birth in 1980 was the occasion of intense media interest, including several revivals and a televised adaptation of his *Autobiographies*.[13] His popularity during this period can be understood in the context of the complex response in the Republic of Ireland to the eruption of paramilitary violence in the North of Ireland.[14] From the foundation of the State until the renewed Troubles, the official line on the revolutionary period was one of reverence and glorification. The flood of official celebrations that marked the fiftieth anniversary of the 1916 Rising typified the orthodox attitude. However, the Troubles in Northern Ireland made Ireland's revolutionary period seem a far more troubled, less glorious narrative than hitherto. Inevitably, the renewed IRA campaign, claiming legitimacy from the tradition of armed republican insurrection, provoked a backlash against the mythologies which underran the foundation of the Republic. O'Casey's perceived condemnation of 'senseless violence' and debunking of romantic nationalist mythology had a timely relevance at the moment when nationalist ideology was resurgent in the partitioned six counties. O'Casey, in short, has been acclaimed for espousing that 'common-sense' humanity supposedly lost in the heady nationalist rhetoric that beguiled the revolutionary generation. Not surprisingly, then, O'Casey has figured in recent intellectual and cultural wars in Ireland, with *The Plough and the Stars* regarded as 'a revisionist play before ever the term was coined'.[15] To be sure, he has before been adopted by some ironic sources: militant labour agitator feted by the theatre-going middle-class; hardline Stalinist beloved by a generation of American liberal critics during the McCarthy era. That this ex-IRB man and Gaelic Leaguer should be championed as an anti-nationalist is the latest of many paradoxical allegiances.

Yet there have been dissenting voices. It is significant that literary critics from the north of Ireland, such as Seamus Deane and G. J. Watson, are suspicious of the tendency to graft the politics of O'Casey's trilogy onto the Northern crisis and have found aspects of the plays sentimental and inadequate to a complex political actuality. Though O'Casey has never been short of devotees, there are many critical commentators who find his political thought unsatisfactory and incomplete.[16] The case for the prosecution merits careful consideration. Though they differ in emphasis, these critics perceive a simplistic and distorting opposition between politics and humanism in O'Casey's work, particularly his Dublin plays: the political 'principles' of the men versus the hearth-and-home humanity of the women, hearts of stone opposed to hearts of flesh. As G. J. Watson complains of *Juno and the Paycock*:

> The politics are a deformation of, and a threat to, the human, and O'Casey's suffering women are the authorially endorsed mouthpieces of this view. There is something simple-minded and sentimental about this ... Since 'principles' and 'politics' do demonstrably have such a major impact, it is simple-minded to ignore them, and sentimental to pretend that humanity consists in ignoring them.[17]

According to these critics – and not all would count themselves nationalists – O'Casey does not give politics a fair hearing. If he really wanted to engage in a serious dispute with political and revolutionary thought, it is curious that he failed to include a single serious political thinker in the trilogy.[18] O'Casey's version of politics is a straw target. Since it is seen solely in its destructive element, with no serious confrontation with either a coherent political ideology and only with indirect engagement with the conditions which created the impulse for political revolution in the first place, politics and family life are constructed not only as hermetically separate, but also in direct hostility to one another.[19] Put bluntly, O'Casey paradoxically regards politics as anti-social. For those who distrust this aspect of his work, O'Casey illegitimately presents the family as anterior to the structures that organize society and more particularly does not recognize, for all his keen awareness of the material plight of the Dublin poor and his own erstwhile political radicalism, the causes of poverty in political terms. Since in his prose writings he insists that the roots of human suffering are secular and since for most of his life he was proud to be associated with the hard left, it is odd that he remains in the trilogy, if not in his real-life activities nor in his later plays of didactic communism, so resolutely apolitical. The hostility to nationalist rhetoric, displayed in the trilogy, is often indistinguishable from a distaste for politics as a whole, downgraded to so many dry, dangerous 'principles'. Like his great hero Charles Dickens, O'Casey caricatures all organized political movements as an anti-humanist scourge – a source of dogmatic ideology that is the enemy of true human relations.[20] This leads to the assumption that the private is in some way accessible in an unmediated state, that the family has a natural existence prior to or untainted by its social role. This leads to simplistic and sentimental ideas about subjectivity and the programmatic tendency to suspect all programmatic tendencies, to be hostile to all systems of thought, all political ideologies, all 'isms'.[21] O'Casey seeks to debunk seductive metanarrative with emotive – and seductive – specific-narrative, which can quickly become an equally totalizing force. His blistering parodies of political rhetoric leave no room for an alternative politics, but only an anti-politics, which is not only at odds with most of his avowed beliefs but also leave an instability in his drama.

Thus goes the case for the prosecution and, indeed, there does seem to be a sense that politics is kept, like Johnny Boyle, largely offstage. The anti-political humanism of the trilogy may, as Raymond Williams held, be partly ascribable to the exigencies of the naturalist form, which makes politics (as opposed to domesticity) hard to dramatize: 'As a direct action it is on the streets, and the people crowded in the houses react to it, in essential ways, as if it were an action beyond and outside them.'[22] In other words, realist drama, because it presents home life in a close often intimate way, tends to be biased in favour of the domestic over the political. It is true that the naturalist form focuses our gaze on the living room and that wider political and social forces remain largely off stage. However the anti-political import of these plays can only partly be explained by this formal bias. There seems to be a polemical insistence, a thematic as well as stylistic fore-grounding, of the intrusion of politics into domesticity.

Moreover, attempts to hammer out a consistency between O'Casey's life and art by arguing that the trilogy is in line with his anti-national-ist socialism do not convince.[23] O'Casey may have left his beloved Irish Citizen Army under James Connolly's leadership because of its lurch towards the Green banner. He may have spent most of his life as a staunch communist and unwavering supporter of the Soviet Union. Yet for all his personal commitments to the labour movement, and in contrast to later propagandistic plays, the socialists in *Juno and the Paycock* and *The Plough and the Stars* are as deluded and conceited as the nationalist braggarts. Jerry Devine and the Covey mouth static dogmas and dead shibboleths but neither contribute anything to ame-liorate the practical sufferings of the heroic women. Furthermore, even if the military violence *was* in the service of a cause that O'Casey con-sidered justifiable, it would not make that much difference to the dra-matic action. It is an important feature of the Dublin trilogy, not often remarked upon, that even if the trouble in the streets was not, as Juno thinks, down to the stupidity of men, even if they were fighting just or heroic battles, the tragedies of these families would still unfold. The braggadocio and delusions of the characters could have thrived equally in a 'just' as much as an 'unjust' or futile War. There were, no doubt, cowards like Donal Davoren, traitors like Johnny Boyle, or martyrs like Jack Clitheroe in the Spanish Civil war, the French Resistance, or – close to O'Casey's heart – the Russian Revolution. Similar plays, with similar dramatic power and a similar tragic action of families torn apart, could have been written about these violent eruptions. The plays do not really engage in political critique at all (save for their antipathy to political rhetoric), rather drawing their energy from the human suf-fering that all war brings. Whatever one's stance on the events in Dublin during these turbulent years, the truth is that these plays in the last reckoning do not have too much to say about Irish politics, only about war in general which, it will come as no surprise, is hell.

However, simply to conclude that the politics of O'Casey's drama is coarse and simplistic and to leave it at that obscures important, rich seams in the trilogy and the tragic vision it expresses. Many elements in his drama brush against the humanist dogma, taken on so credulously by both supporters and detractors alike. His effort in the trilogy to replace nationalist politics with the mythic 'Family' is an uncomfortable transition, which leaves the way open for an intrusion of indeterminate, impersonal historical forces, or 'chassis'. Yet even as it brushes against and fragments the drama's governing polemic, this intrusion and instability can offer suggestive and dramatically effective tensions and conflicts. However, most productions, in their emphasis on naturalist coherence and a neat opposition between domestic integrity and destructive political ideology, have glided over this potential and filtered out the alternative voices. As Maik Hamburger argues:

> the dramatic unity even of the early plays is a unity of heterogeneously contrasting elements that only become effective on the stage if these elements are allowed to maintain their autonomy within the whole. It is the task of the theatre to make these structures 'talk', and it is a debatable point whether the theatre has hitherto evolved a type of acting that can bring out the full richness of these early plays.[24]

The multiple tonal register in the plays – shifting from comedy to tragedy, realism to expressionism, melodrama to vaudeville – could highlight the anguish and dissonance behind the inconsistency and uncertainty of the politics. For instance, the party scene in *Juno and the Paycock*, where the pathos of the Tancred funeral rebukes the revelry in the Boyles' living room, could be presented as the fissured, guilt-ridden, incompatible confrontation it potentially is. However, smoothness and consistency in the dramatic production render it a much more passive, toothless affair. This emasculates the full dramatic effect, the incommensurability and the conflict that would emerge in a production that, instead of reproducing cosy verisimilitude, was attuned to the restive expressionistic undercurrents of the play.[25]

Juno and the Paycock and *The Plough and the Stars* are ultimately not so sanctimoniously polar in their opposition between family and politics, women and men, as their ostensible messages, highlighted by most productions, would suggest. O'Casey's detractors have unwittingly replicated the erroneous oppositions for which he is praised by his admirers. O'Casey does not just comment impartially on his times, he is a symptom of them. Far from transcending or debunking the rhetoric of 'isms', O'Casey is traumatized by it. A gung-ho advocate of political transformation all his life, O'Casey wrote his most famous tragedies when the Irish revolutionary dream had turned into the nightmare of Civil War. The effects of historical disillusionment deeply disturbed his instincts to find a secular remedy to the problems generated by social and political conditions. However, O'Casey maintains a veneer of moral coherence to gloss over these thematic cracks. Discarding his political radicalism for the domestic haven of naturalist drama, he reaches for a humanistic indictment of dangerous delusion, aimed at gullible guttersnipes who believe the bombastic rhetoric visited on them by starry-eyed ideologues. Yet what makes these tragedies interesting is the effect of dissonance, the tensions that emerge when the subterranean pessimism contradicts the overt humanistic fervour. Confusion and embitterment stalk O'Casey's comic and satirical portrayals of Dublin life, as he strives for an idiom to render a disintegrating society cognitively coherent. He keeps a tight grip on the dogma of political remediability, even when he has become disillusioned with politics in action. However much we may admire O'Casey's tremendous energy, his heroic achievement in self-education, his unstinting industry and ceaseless, high-minded fight for justice, there is in his drama a counteractive impulse of dejection, disenchantment and political passivity that he represses and often redirects into moral high-mindedness and sentimentality. However, if there are infelicities in O'Casey's moral and political thought as expressed in the trilogy, they have been engendered by the contemporary political situation. The incompleteness of O'Casey's aesthetic engagement with politics – apart from the exigencies of the naturalist form, of which, given his later experimentation, he seems to have been aware, even if he was not wholly successful in finding a formal solution – is not just due to lack of sophistication on his part. Modern critics have too briskly taken on this rather condescending, quasi-Yeatsian assumption about O'Casey. Rather, it is symptomatic of deeper lacunae, and deeper flaws. It is not, as O'Casey's detractors often maintain of the Dublin trilogy, simply a failure to give politics a fair hearing; his fraught confrontation with social circumstances is not just a refusal of ideology, it is an *alienation* from it. That is to say, his attitude in the trilogy is not, as it has sometimes been regarded, simply an affirmation of humanism and the values of hearth and home against the deleterious intrusions of politics and ideology; it is a renunciation of the idea of political system altogether. The politics of his Dublin trilogy is not just a criticism of his supposedly self-deluding characters, nor is it principally an attack on changeable political and social conditions. For all the attempts to personalize the suffering, to de-mythologize the national tragedy, the domestic story chronicled in these plays is also the tragedy of Ireland in the nineteen twenties, the story of O'Casey's own political genesis. Behind O'Casey's depiction of political rhetoric as a dangerous delusion preying on credulous individuals is a palpable sense of his own profound disillusionment with politics.

So the Dublin plays, for all the comic overtures, sound a sombre note of confusion, guilt and disappointment. Desmond Greaves argues that the historical events that the three Dublin plays treat are regarded retrospectively through the disenchanting perspective of the Civil War: 'O'Casey's three great Dublin plays were written in pain, anger and disillusionment. All the high hopes of the past, even things thought secure and eternal came crashing down.'[26] This notion of 'disillusionment' is significant, given that the three plays are usually read as tragedies set on course by the dangers of *delusion*. In contrast to Synge's Christy Mahon or the Douls, whose delusions of grandeur and heroism give them some dignity and imagination in the teeth of an anaemic community, when O'Casey's characters blind themselves to the 'real world' of domesticity and family obligation, they set about a train of events that ends in terrible tragedy. The exposure of dangerous delusion – as a perversion of natural, family values – might seem a directly contrary motivation to the dramatization of a painful disillusionment. The first implicitly espouses the 'real world' as an antidote to the perils of dream, the second laments the real world as the enemy of hope. Delusion suggests a firm normative reality that is dangerously denied; disillusionment, by contrast, suggests the frustration of a worthwhile struggle, the exposure of a cruel illusion at the heart of a noble aspiration. Hence 'delusion' and 'disillusionment' deal in the same thematic currency with directly opposing value systems. In a delusory scene, the delusion creates the tragedy; in disillusionment, the regrettable return of a brutal, recalcitrant reality creates it. Typically, delusion ends in recognition; disillusionment begins with it. O'Casey conflates the two, choosing to indict a delusory politics, which he projects onto his starry-eyed, credulous male characters, as a mask for political disillusionment. Fortunately this is only a partly successful enterprise. The veneer of anti-ideological polemic has enough cracks to allow contesting discourses to come into dramatically productive conflict.

The Dublin trilogy: disillusionment to delusion

Reading the trilogy in the terms suggested above, as a conflict between O'Casey's own political disillusionment and his compensatory condemnation of political delusion, casts his putative anti-politics in a new light. The first of O'Casey's Dublin trilogy, *The Shadow of a Gunman*, performs a subtle reenactment of this transmutation from disillusionment to the indictment of delusion: the effective rehabilitation of a delinquent politics into a renewed missionary zeal. Here, delusion and disillusionment – the respective flaws of Minnie and Donal Davoren – vie for thematic dominance as the chief target of the play. Significantly, however, and unlike the later two tragedies, Davoren's pseudo-poetic disillusionment comes in for O'Casey's most withering scorn. Though a backward projection to the War of Independence, the play bears many disconsolate marks of the Civil War during which it was written. Often regarded as less accomplished than the other two, it is, nonetheless, in one sense the darkest play of the trilogy, second only to *The Silver Tassie* in O'Casey's entire corpus. All the characters, save Minnie, are contemptibly cowering and selfish; and all, save Seumas, entwine themselves in a communal heroic fantasy, which masks their true natures. Many commentators have perceived an affinity between this play and Synge's *The Playboy of the Western World*.[27] The outsider is led to self-discovery through the imaginative projections of the natives, who seek to turn him into a violent hero as a foil for their own stagnancy and frustration. However, if Christy Mahon's role as a false hero inspires him to action and enables him to unlock a previously suppressed sense of self-worth, Davoren's conceited exploitation of other people's credulity is of wholly destructive effect. Unlike Christy, Davoren looks down on the people around him and is too complacent in his effete despondency to allow their projections to ignite his imagination or unlock his powers of self-realization. Compared to Davoren's world-weary posturing, and to the corrosive, self-serving cynicism of Seumas Shields, Minnie Powell's naive valour appears almost heroic. Certainly, her self-sacrifice in taking the bombs, however misconceived, is the noblest action of a drama populated almost exclusively by braggarts and cowards. The 'accidental' nature of her death, however, is worthy of note. Like that of Bessie Burgess it comes from a mishap, a misunderstanding rather than something fatally predestined or set inexorably in train by a fatal flaw. It has all the miserable, haphazard pointlessness of the death in the road accident that we considered in the Introduction. The sheer avoidability of her death, however, is only partly related to her gullibility and political idealism. The random element, here and elsewhere in O'Casey's depiction of death and suffering, is significant because it suggests an aspect which slips outside O'Casey's purely *social* critique. It is unnecessary, unpredictable and undeserved, but no less tragic for all that.

The play's most intriguing feature is the disorientation in the dialectic between disillusionment and delusion, despair and false hope. Davoren's carefully cultivated 'dejection', elevating him in his own mind to a lofty Shelleyan sphere, is just another form of posturing self-deception. Despite his self-assurance at the end of Act I, Davoren bitterly comes to realize the great danger in being the shadow of a gunman. The recognition, however, brings no catharsis or renewed societal integration because Davoren's paraded self-knowledge is ultimately fraudulent. It is a parody of tragic *anagnorisis*:

> Ah me, alas! Pain, pain, pain ever, for ever! It's terrible to think that little Minnie is dead, but it's still more terrible to think that Davoren and Shields are alive! Oh, Donal Davoren, shame is your portion now till the silver cord is loosened and the golden bowl be broken. Oh, Davoren, Donal Davoren, poet and poltroon, poltroon and poet! (TP, 130)

His new self-knowledge, of his own terrible cowardice, is all too easily assimilated into his practised linguistic rituals; the pretence of brave confrontation, filtered through poetry and melodrama, ironically protects his calloused sensibility. By this point in the play, his bogus poetry and affected despondency ring false, as does his repetition of morose Shelleyan fragments – 'Ah me, alas! Pain, pain, pain ever, for ever!'. Even as he strives for melodramatic import, his high-flown rhetoric indicates that he is hiding behind his pessimism, rather than confronting his pretentious vanity and culpable passivity. In a curious imbrication of the two dominant yet ostensibly opposing themes, Davoren's despair is *itself* cast as a form of comforting delusion. The 'poet' in Davoren helps to delude the poltroon. The recognition of guilt, couched in this over-rich idiom, becomes a mockery of itself. Paradoxically, poetic confrontation of truth becomes a means of distorting it. Davoren replaces bogus and pseudo-poetic self-delusion with bogus and pseudo-poetic self-knowledge.

Despite their unflattering portrayals, the figures of Davoren and Shields clearly manifest many characteristics of their author.[28] Shields, like O'Casey, has a militant republican past, but the experience of actual violence has disabused him of Cathleen ní Houlihan and her guerrilla charms:

> *Davoren.* I remember the time when you yourself believed in nothing but the gun.
> *Seumas.* Ay, when there wasn't a gun in the country; I've a different opinion now when there's nothin' but guns in the country ... . An' you daren't open your mouth, for Kathleen ni Houlihan is very different now to the woman who used to play the harp an' sing 'Weep on, weep on, your hour is past', for she's a ragin' divil now, an' if you looked crooked at her you're sure of a punch in th' eye. (TP, 110)

In case we were in any doubt that Shields is following O'Casey's own military career path, including his one-time fondness for the imagery of Cathleen ní Houlihan, he gets to utter the play's main moral message – if so uncertain and vacillating a play as this can be said to have a moral: 'I draw the line when I hear the gunmen blowin' about dyin' for the people, when it's the people that are dyin' for the gunmen!' (TP, 111). Similarly, Davoren follows O'Casey in his fondness for Shelley – the genuinely revolutionary Shelley operating as a counterpoint to Davoren's impotence and passivity – and also in his mistrust of the mythology of Romantic nationalism: 'Oh, we've had enough of poems, Minnie, about '98, and of Ireland, too' (TP, 90). These attitudes make his exploitation of Minnie's over-eager Romantic nationalism all the more culpable.

Perhaps the facet of Shields and Davoren where we can most clearly discern an uneasy and guilty projection of their creator is in their lack of military courage. For all their world-weary fatigue with the myths of nationalism – and in contrast to a later heroine like Bettie Burgess – neither has the human courage to prevent Minnie from taking the bombs from the room or to intercede when she has been apprehended by the Black and Tans. O'Casey, it seems, suffered from similar timorousness. Though his *Autobiographies* could scarcely be accused of self-effacement, the one failing to which O'Casey continually admits is his fear in the face of military danger. This aspect of his personality surely contributed to the vividness with which he later characterized Johnny Boyle, living out his final days in terrified anticipation of his coming execution. O'Casey honestly recounts his terror when the police horse-charged the labour demonstration in Parliament Street and, later, during the union scuffles with the police on O'Connell Street. He envisages the results of violence in highly graphic terms. Seeing a phalanx of police confront a union gathering, he feels a rush of nausea: 'for in his mind's eye he could see the swiftly rising arm, the snarling face, and feel the broad bone of his skull caving in on his brain, with the darkness of death beside him' (A1, 579). Repeatedly, during violent street scuffles, the belligerence of his written word deserts him: 'Sean shivered, for he was not a hero, and he felt it was unwise to have come here' (A1, 582). O'Casey's admission that he was no hero is extraordinarily anomalous in the context of the autobiographies as a whole; it could only appear, as here, where violence or the fear of violence was involved. Even when castigating his detested, drunken brother Michael, Sean ascribes to him a physical bravery that he knows he does not himself possess: 'And yet, not so long ago, Sean had seen that perished face lit up with a courage that he could never summon to himself' (A2, 36). He must have been acutely aware of this failing during the Easter Rising, when many of his old friends were combatants.[29] As his biographer puts it, 'O'Casey's emotions in 1916 were volatile, he was both moved by and excluded emotionally from the rebellion: how could he not feel his own cowardice – with a deep, self-consuming bitterness that the revolt had not followed the path he wanted in the face of so much heroism.'[30] In retrospect, however, he can recast his non-involvement in the rebellion in terms of his later anti-nationalism. He can also mitigate the guilt, made more pointed by the deep political commitment of his adult life, by filling his sense of political vacuity with artistic mission. Nonetheless, O'Casey's move from active militarism and politics into a more rarefied poetic realm is underwritten by doubt and feelings of impotence at his passivity and bitter disenchantment with the course of Irish politics. Donal Davoren, sophisticated, poetic, pretentious and passive, is a sublimated expression of this guilt and this frustration. *The Shadow of a Gunman*, though it lacks the breadth and ambition of the later two trilogy plays, is unique in its self-doubt and embitterment. Moreover, the efforts to transmute harsh disappointment and disillusionment into a meaningful and moral exposure of delusion – the governing motive of the trilogy – is here most strongly encoded in the action. Ironically, the relative inexperience with which O'Casey wrote *The Shadow of a Gunman* is, in one sense, its strength. *Juno and the Paycock* and *The Plough and the Stars* are more accomplished in the concealment of the suppressed motivations behind their construction, smoothed over by a more finessed realist coherence (exacerbated, as I have suggested, by productions that suppress those elements which fragment this coherence).

Critics have tended to read the trilogy as a monolith, gliding over major differences that exist between the three plays. This is particularly true of *Juno* and the *Plough* where the anti-revolutionary didacticism of the latter is often read back into the former. To be sure there is a horror of war in *Juno* but it is of a far more complex, tentative order than many commentators – old and new, supporters and detractors – have allowed. *Juno* is set during the Civil War, a much less glorious enterprise than the Easter Rising by any standards. Hence the waste which the play expresses does not need the same degree of polemical insistence and satire with which O'Casey festoons *The Plough and the Stars*. *Juno and the Paycock* deals in broken dreams. The narrative uses a stock melodramatic plot – fortune supposedly inherited, then lost – as a mockingly blunt allegory for the disappointments of post-Independence Ireland.[31] The conventional interpretation of the play elevates Juno as the humanist heroine, who keeps house and home together despite the drunken irresponsibility of her feckless husband. Again, however, there is much in the play that queries Juno's opposition between hearts of stone and hearts of flesh, or at least undermines her status as the play's pragmatic heroine. G. J. Watson rightly regards the depiction of Boyle and Joxer as undermining Juno's allocated role as heroine, yet this need not be a flaw.[32] The comic allure of Captain Boyle and Joxer corrodes the moral authority of Juno who, for all her pragmatic forbearance, often strikes the spectator as something of a killjoy. The verbosity and imagination of the two men, though parasitic and culpably irresponsible, is often more attractive than Juno's dour conformity. As Boyle remarks, "'Tisn't Juno should be her pet name at all, but Deirdre of the Sorras, for she's always grousin'" (TP, 11). The paycock has the finer plumage. We know that it is Juno who keeps the family together and we admire her for her fortitude and compassion, particularly at the end of the play. Poverty means she can afford the luxury of neither imagination nor politics. However, despite his irresponsibility, the Captain's shenanigans sparkle long after the curtain has dropped. To be sure, we also witness his selfish, vainglorious bluster in its less attractive manifestation and his hopelessly weak, inadequate and immoral rejection of Mary at the end of the play.

However, the ambivalence of the audience response need not indicate wholesale dramatic weakness, but could feasibly engender a healthy confusion – an antidote to the polemicism for which O'Casey is notorious. An astute production might well turn the convolution and confusion into an enabling feature, reinforcing the 'dehiscence', disintegration and chassis which, Beckett reminds us, is the play's tragic import.[33] After all, for all the dogmatism of O'Casey, the conflictual register in his dramatic method is geared to generate precisely this sort of ambivalence. *Juno* shifts from high tragedy to low farce with such facility that we are often discomfited; yet we are also enabled, appropriately circumspect and cautious about the response the play seems to be demanding. Part of us feels we ought to spurn Boyle, yet we cannot help being lured by his scandalous behaviour, just as we cannot help being somewhat irked by Juno's tedious good sense. We are right to be equivocal about Boyle and Juno. We feel we should admire Juno, but we cannot help preferring the Paycock and his roguery endures longer than her responsibility.

Furthermore, Juno is not always the put-upon 'heart of flesh'. A certain scorn for her is inculcated early on in the action. When Mary asks her advice on what ribbon she should wear in her hair, her response, though schooled in the pragmatics of survival, seems troublingly acquiescent: 'I don't know what a girl on strike wants to be wearin' a ribbon round her head for, or silk stockin's on her legs either; it's wearin' them things that make the employers think they're givin' yous too much money' (TP, 7). This is a cowering, dispirited sort of advice which, though it may help Mary keep her job, is ultimately self-defeating, for it espouses the sort of forelock-tugging on which unjust labour conditions thrive. It is certainly not an attitude that O'Casey, dismissed from an early job for refusing to take off his cap when collecting his pay, would endorse.[34] It suggests that Juno's anti-politics is not so unblinkingly heroic as might be supposed. Her instinct for family preservation seems admirably pragmatic when opposed to windy nationalist rhetoric, yet it does not seem so noble when it comes into visible conflict with the interests of others. She criticizes Mary's solidarity with her victimized fellow worker, Jennie Claffey, on the grounds that, before the strike, Mary 'never had a good word for her' (TP, 7). Mary's justification for her action – 'a principle's a principle' (TP, 8) – seems solid enough here, however shallowly rehearsed this refrain later becomes. Not all principles are just bombast, as O'Casey's life often admirably attests. Whatever her practical compassion for Mary and down-to-earth realism at the end of the play, there is an element of inefficacy in Mrs. Boyle that cannot simply be put down to the vagaries of external forces and unreliable men. Her cures for suffering often do not work. She is signally inadequate in comforting Johnny:

> *Mrs. Boyle.* There, now, go back an' lie down again an' I'll bring you a nice cup o' tay.
> *Johnny.* Tay, tay, tay! You're always thinkin' o' tay. If a man was dyin', you'd thry to make him swally a cup o' tay. (TP, 8)

Juno's relations with Johnny, here and throughout the play, merit close analysis. Having failed to dissuade him from military action, she is unable to assuage the trauma he now endures. She can only say 'I told you so'. This inefficacy stands in signal contrast to her clear-sighted support of Mary in her more 'social' crisis at the end of the play. In her relations with Johnny, at least, there is no reason to suppose that Juno's anti-politics is a strength. Nor is there any reason to take on board her description of Johnny's soldiering as 'makin' a fool of himself' (TP, 9). If Boyle's talk of 'doin' his bit' in Easter Week is fraudulent bluster, his son's claims to have done enough for Ireland may well be merited. The Captain's comic pretensions to heroism are hardly any more dubious than Juno's dismissal of authentic heroism. Johnny is a complex figure whose story is only glimpsed aslant, just as he spends most of his tormented time in the adjacent room, off stage. Yet his significance should not be underestimated.[35] One should pause before believing Juno's evaluation of his activities in Easter Week. Her view that Johnny lost his 'best principle' when he lost his arm may be no more reliable than her impatience with Mary's principle to strike in support of her fellow-worker, despite a personal animosity towards that individual. Watson, in dismissing Johnny as 'a fool' in politics, too readily subscribes to Juno's attitude to her son. Though given to nationalist sloganizing, he is not, as Watson claims, 'clearly from the same stable as Tommy Owens in *The Shadow of a Gunman*'[36] – not least for the reason that he actually *did* do his bit in Easter Week. After the bogus posturing of Davoren, Johnny is not just the shadow of a gunman – he has been a real soldier, however physically and psychologically shattered he has become. He is not a fool, but a broken man, metaphorically and literally. He is the figure who most represents the Ireland of which, and from which, O'Casey writes. Crushed by Civil War and haunted by the guilt of betrayal of his comrade, which is also a betrayal of his own political idealism, Johnny's greatest hope is of escape. News of the legacy provides him with this prospect. Whatever mysterious impulse caused him to betray Robbie Tancred, his old comrade, is never disclosed. The betrayal, however, is a pained glance at Civil War Ireland, too traumatic to be more than obliquely incorporated into the main action of the play.

Towards the end of Act II, in a scene already referred to, the Boyles throw a party to celebrate their inheritance. Just as the audience begins to settle down in its enjoyment of the comic spectacle of song and repartee, the gathering is interrupted by Mrs. Tancred with the procession for her dead son's removal to the church. The harmony is disrupted by a scene of woeful grief and tragedy in the face of which the rejoicing of the Boyles, Joxer and Mrs. Madigan seems troublingly discordant. Previously, the intrusion into the comic antics of Boyle and Joxer was economic, represented by Juno's concerns. Now it is political. Faced with the grief-stricken Mrs. Tancred, Mrs. Boyle and Mary offer words of consolation and compassion (though Juno's exhortation to the bereaved mother to come in for a hot cup of tea echoes Johnny's earlier rebuke that his mother's answer to every problem is 'a cup o' tay'). The men, by contrast, prove dreadfully inadequate. Bentham's view is that 'the only way to deal with a mad dog is to destroy him' (TP, 46) and Captain Boyle disowns all involvement and responsibility: 'We've nothin' to do with these things, one way or t'other. That's the Government's business, an' let them do what we're payin' them for doin' (TP, 47). As with Johnny's mainly private trauma, the ugliness happens offstage, the open door an aperture through which it is witnessed – by the protagonists, not us – from the all-too-fragile domestic setting. The door closes and the gathering seeks to return to its entertainments, troubled now by awareness of events outside their window. It is Johnny, significantly, who is most eager to put on the gramophone. He, more than anybody, needs distraction from the mournful procession in the street. Their revels now restarted, the officious Needle Nugent makes an indignant intervention into the room to complain about the disrespect being shown to the funeral outside. Juno's response suggests that she shares her husband's tendency to eschew community obligations: 'Maybe, Needle Nugent, it's nearly time we had a little less respect for the dead, and a little more regard for the livin'' (TP, 49). The feature of Juno often admired as her greatest strength – her unshakeable commitment to her family – is also, on occasion, her weakness, particularly when it comes into conflict with wider social imperatives. Her concern for her family – at the expense of society, now represented by the procession – leads to her self-reproach at the end of the play: 'Maybe I didn't feel sorry enough for Mrs. Tancred when her poor son was found as Johnny's been found now' (TP, 71). If the play regards Juno's hostility to politics as a humanistic virtue, the same quality could be said to erode her commitment to her community, to the other mothers in the tenement.

The ambivalent depiction of Juno complicates David Krause's claim that the governing vision of O'Casey's Dublin trilogy is anti-heroic.[37] The import of *Juno and the Paycock* could more accurately be described as anti-betrayal – an opposite tendency really because, as in Johnny's case, the betrayal can be a betrayal of his own erstwhile heroism. There are a web of betrayals in *Juno*, extending from the neglect and idleness of Captain Boyle to the political intrigues of Johnny to Bentham's scandalous desertion of Mary. The advantage of the concept of betrayal for the disillusioned political thinker is that a clear target, a temporal cause, emerges from the mess of historical process. A traitor, or a treacherous tendency, in explaining the failure of a revolution, can provide a reassuring coherence for one who has invested so much in the idea of revolution. As already seen in *The Shadow of a Gunman*, the search for a target, for temporal causes, is often the motivation behind O'Casey's robust insistence on the 'stupidity o' men'. He seeks a coherent cause for his own disillusionment, the solace of something to blame. The wider view of O'Casey's life reveals his disposition as anything but anti-heroic, as his lifelong totemization of Jim Larkin testifies. There are more villains than heroes in his life-story, but the model, albeit inverted, remains fundamentally the same.

O'Casey's anxious transference of the irreparable into the reparable is not always successful, and the materialist, temporal and political idiom is occasionally punctuated by the cosmic and fatalistic. The most obvious area where this occurs is, ironically, politics itself, which seems to be driven by fate, not by human agency. As Seamus Deane puts it: 'what O'Casey has done here is to cast politics in the role of an inexorable fate which exploits the flaws in men's characters for the sake of destroying them.'[38] Of course, it is paradoxical that political agitation – inflamed by the possibility that power can be more fairly distributed, that 'self-determination' is a realizable goal – becomes the very source which robs the tenement dwellers of their agency, trapping them in a fatalistic spiral. O'Casey is led to this contradictory conclusion because he is unwilling to yield up the idea that suffering is *avoidable*, but has abandoned the notion that communal suffering might, politically, be *reparable*. Though O'Casey instinctively searches for a temporal, secular cause for the suffering he depicts – an insistence that masks his own morose disenchantment with meliorism – he often ends up inadvertently falling back on a discourse of irreparable tragedy.

The oscillation between avoidable and irreparable suffering pervades the play. On the one hand, we have the indefatigable Juno ascribing the suffering her family endures to human not divine sources: 'These things have nothin' to do with the Will o' God. Ah, what can God do agen the stupidity o' men!' (TP, 70). On the other hand, we have a sense of unravelling tragic destiny, a sense that the family's fate is as mysterious and inscrutable as the stars at which Boyle so eerily and poignantly gazes. In Act I, Boyle's fantasies on his glamorous seafaring past, comically encouraged by the unctuous and entirely disbelieving Joxer, drift into one of the most famous and moving speeches of the play:

> *Boyle.* … Ofen, an ofen, when I was fixed to the wheel with a marlin-spike, an' the win's blowin' fierce an' the waves lashin' an' lashin', till you'd think every minute was goin' to be your last, an' it blowed, an' blowed – blew is the right word, Joxer, but blowed is what the sailors use… .
> *Joxer.* Aw, it's a darlin' word, a darlin' word.
> *Boyle.* An' as it blowed an' blowed, I often looked up at the sky an' assed meself the question – what is the stars, what is the stars?
> *Voice of Coal Vendor.* Any blocks, coal-blocks; blocks, coal-blocks!
> (TP, 23)

In contrast to Juno's pragmatism, Boyle's speech seems to place the architecture of the universe beyond the knowledge and power of humankind. The contrast of the coal vendor's toil-worn cries at once undercuts and reinforces his meditation. This clash of the secular and quasi-spiritual, an opposition related to the remediable and the fatalistic, is reflected in other dichotomies in the play. It is evinced, for instance, by the incursion of the supernatural. Johnny, like Macbeth, has a vision of the blood-boltered victim of his treachery: an omen of the retribution to be visited on himself. It is represented on another level by Charles Bentham and Jerry Devine. (The names are ironically inappropriate: no one is less divine than the atheistic Devine, no one less utilitarian than the idealist Bentham.) Devine's dogmatic socialism is scarcely less reprehensible than Bentham's self-indulgently over-abstract and ultimately self-serving theosophy. As Boyle remarks on the contrast: 'The two o' them ud give you a pain in your face, listenin' to them; Jerry believin' in nothin', an' Bentham believin' in everythin'.

One that says all is God an' no man; an' th'other that says all is man an' no God!' (TP, 33).

There is, then, a counterpoint in the play between the ethereal and the all-too-real, between the pretentiously elevated and the obstinately material. This opposition is not surprising in a text which continually entwines inflated language with squalid reality. As always, the joyful, imaginative principle represented by Boyle leans on the labours of others: his metaphysical musings, like his self-pampering, must suspend the pressing drudgery of material survival. In this respect, Boyle and Joxer are characters in the tradition of the Douls in Synge's *The Well of the Saints* – they provide a seductive alternative which, for all its comical and imaginative appeal, has nonetheless a germ of pathos because it is ultimately fraudulent and parasitic. Just as the characters' verbal eloquence and loquacity mask an oppressive, claustrophobic inability to act, so do imagination, joy and entertainment survive only by covering over a harrowing political and material reality. Another master of the claustrophobic mood, Samuel Beckett also uses the technique, albeit in a sparser, more pointed way: Estragon and Vladimir strive to block out an intolerable reality through inventive, if pointless, verbal exchanges and the distractions of empty ritual and habit. In their attempts to evade an intolerable reality, they stand alongside Joxer and Boyle and Martin and Mary Doul.

The oscillation between reparable and irreparable discourses, between materialism and idealism, finds a parallel expression in the formal incompatibilities of tragic and comic modes. The comic moments attempt to evade but are ultimately undercut by intractable tragic reality, be it Juno's economics or Johnny's politics. O'Casey's earlier critics fretted about the generic properties of his work: whether it should be regarded as comedy or tragedy. For writers like O'Casey, concludes David Krause, 'life is at the same time too brutal and too beautiful to be treated with undisguised agony or idealism. For them, the double mask of tragi-comedy reveals the polarity of the human condition.'[39] This idea that the mixed genre of 'tragi-comedy' possesses a high 'truth-value' through its treatment of the essential 'polarity of the human condition' is common amongst apologists for the genre. It may be tempting to go along with Krause in regarding O'Casey's conflicting moods as, simply, indicative of this duality – a realistic depiction of a world governed by the polar forces of good and evil, joy and sorrow. However, on closer analysis, O'Casey's form of tragi-comedy, like Beckett's, is no happily complete combination of the two halves of human experience. It is not just a question of contrast or literary chiaroscuro. The comic and tragic moments in O'Casey's work – the humour and the pathos – do not simply collude, they also, at their most poignant, collide. There is discordant incongruity here, not just contrast or complementarity. The Boyles' celebrations do not contrast with Mrs. Tancred's grief, rather they blaspheme against it, just as Captain Boyle's endearingly comic bluster is a betrayal of his familial duties. J. W. Krutch is unusual in recognizing this deeply anomalous nature of O'Casey's comic tragedy: 'O'Casey makes no effort to harmonize these elements [the tragic and the comic]. The most striking, indeed the almost unique characteristic of his plays is the fact that they are one long unresolved dissonance.'[40] As already argued, that critics can regard the conflict in terms of simple dramatic duality may derive from the limitations of the realist form which, by imposing naturalistic coherence on the proceedings, irons out the clash of moods and evaluative demands, creating a spurious holism. That dramatic productions of the trilogy have tended to reproduce, rather than to challenge, the domestic verisimilitude has regrettably limited the potential for the comic and tragic motifs to emerge as conflictual, not just contrasting.

The antagonism between the comic and the tragic reaches its zenith in the final act of *Juno*. All has been undone: the newly acquired trappings of wealth removed, Mary disgraced and deserted. With the exception of Juno's support for Mary, all are caught in a web of betrayal and recrimination. In a hollow irony, Jerry assures Mary that 'Humanity is above everything', before he realizes the full extent of her crisis. The verses Mary recites, 'Humanity's Strife with Nature', which Jerry read at the Socialist Rooms earlier in their courtship, powerfully bring home the sense of loss and disenchantment which permeate the play, and the historical events that formed it. The optimistic idea of human supremacy over the natural forces of perversion and destruction now seems painfully distant. Moreover, O'Casey's supposed demystification of heroism and ideology falls apart to reveal the disillusionment which it served to mask:

> An' we felt the power that fashion'd
> All the lovely things we saw,
> That created all the murmur
> Of an everlasting law,
> Was a hand of force an' beauty,
> With an eagle's tearin' claw.

> Then we saw our globe of beauty
> Was an ugly thing as well,
> A hymn divine whose chorus
> Was an agonizin' yell;
> Like the story of a demon,
> That an angel had to tell;
>
> Like a glowin' picture by a
> Hand unsteady, brought to ruin;
> Like her craters, if their deadness
> Could give life unto the moon;
> Like the agonizing horror
> Of a violin out of tune. (TP, 67)

These verses are a curious addition to O'Casey's play and merit attention. Against his usual meliorism – and in contrast to Jerry's socialism – they express a profoundly Manichaean view of the universe. Evil and discord coexist with goodness and harmony, not just because of the 'stupidity o' men', but as a fundamental part of the divine signature. Disenchanted with Jerry's *faux* socialist meliorism, Mary has come to the pessimistic view that human suffering is caused by a fundamental perversion of nature. Her poem corresponds with a post-lapsarian iconography: all the beauties of the created world are marred by a fundamental discontent. The implication is conservative: human agency, and hence political reform, is invariably limited by the in-built flaws of nature. As we have seen, O'Casey's prevailing instinct is to subscribe to Juno's belief that the flaws of society are wholly 'man'-made. This is the unambiguous implication of his pre-Civil War political stance and the socialist optimism of most of his later plays. In the trilogy, however, he is forced to negotiate the supreme let-down brought on by the course of Irish history. O'Casey's belief in reparability is vitiated in the trilogy – it is his desperate efforts to regain the social element that sometimes leads to the confusion and polemicism of which critics such as Watson and Deane have complained. However, if we read these plays against the grain of their overt polemic, we can observe O'Casey writing not as an impartial observer or a bitter satirist of his country's tragedy, but as a symptom of it.

The final scenes of *Juno* bring the contesting meliorist and pessimistic philosophies into even sharper relief. On learning of Johnny's death, Juno repeats Mrs. Tancred's threnody for her son. This speech alternates from an accusation of divine desertion to her earlier humanist sense that suffering is brought on through the stupidity of men:

What was the pain I suffered, Johnny, bringing you into the world to carry you to your cradle, to the pains I'll suffer carryin' you out o' the world to bring you to your grave! Mother o' God, Mother o' God, have pity on us all! Blessed Virgin, where were you when me darlin' son was riddled with bullets? Sacred Heart o' Jesus, take away our hearts o' stone, and give us hearts o' flesh! Take away this murdherin' hate, an' give us Thine own eternal love!' (TP, 71–2)

This is a scene of supreme pathos in which Juno's eloquence and dignity lend her heroism, not a heroism of idealism or high grandeur but of practicality and family loyalty. She is not a visionary, but is clear-sighted and compassionate. However, its eloquence is not matched by consistency. The plea for pity from the Blessed Virgin contrasts with the Job-like accusation of the ensuing sentiment. Trust in God shifts to feelings of loss and divine abandonment – echoing all the other betrayals in the play. Finally, the suffering is blamed on the 'hearts o' stone': political suffering is brought about by human callousness.

The play might well have ended at this point, but O'Casey adds a scene which places the tragic conflict in a new relation to the comic incongruity. This collision can, at its most violent, increase the dehiscence and disintegration and move to a point beyond tragedy, beyond the conflict between the family and society, humour and pathos. Nowhere is this inconsistency and strange interpenetration of comic and tragic modes more brilliantly realized than in the final scene of *Juno*. The re-entrance of Boyle and Joxer is a flourish which restructures their erstwhile relation to the tragic action. Their verbal escapism no longer sweetens the sourness of the slum dwelling. Drunkenness has corroded language to near incoherence and now, in contrast to their earlier antics, the self-delusory consolations of the pair only add to the disintegration and degradation of the scene. Gabriel Fallon praises their re-entrance for striking 'a note beyond tragedy, a blistering flannel-mouthed irony sears its maudlin way across the stage and slowly drops an exhausted curtain on a world disintegrating in chassis'.[41] The uneasy counterpoint between the humour and the pathos is here unstitched, and the comic and the tragic become uncomfortably indistinguishable. This is the disintegration that Beckett praised in the play. It is a chaos in which, crucially, the forms of drama are themselves caught up. We have seen that Davoren's final speech in *The Shadow of a Gunman* is a mockery of conventional tragic recognition or *anagnorisis*. *Juno and the Paycock* similarly flouts the genre.

Following on Juno's final speech, the confrontation between the Captain and Joxer refuses the culmination of conventional dramatic tragedy. Rather than resolution or final closure, it imparts a Beckettian sense of wind-down, of things falling apart. Like a Beckettian pair, the two talk to keep out the chaos. Finally, however, the 'chassis' is dominant.

We see a similar confusion in the final play of the trilogy, though the polemically anti-nationalist tone has increased. However, the hostile attitude to the 1916 Rising expressed in *The Plough and the Stars* was not always held by O'Casey. Many have assumed, based on the denigration of the Irish Volunteers in his *Autobiographies* and in his 1919 pamphlet *The Story of the Irish Citizen Army*, that after a short-lived flirtation with nationalism in his twenties, O'Casey consistently felt an aversion to Romantic nationalism. But he tended to read back a consistency into his political position that was not there at the time, giving himself a political stance – international socialist – that belies his erstwhile nationalism. However, between 1900 and 1926 O'Casey's political loyalties underwent many mutations. In February 1913, he was defending Irish nationalism against 'Euchan', a columnist in the *Worker*, who argued, as O'Casey was later to argue, that the future political battle in Ireland would be between Capital and Labour. O'Casey's tone is intriguing:

> The delivery of Ireland is not in the Labour Manifesto, good and salutary as it may be, but in the strength, beauty, nobility and imagination of the Gaelic ideal. I am one of those who has entered into the labour of our fathers; one of those who declare – by the fame of our forefathers; by the murder of Red Hugh; by the anguished sighs of the Geraldine; by the blood–dripping wounds of Wolfe Tone; by the noble blood of Emmet; by the death-wasted bodies of the famine – that we will enter into our inheritance or we will fall one by one. Amen.[42]

So much for the Plough and the Stars or, indeed, *The Plough and the Stars*. This attitude had not entirely disappeared by Easter Week. Garry O'Connor concludes that 'O'Casey's emotions in 1916 were volatile, he was both moved by and excluded emotionally from the rebellion: how could he not feel his own cowardice – with a deep, self-consuming bitterness that the revolt had not followed the path he wanted – in the face of so much heroism'.[43] Notwithstanding the testimony of his autobiography, where he claims to have sought to prevent the insurrection, it is evident that, as late as 1917, O'Casey was glorifying the Rising. His *Lament for Thomas Ashe*, for example, contains many strongly nationalist sentiments, reminiscent of the O'Casey of 1913. He says of the Rising: 'men fought and fell with the glow of burning buildings on their faces, and the glow of enthusiasm lighting their hearts in the effort to establish an Irish Republic.'[44] Greaves thinks that O'Casey's later condemnation of the Rising – he describes it in his *Autobiographies* as a 'rare time for death in Ireland' (A1, 661) – originates in a disillusionment with the currents in Irish politics and a retrospective justification for his own non-involvement in the insurrection. But whether or not one agrees that a sense of personal guilt for not taking part in the Rising is 'the emotional fulcrum of *The Plough*',[45] one must acknowledge the element of disillusionment informing O'Casey's retrospective depiction in his play. The revolutionary ideals of the Rising had been corrupted into the carnage of Civil War. As he puts it in his *Autobiographies* (somewhat cornily), 'The terrible beauty was beginning to lose her good looks' (A2, 72).

Ostensibly, *The Plough and the Stars* is a rebuttal of the myths – especially the Cathleen ní Houlihan myth – underlying the Rising. Elevating love for Ireland above love for a woman is presented as unnatural and inhuman, equivalent to elevating an abstract, bloodless idealism above the flesh and blood familial concerns of hearth and home. Again, however, the effort to debunk the mythology of nationalism really turns out to be its inversion, just as O'Casey does not abolish Cathleen ní Houlihan but turns her into Shields's old crone in *The Shadow of a Gunman*. Even more than the previous two plays, *The Plough* has strains of nihilism beneath its surface. Mrs. Gogan, who can claim to be the most visually imaginative character in the play, has a morbid, macabre fascination with funerals and death. She gets pleasure from the fact that she is not experiencing the suffering she is witnessing: 'It always gives meself a kind o' thresspassin' joy to feel meself movin' along in a mournin' coach, an' me thinkin' that, maybe, th' next funeral'll be me own, an' glad, in a quiet way, that this is somebody else's' (TP, 141). She behaves like the spectator in Edmund Burke's conception of tragedy, enjoying the spectacle of suffering precisely because it makes her feel her own comparative safety. At every opportunity, she revels in the grisly details of violent death. In the second act, on admiring the ostrich feathers in the Foresters' uniforms, she gratuitously dwells on the physical mechanics of execution: 'When yous are goin' along, an' I see them wavin' an' noddin' an' waggin', I seem to be lookin' at each of yous hangin' at the end of rope, your eyes bulgin' an' your legs twistin' an' jerkin', gaspin' an' gaspin' for breath while yous are thryin' to die for Ireland!' (TP, 167). Her grim fantasies contrast with the rhetorical glorification of death and bloodshed made by the Speaker in the Window, but she is no less fascinated by the prospect of spilt blood.

Mrs. Gogan's story of poverty, hardship and bereavement, like that of her daughter Mollser, is only glimpsed aslant. However, she governs the opening scene of the play and gives us crucial initial information about the character of Nora Clitheroe and her relationship with her husband. All is not well with the Clitheroe household, even before politics intrudes its ugly head. Mrs. Gogan – an informed and curious observer, for all her faults – recognizes Nora's 'notions of upperosity' and the rapaciousness with which she sets about her programme of self-improvement: 'She's wipin' th' eyes of th' Covey an' poor oul' Pether – everybody knows that – screwin' every penny she can out o' them, in ordher to turn th' place into a babby house' (TP, 138). On the one hand, Nora's upwardly-mobile ambitions to take her family out of the slums – 'She's always grumblin' about havin' to live in a tenement house' (TP, 138) – is an understandable and pragmatic aspiration, to be distinguished from the nebulous idealism of the men. However, as was the case with Juno, it is often difficult to reconcile Nora's material ambitions with her duties to her immediate community. A point sometimes missed is that Nora's much admired rejection of politics is contingent on a parallel rejection of her society and of her neighbours. It is, then, highly significant, as a recently discovered production notebook has shown, that O'Casey initially intended the Clitheroes to be a middle-class family, with Jack as a clerk rather than a bricklayer. He was dissuaded by Yeats and Lennox Robinson, who were convinced that his talents were best suited to depicting proletarians.[46] Like Juno, Nora's devotion to her family is often not just anti-political, it is anti-social. For all her own assumptions of independence, and the assumptions of later liberal-minded critics who espouse the idea that Nora represents an uncomplicated family ideal, Nora's ambitions bear the disavowal of community characteristic of the middle-class values. Her loyalty to her immediate family is founded in an atomized individualism, based in a denial of societal structure and community obligation. The critically repressed facet of the play is that Nora seeks to dissociate from her immediate environment by denying her connection with it. In Act III a distressed Nora returns with the heroically brave Fluther who has rescued her from the streets. Here she reveals a selfishness contrary to the put-upon benevolence for which she is celebrated. 'I can't help thinkin' every shot fired at Jack'll be fired at me. What do I care for th'others? I can think only of me own self... .' (TP, 184). It is true that Nora is traumatized here, but the remark illustrates that her anti-heroism is not always a virtue.

When she physically tries to impede Clitheroe from proceeding with his comrades, including the gravely wounded and dependent Langon, the audience has an appropriately ambivalent response. Where does Clitheroe's duty lie? Nora claims, with the agreement of many critics of the play, that she is his 'dearest comrade' (TP, 195). But where does this leave his duty to the wounded Langon? His obligations to his friends and fellow-soldiers are now pressing and real, no longer abstract, rhetorical and ideal. The choice is not now between a vainglorious militarism and domestic reality, but between two conflicting and immediate duties. This is a far more pointed, painful dilemma, for the audience as much as for Clitheroe himself. It certainly gives the lie to the callow opposition often read into the play: 'Clitheroe puts Ireland before his wife. That is the real tragedy: death before life. Faced with a choice, the Irishman accepts Thanatos before Eros, and so the purpose of life is defeated.'[47] Luckily, from the point of view of interesting drama, the choice is not so simple. The dramatic opposition between Nora's powerful entreaties for Jack to remain with her, and Langon's agonized pleas that the three soldiers move on, generates a powerful urgency. Performed in a manner sensitive to the pressing conflict, the scene can be powerfully tragic – briefly incarnating the incompatible moral imperatives which war and revolution create. Such moral complexity counters the play's polemical pacifism and simplistic polarities that the play's detractors distrust.

Other significant slippages in the play occur in the presentation of the Clitheroe marriage. The relationship between Nora and Jack is a good deal less harmonious than we might suppose, even in the apolitical, domestic sphere that is supposedly the play's idealized realm. Consistently in the play, as befits this version of the Cathleen ní Houlihan myth, love for Ireland is configured in terms of love for a woman and vice versa. This reaches its parodic zenith in Act II, when Rosie the prostitute realizes regretfully that the men are so infatuated with the Nation that there 'isn't much notice taken of a pretty petticoat of a night like this' (TP, 161). Yet Nora and Jack's relationship raises serious issues about the nature of desire that remain disturbingly unresolved. Mrs. Gogan strikes a significant note when she observes of

Jack that, despite his earlier ardour – '[t]he pair o' them used to be like two turtle doves always billin' an' cooin'' – he is now

> beginnin' to take things more quietly; the mysthery of havin' a woman's a mysthery no longer... . She dhresses herself to keep him with her, but it's no use – afther a month or two, th' wondher of a woman wears off.
>
> *Fluther.* I dunno, I dunno. Not wishin' to say anything derogatory, I think it's all a question of location: when a man finds th' wondher of one woman beginnin' to die, it's usually beginnin' to live in another. (TP, 138)

The suspicion is planted that Cathleen ní Houlihan has not lured Clitheroe away from Nora – he was already disenchanted. Fluther disagrees with Mrs. Gogan's rather cynical view of sexual relations. He believes that Jack's new coolness to Nora comes from infatuation with another woman; the audience, by implication, intuits the rival to be the feminized Ireland of familiar myth. Nonetheless, the issue of whether Clitheroe was lured into figurative infidelity – delusion – or was already predisposed for it – disillusionment – is left unanswered. Later in the act, a love scene takes place between Nora and Jack that supports Mrs. Gogan's diagnosis of their relationship. We learn that, during their courtship, Nora beseeched Jack to go to the Citizen Army meetings, but he refused, saying he felt lonely without her. Less than a month into their marriage, he 'couldn't keep away from them' (TP, 153). Now when Jack kisses Nora she rebuffs him, confirming Mrs. Gogan's suspicions that he has lost a much of his ardour: 'Jack, Jack; please, Jack! I thought you were tired of that sort of thing long ago' (TP, 154). Nora is well aware of Jack's fickleness. She is disturbed by the worrying facility with which his desire shifts from her to his political ambitions, and she pinpoints a feature not just of Jack's love, but of desire and satisfaction in general: 'It's hard for a body to be always keepin' her mind bent on makin' thoughts that'll be no longer than th' length of your own satisfaction' (TP, 154). It seems that, once satisfied, desire drifts wayward. It is not the charms of Cathleen ní Houlihan which lure Jack away, but a prior sense of dissatisfaction. In the light of her earlier perceptive remarks on the Clitheroe marriage, Mrs. Gogan's consolation to the distraught Nora in Act III has a sinister double meaning: 'If you'd been a little longer together, th' wrench asundher wouldn't have been so sharp' (TP, 185). It suggests, again, that their desire, if satisfied, becomes dormant. The implication is that romantic love, and with it the bonds of new marriage, may be as delusory – or as real – as the romantic nationalism against which it is placed as a healthy alternative. So, if on one level O'Casey's play shows political idealism intruding into domestic reality, on another it presents them as covert doubles.

The Silver Tassie: holy war?

However wavering and uncertain the Dublin trilogy's espousal of hearth and home as an alternative to destructive warfare, *The Silver Tassie* refuses even these meagre consolations. O'Casey's supposed political meliorism and Shavian belief in the life-force are scarcely evident in this bleak, nihilistic work. Yet he labels the play a 'tragicomedy' rather than a 'tragedy', even though the Dublin plays, with vaudevillian antics alongside supreme pathos, suit this designation far more obviously. On the other hand, the hybridity implied in this subtitle befits a play of such shifting registers and heterogeneous styles, slipping as it does from naturalism to expressionism, from banality to symbolism, from the ecstasies of triumph to the agonies of impotence. Though the play has faults, it is nonetheless a formidable achievement. Mindful of the inadequacy of realistic representation of the First World War, it boldly seeks a more fittingly recalcitrant, less beguilingly coherent dramaturgy to stage the horrific chaos and senseless slaughter.

That the play deals with the Great War is possibly one of the reasons why it was rejected by the Abbey. For Yeats, modern warfare, if not the Homeric or the Ossianic variety, was innately opposed to the authentic tragic spirit. Having refused to accept the war poets for his Oxford anthology of poetry, Yeats was notoriously hostile to artistic treatment of the First World War, claiming, 'If war is necessary, or necessary in our time and place, it is best to forget its suffering as we do the discomfort of fever.'[48] The social forces which Yeats would disallow in the 'tragic' canon are dismissed not, as we might have thought, because of their secular fickleness, but for a sort of inherent fatalism, 'necessary in our time and place'. It is, however, the fatalism of the mundane, which Yeats sees exemplified in the common fever. Yet why should Fate, conventionally the starting point of tragedy, be drained of mythic significance and relegated to mere 'necessity' on entering modern history? The difference between 'Fate' and 'Necessity' is that while fate is pre-ordained, necessity seems simply contingent on the confluence of other circumstances. Or perhaps, necessity is just a modern, secular notion of fate: leached of transcendental significance, fate becomes mere determinism, theology reduced to mechanics. The reason why Yeats dismisses 'necessary' suffering as artistic material is because of the implied absence of human agency. He cannot consider supposedly 'passive suffering' as truly tragic. Since, for Yeats, no great deed or hubristic exertion leads to modern warfare, its origin lacks tragic conflict – however disastrous its effects are, they are brought on by the activities of anonymous forces, outside the control of human endeavour. This derives from a Romantic notion of tragedy that emphasizes selfhood, *hubris*, and heroism. Yet the idea that modern warfare derives from mere 'necessity' indicates some dangerous assumptions. The protagonists of a war, aggressors and defenders alike, are implicitly stripped of all control. This denial has obvious conservative implications: tyrants are spared their culpability; heroes robbed of their valour. Ironically, human control, and hence politics, is brushed over: 'history' becomes inhuman, something which, like Haines in Joyce's *Ulysses*, we can blame, while at the same time disowning all responsibility.[49]

The reasons for the Abbey rejection are worthy of investigation.[50] As many critics have remarked, Yeats's famous rejection letter was at best tactless, particularly given what he must already have known about O'Casey's pugnacious character and likely response. O'Casey had contributed three of the Abbey's finest plays, and would at this stage have had good reason to think himself Yeats's dramatic peer rather than apprentice. For O'Casey, Yeats's tone revealed his assumption of 'Zeussian infallibility'.[51] However, Yeats's hostility to O'Casey's obtrusive 'opinions', even if we disagree that these opinions are fatally destructive of the *Tassie*'s merits, are all-too prescient of O'Casey's later blasts and benedictions. O'Casey, however, is right to be dismissive of Yeats's injunction that he needs to write about direct experience – that he should write only about Dublin slums because that is what he 'knows' – a stricture that does originate in class condescension towards 'Casey'[52:]

> But you are not interested in the Great War; you never stood on its battlefields or walked its hospitals, and so you write out of your opinions. You illustrate those opinions by a series of almost unrelated scenes as you might a leading article; there is no dominating character, no dominating action, neither psychological unity nor unity of action, and your great power of the past has been the creation of some unique character who dominated all about him and

was himself a main impulse in some action that filled the play from beginning to end. The very greatness of the war has thwarted you; it has refused to become mere background, and obtrudes itself upon the stage as so much dead wood that will not burn dramatic fire. Dramatic action is a fire that must burn everything that does not belong to it; the whole history of the world must be reduced to wallpaper in front of which the characters must pose and speak. Among the things that dramatic action must burn up are the author's opinions ...[53]

However, the discontinuities in the play – 'the unrelated scenes' – could be regarded as a bold anti-naturalist move, an attempt to reproduce the rebarbative face of war on a formal level, rending fissures and caesura in the dramatic surface the better to disorientate and shock an audience used to reassuring narrative coherence. That Yeats sees them as a symptom of journalistic 'opinion' is ironic for this is the least opinionated of O'Casey's plays. Though there are occasional moments of heavy-handed satire – Susie's 'tambourine theology' or the blimpish Visitor to the front, for instance – the stylistic departures generally foreground opacity and incoherence, not authorial polemic. Again, this is due to the tragic subject matter, which threatens the synoptically confident perspective from which dogmatic edicts or objective declarations of value can be handed down. Some of O'Casey's later plays, which celebrate a Utopian alternative to the restrictive norms and life-denying orthodoxies of Church-controlled Ireland, would merit Yeats's censure for 'opinions' far more than the discontented and fragmented incantations of *The Tassie*.

Yeats's objection that the War obtrudes into the drama is, in fact, one of the plays great virtues. The strength of this play over the Dublin trilogy is that the more overt entwining of expressionist with naturalist modes allows O'Casey to address the public realm in a way he has never before achieved. The domestic haven here is not just unsettled by intrusive political forces from offstage; we confront the destructive force of war far less tangentially. Part of this effect is achieved by the strategic deployment of audience alienation. In *The Silver Tassie*, the familiar naturalistic setting of the first act generates an empathy with the characters that makes the estranging atmosphere of the second act all the more effective. In this it resembles *Ulysses*, where the reader's empathy with Bloom and Stephen in the opening chapters is assaulted by the alienating stylistic experimentation of the ensuing episodes. Yet because the initial connection has been established, we keep faith with the characters and our concern survives the formal onslaught. Apart from Barney, strapped to a gunwheel for stealing a cock, the soldiers in the second Act are reduced to anonymous numbers, their humanity erased by the terrible mechanics of the war. Yet their ritualized incantations, and poetic evocations of home, contrast with the arid officialese of the Staff Wallah, with his barked injunctions and regimented inhumanity.

Significantly, this assault on recognizable character is one of Yeats's principle objections to the play, as his rejection letter demonstrates. Even if, as Lady Gregory was the first to claim, O'Casey's strength lay in characterization, it is notable that Yeats's call for a great character who dominates everything around him contradicts his definition of tragedy, where he espouses the eradication of specific characteristics in the interests of universality. In his 1910 essay 'The Tragic Theatre', Yeats distinguishes tragedy and comedy by claiming that the latter develops character and difference while 'tragedy must always be a drowning and breaking of the dykes that separate man from man, and it is upon these dykes comedy keeps house'.[54] It seems that tragedy, in probing beyond surface character to a deeper human unity, is the more profound theatrical experience: 'Tragic art, passionate art, the drowner of dykes, the confounder of understanding, moves us by setting us to reverie, by alluring us almost to the intensity of trance. The persons upon the stage, let us say, greaten till they are humanity itself.'[55] It may have been that O'Casey in breaking down the dykes that separate man from man, was trying to write tragedy of a Yeatsian tone, albeit tuned to a historical rather than a universal key. In O'Casey's caustic reply to Yeats's letter, he focuses particularly on this issue, claiming that it is precisely his attempt to get beyond the circumscription of character that makes *The Silver Tassie* more accomplished than its predecessors:

> Now is a dominating character more important than a play, or a play more important than a dominating character? In *The Silver Tassie* you have a unique work that dominates all the characters in the play... in my opinion – an important one – *The Silver Tassie* because of, or in spite of, the lack of a dominating character, is a greater work than *The Plough and the Stars*.[56]

In this respect *The Silver Tassie* strives to be a tragedy in the Yeatsian mould. However, O'Casey wishes to get beyond character not to express the essential archetypes of 'humanity itself' but rather to reveal something at the heart of a specific historical and political trauma.

As already suggested, through the formal disruptions of the second act of *The Tassie*, we have a more substantial engagement with the public intrusion into the private than the more realistic methods of the trilogy could effect. As if in indication of this opposition, the scene of each of the four acts contains within the set an aperture into the larger world through a window or door. In Act I we see through the window the ship that will bring the combatants back to the fray. The broken shell of the monastery in Act II not only evokes the persistent religious theme, but also provides a view of the 'country stretching to the horizon where the front trenches are' (ST, 41). Nowhere in O'Casey's work is private life and human subjectivity more thoroughly compromised by cold instrumentalism and publicly sanctioned barbarism. The setting, which shows the Red Cross hospital and the monastery as the most fragile of havens, is fitting for this conduit between public and private, as the traumatized and wounded soldiers are brought onstage. The distinction between the two is violently dismembered in the final, frenzied tableau of this act, as the enemy break through and the soldiers run to man the gun to which they have just prayed. The erstwhile haven becomes the battlefield. Acts III and IV also provide a physical view offstage: to the hospital garden and to the dance at the sports centre. In each act, the crippled Harry Heegan passes in and out. The point is that while *The Plough* provided only a shadow of the speaker at the window and while *Juno* and *The Shadow of a Gunman* allowed us to hear, but not see, the ructions outside, the stage setting of *The Silver Tassie*, as if in parallel to its departures from dramatic naturalism, gives us a physical spectacle of the world outside the immediate setting in each act.

Though ostensibly the play follows a familiar dramatic trajectory of domestic life destroyed by intrusive, destabilizing and futile political violence, it is a common error to see it simply as an anti-war play. It is usually assumed that the barbarism of the battlefield causes the disharmony of Acts II and IV. Only one or two critics have pointed out that the corruptions and latent violence of the Dublin homes have been there since Act I and, perhaps, the war is a *result* of the prevailing social structure, rather than vice versa.[57] If, as I have argued, reading the trilogy in terms of the simple opposition between politics and humanity underestimates the tensions and discontents in the domestic scene before the political upheavals, then in *The Silver Tassie* these tensions are far more evident. The dissonance, disharmony and violence are not just brought in by the War, they are there from the start. The first Act, for all its colourful characters and playful antics, depicts a truly despicable community of braggarts, bullies and poltroons. Indeed, in an unlikely turn, and in contrast to the Dublin trilogy, the men's return to the front brings *relief* to the women left behind. Far from the pacifist and pragmatic females of *Juno* and the *Plough*, we have the evangelical Susie polishing Harry's rifle, in a symbolic fusion of beauty, religion and violence. Yet the women's wish for the men to leave them is not just the idealism of a Minnie Powell. It is based in self-interest which if, as in the case of Mrs. Foran, is understandable, it is often squalid and greedy. Far from the affirming compassion of Juno, Harry's mother is obsessed with her separation money, a singular concern that persists through the play. Given O'Casey's usual cherishing of motherhood, this characterization is worthy of some attention. We saw in the last chapter how in *Riders to the Sea* the language of economics was incompatible with the language of individuation and subjectivity. Here we have another commercial retelling of the Cathleen ní Houlihan myth, but with a far more cynical spin. Mrs. Heegan waits outside in the shivering cold not in anticipation of her son's arrival home from the front, and not to persuade him to stay, but rather to ensure that he returns from the football game in good time to catch the ship back to France. In a bitterly parodic inversion of the maternal role in Irish drama, her motives are purely selfish and mercantile:

> MRS. HEEGAN. The chill's residin' in my bones, an' feelin's left me just the strength to shiver. He's overstayed his leave a lot, an' if he misses now the tide that's waitin', he skulks behind desertion from the colours.
> SUSIE. On Active Service that means death at dawn.
> MRS. HEEGAN. An' my governmental money grant would stop at once.
> SUSIE. That would gratify Miss Jessie Taite, because you put her weddin' off with Harry till after the duration of the war, an' cut her out of the allowance. (ST, 19–20)

Even in the final act, when many of the characters have changed, Mrs. Heegan's concern, true to form, is Harry's disability allowance and, rather than sympathizing with him over Jessie's preferment of the now more potent Barney, she maliciously decries his earlier courtship: 'plungin' every penny he could keep from me into presents for the consolation of the courtship!' (ST, 128).

Mrs. Heegan is not the only unattractive character. Susie's 'tambourine theology' grates on us as much as on the feckless Sylvester and

Simon. Her puritanism – no less than her later wantonness – is self-serving and cowardly, as evinced by her inadequacy when Mrs. Foran seeks her aid: 'Even the gospel-gunner couldn't do a little target practice by helpin' the necessity of a neighbour' (ST, 18). Regardless of the war, the Foran marriage was not made in heaven and Teddy's domestic violence is genuinely shocking: an anticipation of the destruction on the battlefields in the next Act, just as the wedding bowl he smashes is the double of the Silver Tassie and the broken promises it will come to represent in the last act. It is also important that Harry, if a sporting hero here, is not unambiguously celebrated. O'Casey often valorized the physicality and youthful life-force represented by the likes of Harry and Jessie in Act I, but one feels that here his endorsement is heavily qualified. Just as Jessie's affections prove to be unnervingly fickle when Harry's prowess and status are lost, so his self-identity and self-assuredness seem far too heavily reliant on external validation. He is far more of an egotist than a hero, encouraging toadies like Barney and indifferent to the hurt he causes others, like the spurned Susie. 'Napoo, Barney, to everyone but me!' (TP, 35) is his all too telling refrain.

Act II, though often conceived as a radical departure from Act I, is rather embryonically contained within it. All these acts are far more porous with each other than first appearances – or Yeats's 'unrelated scenes' – would suggest. The incantatory mode that Sylvester and Simon often slide into anticipates the nightmarish rituals of the ensuing act, just as the ructions and disruptions, the arrival of the sportsmen and the violence of the Forans, augur the ensuing bloodshed and militarism. Relatedly, there is a macabre symmetry to the introduction of military motifs into civilian life – Harry and his teammates clad in fatigues – and the introduction of civilian motifs – the 'Visitor' – into the war. The area where the continuity is, perhaps, most deserving of notice is the obsessive foregrounding of religious iconography. Susie's biblical fervour in Act I (though her later licentiousness explodes her initial prim evangelism) anticipates the obsessive religious allusions of Act II. However, just as the monastery is a bombed-out shell, there is something perverse, empty and formulaic about the religious element here. As with the soldiers and their bewildered chanting, we sense an ominous exhaustion and impotence in the religious consolation offered in this 'valley of dry bones'). One feels that God has deserted these sufferers, much though they need his presence: 'There's a Gawd knocking abaht somewhere' (ST, 57). They totemize graven images: first, the broken crucifix but, at the end, the howitzer gun to which they eagerly and eerily pay religious homage: 'We believe in God and we believe in thee' (ST, 67, 68). As so often in O'Casey's tragedies there is a blending of the spiritual and the material. The urge to find a consoling cause or explanation for the confusion and suffering oscillates between the religious and the secular, the universal and the historical. Again, there is a need for meaning, a persistent questioning of where this desperate condition originates. Does it come from the will of God or the stupidity of men? Or is it a meaningless, random situation, based only in absurdity? The pressing question is put by the soldiers themselves: '1ST SOLDIER: ... But wy'r we 'ere, wy'r we 'ere – that's wot I wants to know!'. The answer is elusive. Whether it lies in divine or in military authority, it will not be shared with the soldiers: '2ND SOLDIER: God only knows – or else, perhaps, a red-cap' (ST, 46). One response comes through the dry language of military authority, which rather than answer the question resorts to the cold logic of allocated roles. The staff officers, they conjecture, would tell them they are there because they are soldiers: '1ST SOLDIER (*chanting*). Tabs'll murmur, 'em an' 'aw, an' sy' 'You're 'ere because you're / Point nine double 0, the sixth platoon an' forty-eight battalion ...' (ST, 46). The priest, the soldiers infer, would offer a less circular, but similarly clichéd explanation:

> 1ST SOLDIER. (*chanting*). The padre gives a fag an' softly whispers:
> 'Your king, your country an' your muvver 'as you 'ere
> An' last time 'ome on leave, I awks the missus:
> 'The good God up in heaven, Bill, 'e knows,
> An' I gets the seperytion moneys reg'lar'.
> (*He sits up suddenly*)
> But wy'r we 'ere, wy'r we 'ere, – that's wot I wants to know?
> THE REST (*chanting sleepily*). Why 's 'e 'ere, why's 'e 'ere – that's wot 'e wants to know! (ST, 47)

The addition of 'muvver' to the predictable king and country pairing is notable. It is certainly a long way from Juno Boyle and the pacifist women of the trilogy. The passage would seem to hark back to Act I, where Harry's mother is disconcertingly eager for him to return to the fray and, like the speaker's wife, is more concerned with her separation money than understanding the war. Barney, significantly the only character from the first Act who survives the formal mutation to the second, silences the men's anxious queries: '(*singing to the air of second bar in chorus of "Auld Lang Syne"*). We're here because we're here, because we're here, because we're here!' (ST, 47). The soldiers, Barney seems to suggest, can only come up with circular responses that beg the question they are striving to answer. The stretcher-bearers who enter near the end of the Act have a more childish, repetitive and petrified chant than the Old Testament allusions of the Croucher or the questioning and nostalgic incantations of the soldiers. They know that they will never understand the reasons for human suffering in the secular realm:

> Carry on – we've one bugled reason why –
> We've 'eard and answer'd the call, call, call.
> There's no more to be said, for when we are dead,
> We may understand it all, all, all.
> There's no more to be said, for when we are dead,
> We may understand it all. (ST, 61)

Only after death will the answer that all the soldiers seek be revealed. Here on the battlefield, meaning, so desperately needed, is cruelly withheld. And, in a sense, the audience share in the confusion, disorientated as they are by the affecting formal fragmentation and ritualistic language.

The poignant cry – 'why are we here?' – is given added resonance by the allusions to that archetypal tragic tale, the Book of Job. The Croucher of Act II is one obvious Jobian figure, but the evocation is at its most explicit in the final exchanges of the play between the paralysed Harry and the blind Teddy. Surrounded by the mundane and crass celebrations of the community – which, selfish and insensible as ever, seems to have learned nothing from the war – the two crippled men contemplate their fate in the now familiar incantatory language. They are left with Job's comfort – God's will is inscrutable:

> HARRY. I can see, but I cannot dance.
> TEDDY. I can dance, but I cannot see.
> HARRY. Would that I had the strength to do the things I see.
> TEDDY. Would that I could see the things I've strength to do.
> HARRY. *The Lord hath given and the Lord hath taken away.*
> TEDDY. *Blessed be the name of the Lord.* (ST, 119–20) [My emphasis]

The final couplet is ritualistically repeated in a similar exchange a few moments later. But lest we think the men find some answer to the problem of human suffering in the incomprehensible divine schema, we are given a socialist version by Harry as his very last lines onstage: 'The Lord hath given and *man* hath taken away! [My emphasis] /TEDDY. (*heard from the garden*). Blessed be the name of the Lord!' (ST, 130). Hinging between the secular and the religious, history and fate, no final answer to the problem of suffering is provided by the play. Once again, do we ask with Juno, 'what can God do agen' the stupidity o' men?', or do we find the explanation in Mary Boyle's Manichaean verses, which suggest that corruption lies inherent in creation?

Yet to provide too pat an answer, to ascribe all human suffering to a neat catch-all – God's will, human folly, basic absurdity – would undermine the moving elegiac quality of the play, which derives its dramatic virtues from its humane, bewildered ambivalence, its resistance to 'explaining' the causes of the slaughter. Harry's final words leave the door open to a melioristic response – that human agency is responsible for suffering – but avoid sinking into an anti-war rant. With the interdependence of the crippled Harry and the blind Teddy, we have a pairing that chimes across modern Irish drama from Yeats's *On Baile's Strand* to Beckett's *Endgame*. For all Harry's bitterness and pessimism, his suffering leaves room for fellow-feeling, the sort of moving kindness that we sometimes see between Beckett's vagrants. This is the one solace we can take away from this harrowing play. There are other Beckettian touches in this drama which so often teeters on the edge of absurdism. Some lines could be lifted straight from a Beckett play, with all the economy and poignancy intact: '2ND SOLDIER. Perhaps they have forgotten./ 3RD SOLDIER. Forgotten./ 4TH SOLDIER. Forgotten us' (ST, 53–4). One could well imagine Hamm claiming, like Harry, to feel 'the horrible sickness of life only from the waist up' (ST, 81).[58] As with Beckett, the depiction of appalling suffering, a suffering which destabilizes and strains the mechanics of dramatic representation, sometimes brings out the humane and the compassionate, even as it demolishes the conventional affirmations of liberal humanism.

But *The Silver Tassie* evokes Beckett more than any other of O'Casey's plays for a deeper reason than the stylistic fragmentation and incantatory language. Ironically, and despite Yeats's castigation of O'Casey's 'opinions' in the play, this is the least thematically or polemically sure-footed of any play he wrote and in this it reflects the poignant bewilderment that we often find in Beckett's world. In the second Act, O'Casey manages to generate an overwhelming, opaque sense of dark perverse ritual. The subterranean tensions, ambivalences and contradictions of the Dublin trilogy – between the secular and the spiritual, the melioristic and the fatalistic, the comic and the tragic –

are less concealed beneath naturalistic coherence. And here, more than anywhere else, O'Casey expresses the bewilderment and disillusionment which he strives to repress, but which generate the dramatic conflict in these early plays. Productions of the trilogy need to be alert to these conflicts and inconsistencies, to resist the reassuring moral messages that slide all too easily from plays performed in a cosy naturalistic setting. O'Casey's best work came from confusion, not didactic certainty. And, as a later Irish playwright will remind us, 'confusion is not an ignoble condition'.[59]

4
Beyond Tragedy: Samuel Beckett and the Art of Confusion

Tragedy is not concerned with human justice. Tragedy is the statement of an expiation, but not the expiation of a codified breach of local arrangement, organized by the knaves for the fools. The tragic figure represents the expiation of the original sin, of the original and eternal sin of him and all his 'soci malorum', the sin of having been born.

– Samuel Beckett

Absurdity for Beckett is no longer diluted to an abstract Idea of Existence to be illustrated in a Situation. The poetic process abandons itself to absurdity without a guiding intention.

– Theodor W. Adorno

I think anyone nowadays who pays the slightest attention to his own experience finds it the experience of a non-knower, a non-can-er (somebody who cannot). The other type of artist – the Apollonian – is absolutely foreign to me.

– Samuel Beckett

Introduction: Beckett and tragedy

So far as conventional or strictly Hellenic conceptions of the genre go, Beckett appears an unlikely tragedian. His aesthetic is founded on anti-heroism rather than heroism, inaction rather than action, and narrative irresolution rather than the grandiose sense of closure one might expect in traditional tragedy. As Vivian Mercier puts it:

> where in fact is the tragic to be found? Beckett cannot believe in, or at least cannot create, a genuine tragic hero – powerful, proud, yet

essentially good save for the tragic flaw. Beckett's anti-heroes do not aspire, so they can never fall.[1]

Even if we bypass – as we must for most 'modern' tragedy – the traditional search for heroism, *hamartia*, the 'unities' and all the other classical trappings, Beckett still seems something of a misfit. Commentators hospitable to modern manifestations of the genre can bend or ignore Aristotelian prescription to include Ibsen and Miller along with Shakespeare and Sophocles, but Beckett's work is too indeterminate and uncertain, lacking, even, a stable human subject around which tragic loss could cohere.[2] Therefore even the most ecumenical definitions of tragedy are liable to have difficulty with Beckett's drama, which seems too diffuse, too concerned with the uncertain and the remorselessly squalid, to reach tragic status.

We saw in the Introduction how the label 'tragedy' is embroiled in questions of literary value and canonicity and, not surprisingly, Beckett's role as the century's foremost poet of suffering, our most discerning connoisseur of whines, has prompted some to search for continuity between his work and the tradition of dramatic tragedy. Since this cannot be achieved through generic similarity with canonical tragedy, emphasis is placed on the content or the impact of his work. To this end, no less an authority than Martin Esslin concentrates on the *effect* of Beckett's work beyond its neutral formal characteristics, and arrives at the opposite conclusion to Mercier:

> It is, moreover, highly significant that this emotional impact, in apparent contradiction to the recondite intellectual content of Beckett's work, is indeed an exhilarating one. How is it that this vision of the ultimate void in all its grotesque derision and despair should be capable of producing an effect akin to the catharsis of great tragedy?[3]

Yet, this affinity can really only be glimpsed at an impressionistic level. The structure of the drama resolutely refuses the closure, resolution or catharsis expressed by great tragedy. This refusal seems intentional. It is as if Beckett is deliberately flouting or denying the consolations offered in the classical form. In Beckett's work, far more even than in Synge and O'Casey, heroism is constantly spurned, pretensions to grandeur, as with the high-flown soliloquies of Pozzo and Hamm, remorselessly mocked. Yet there is a sense, as argued in the Introduction, that the absence of much-yearned-for resolution, the failure of his characters to achieve recognition or *anagnorisis*, the fumbling aphasia and evasion with which they confront their mystifying condition are themselves tokens of a tragic loss: the loss of conventional tragic consolation.

This may be one explanation for the fragmented allusions in his work to canonical tragedy. A critical sifting of *Endgame* (1958), for example, reveals it to be bursting at its intertextual seams. John Fletcher and John Spurling have identified some of the 'heavily conscious reference to most of the heroes of Tragedy: '"Woe, woe is me! Miserable, miserable that I am" (*Oedipus Rex*); "Ah, this is one misery I have not yet endured. What fresh torments still lie in wait for me?" (Racine's *Phèdre*); "As full of grief as age; wretched in both" (*King Lear*); "Appease the misery of the living and the remorse of the dead" (Yeats's *Purgatory*).'[4] Nor is it irrelevant that Jan Kott, Martin Esslin and Peter Brook, amongst others, have all seen fit to direct Shakespearean tragedies in a Beckettian style.[5] Yet these parodic allusions highlight an *absence*: they float around the drama like the flotsam and jetsam of a wrecked tradition. If Beckett is writing tragedy it is of a new sort, eager to embody the speechlessness and inarticulacy engendered by the 'breakdown in the lines of communication' of which he so often speaks. Part of this effect is achieved by a re-imagining of genre, not just on the syntactic, but also on the semantic level,[6] not just in terms of mode, but also in terms of mood.

This disorientation of mood is clear in Beckett's fusion of tragic and comic elements. During the first production of *En Attendant Godot* (1953), he wrote to Roger Blin: 'The spirit of the play to the extent to which it has one, is that nothing is more grotesque than the tragic. One must express it up to the end, and especially at the end.'[7] This declaration occurs in a letter insisting that Estragon let his trousers fall all the way to the ground at the end of Act I – the stubborn or bashful actor playing the part had been reluctant to fully comply with this stage direction. This scene is usually played for a vaudeville laugh and Beckett's instruction would hardly be likely to lessen the humour. It is interesting, then, that Beckett sees the scene as 'tragic'. If his remark were inverted – nothing is more tragic than the grotesque – it would not be so significant. As it is, it suggests that Beckett regards the tragic and the comic as deeply entwined. This may not be surprising, given Nell's insight in *Endgame* that 'nothing is funnier than unhappiness' (CDW, 101) – a remark which Beckett chose as 'for me the most important line in the play'.[8] Similarly in *Watt* (1953), Arsene declares that the highest form of laughter is always directed towards 'that which is unhappy'.[9] The relation between comedy and tragedy in Beckett's work, then, is not one of simple opposition, the comic providing light dramatic relief from the moments of tragic despair. The comic and tragic moments permeate each other in ongoing reciprocity. In its typical debasement of its 'heroes', its often mundane, trivial style, 'tragicomedy' is often highlighted as the dramatic genre most in tune with modern culture. As John Orr puts it, the addition of a comic element is an 'indispensable framework for the tragedy of dissolved identity, the tragedy of the diminished hero who no longer knows who he is, who lives out his life, at times consciously, in a masquerade'.[10] If 'comic relief' is sometimes designed as a respite from tragic bleakness, it can also serve to sharpen its impact. This sense that comedy can intensify the tragic moment, making it less grand and hence more bleak was recognized, in existential terms, by one of Beckett's great philosophical forebears, Arthur Schopenhauer:

> Thus, as if fate wished to add mockery to the mystery of our exis-
> tence, our life must contain all the woes of tragedy, and yet we
> cannot even assert the dignity of tragic characters but, in the broad
> detail of life, are inevitably the foolish characters of a comedy.[11]

From this point of view, the comic element renders the tragic life more irremediable and more poignant just as, contrapuntally, the comic, for Nell, is magnified by unhappiness. Comedy exposes and throws the tragic vision into starker relief. Both, after all, are evoked by a gap between aspiration and actuality: comedy derives from incongruity, tragedy from conflict. So far as Beckett's work goes, the comic, far from an antithesis, is deeply and symbiotically interrelated with the tragic, suggesting that he may well hold, with Ionesco, that 'comic and tragic are one'.[12]

So the comic deflation in Beckett's work, coupled with the ironic incorporation of portentous, 'high tragic' moments, points towards a deliberate refusal or subversion of tragedy which may, in another sense, be its intensification. The Beckettian stage is so moribund and derelict that the consolations of tragedy, its lyrical grandeur or philo-sophical insights, are as depleted as Hamm's painkillers. All versions of tragedy – ancient and modern, aristocratic and proletarian – hinge on a 'loss' of some sort. To be called tragic, that loss must be of some significance or moment and this is only possible in a world of clearly defined values. The loss of a child can be called tragic in a way that the loss of a handkerchief cannot (with all due apologies to Othello). Yet along with the other uncertainties and ambiguities of Beckett's world, the entire category of value is thrown into question. It is a world of profound, unremitting confusion and this, perhaps, is the origin of the refusal of tragedy. As we have seen, one of the traditional benefits of tragedy has long been regarded as the putative insight or revelation it offers. Whether it comes through the moment of *anagnorisis* of a suffering hero or whether the work itself contains some bleak vision or outlook on the world, a major consolation of tragedy rests in its ontological purchase: solace is gleaned from the thought that however bad things are at least they are being confronted. Beckett's work eschews all such certainty and all such knowledge. His drama and prose are so opaque and indeterminate that it seems somehow misconceived to ascribe to them a 'vision' or 'worldview' – 'tragic' or otherwise.

Yet there are changes in the way Beckett registers this confusion. In the pre-war period he espouses the unknowability of the world in philosophical terms, insisting that the vehicles of communication are inaccessible. In his post-war work he spurns the language of ratiocination and strives to demonstrate ignorance and impotence artistically, rather than declaring it abstractly. Yet for all the chaos, disorder and opacity of Beckett's content, his form is characterized by scrupulous precision and stylistic symmetry, evident in the patterned rhythms of his mature prose or the choreographed gestures and movements of his drama. This opposition between form and content offers a useful angle from which to assess materialist, political elements in his work. I argue that Beckett, for all his cosmopolitan refusal of origin (national and otherwise), is deeply attuned to the political structures of his historical context. These structures are both manifest in and subverted by his epistemological scepticism. The second half of the chapter extends these considerations by focusing on a central, exemplary theme in Beckett, germane to his notion of tragedy, that of Original Sin. In his 1931 essay *Proust*, Beckett borrows Schopenhauer's definition of tragedy as originating in the 'sin of being born'. This motif haunts his work. It mutates, however, from the assuredness of his early pessimism to the much more sceptical, aporetic condition of the narrators in the trilogy, where life is depicted as both guilt and punishment, sin and expiation, commingled in a confused, self-sustaining morass. This imbrication, symptomatic of the wider inaccessibility of coherent causal relations, is used to examine the mysterious operations of the 'Law' in Beckett. Referring to materialist ideas of tragedy, the chapter ends by looking at the political dimension to Beckett's depiction of the dynamics of authority, and the epistemological implications of his exploration of bewildered humility.

The anti-philosophical turn

Like most of the decrepit old creatures loitering on Beckett's stage, the eponymous hero of *Krapp's Last Tape* (1958) has only bemused contempt for abstract intellectual speculation or self-analysis. Alone in his den, fumbling through the tape made thirty years before on his thirty-ninth birthday, he wants to relive the evocative, sensually depicted scene with the woman in the punt, the scene of lost love. Much to his annoyance, he thrice stumbles on the bombastic passage of his vision at the end of the jetty, his revelation that 'the dark I have always struggled to keep under' would be the raw material of his art. This epiphany, which critics have regarded as based on a real-life experience of crucial importance to Beckett's artistic development, is greeted with curses and frustration by the elder Krapp, who has only a bitter laugh for the smug theorizing of his younger self: 'Just been listening to that stupid bastard I took myself for thirty years ago, hard to believe I was ever as bad as that' (CDW, 222). Ironically, legend tells us that it was precisely this revelation or epiphany that eroded Beckett's interest in the language of ratiocination, that revealed to him the path of radical scepticism and impotence – man as a 'non-knower' and a 'non-can-er' – that he was destined to explore in his mature writing.[13] Of course, 'revelation' and 'destiny' suggest a world of knowledge and coherence that scepticism itself would deny. How can one trust the absolute revelation that all absolute revelations are bogus? How can one propound as certain knowledge the inaccessibility of certain knowledge? Perhaps it is the danger of the sceptic's embarrassment that fuels the mature Beckett's wariness of philosophical ideas: if it were expressed in the language of abstraction or logic, his view of experience would fail under its own terms. Mindful of these dangers of self-contradiction, he opts for artistic demonstration, rather than abstract declaration. 'I wouldn't have had any reason to write my novels if I could have expressed their subject in philosophic terms', he once remarked.[14] Though 'demonstration' may be too strong a word here, suggestive of too great a degree of intentionality, too harmonious a relation between form and content, for Beckett's enigmatic texts. One would never expect his perplexed people to muster the energy to 'demonstrate' anything as strenuous as a philosophical stance.

It is appropriately ironic, then, that the psychobabble that the elder Krapp derides describes the moment when his hostility to psychobabble was born, the moment when he renounced the rational acquisition of external knowledge, plumping instead for the evacuative and immersive methods of Beckett's mature aesthetic. The scene of Krapp's revelation seems to take place on Dún Laoghaire pier in Dublin and critics have supposed that it was lifted from direct experience. We now know, thanks to James Knowlson's authorized biography, that the actual experience, a sudden realization of ignorance more than a moment of insight, took place in the much less sublime surrounding of the front room of Beckett's mother's house in Killiney in 1945;[15] the raging foam and magnificent granite were always a little too near to Romantic cliché for Beckett to invoke without parody. Like Krapp the elder, it seems the elder Beckett viewed his younger self with embarrassed disdain. He held most of the articles and reviews he wrote before the war in low esteem, only with reluctance agreeing to their publication in the eighties under the less than aggrandizing title, *Disjecta*.[16] These pieces are often remarkably perceptive and intelligent but are also, particularly those from the 1920s and 30s, pedantic, over-written, haughty in tone and *recherché* in method. His 1931 monograph on Marcel Proust, with its heavy theorizing and its often turgid style, embodies many of these qualities and defects. Added to its bleak diagnoses on the destructiveness of time and the insatiability of human desire, *Proust* repeatedly insists on the impossibility of communication and knowledge – both subject and object are in a constant state of flux and any meaningful connection is impossible. Yet the tone of unshakeable authority in the monograph would seem to contradict its overt message. It is riddled with omniscient declarations – 'We cannot know and we cannot be known', 'the attempt to communicate where no communication is possible is merely a simian vulgarity' – declarations of scepticism, voiced in anything but a sceptical tone, that are in danger of falling under their own strictures (P, 66, 63). Later, Beckett will come to artistically *embody* the fractured communication that he can only abstractly declare now. On the title page of a copy of *Proust* unearthed in a Dublin secondhand bookshop several years ago was written in Beckett's hand: 'I have written my book in a cheap flashy philosophical jargon.'[17] This is an overly harsh analysis of his flawed book, but is consistent with how Beckett turned against the language of philosophy that enraptured him in his twenties and thirties.

There is in the mature Beckett an abiding suspicion of abstract thought and the blunt instrument of philosophical theory. When allusion to philosophy surfaces in the trilogy or in the drama, as opposed to *Murphy* and his other pre-war fiction, it usually comes laced with mockery. Although many have scholarly or intellectual backgrounds, it is clear that these poor vagrants, like Krapp the elder, have moved beyond all that shrill theorizing. 'Ideas' seem hollow in the teeth of their dereliction, too cumbersome or remote to be of much comfort in such extreme torment. Typically treated with the disdain and scorn with which the other characters in *Waiting for Godot* (1955) view Lucky's 'think', there is often a conscious effort to distance this work from that sort of idiom. Just as Beckett himself moved from the universal declarations of pessimism we find in *Proust* to a much less sure-footed stance in his later drama and prose, the perplexity and ignorance of Beckett's old, dwindled characters are of a type that comes *after* rather than before knowledge; or, like Krapp, after that assertive knowledge that presumes to explain the self or the world in packaged concepts. Beckett's people embody an exalted, belated ignorance or innocence: the puerility of advanced old age. Hints are often thrown out that they have scholarly or intellectual backgrounds. Like Krapp, many have or had aspirations towards authorship. Yet now they find old certainties to have atrophied and a spirit of confusion and anxious bewilderment reigns.

Dissatisfaction with abstract and philosophical ideas also underpins Beckett's impatience with literary criticism, dismissed rather mordantly as 'hysterectomies with a trowel'. We might remember that, in *Waiting for Godot*, 'Crritic!' is the most shockingly offensive insult that can be hurled between the two tramps (CDW, 70). His hostility, like that of the reformed smoker, is doubtless fuelled by his own early flirtation with literary criticism and immersion in the history of ideas. 'I am no intellectual', he once rather disingenuously remarked, 'all I am is feeling.'[18] Though the young Beckett in particular was excited by certain philosophers – Democritus, Descartes, Geulincx, Schopenhauer and Spinoza amongst many others – the older man consciously sought to evacuate the allure of their theories and opts instead for an aesthetic, stylized appreciation. A glance at his *Proust* reveals how influenced the Beckett of 1931 was by the pessimism of Schopenhauer;[19] later in life he still speaks fondly of the thinker, but his emphasis has turned to the philosopher's *stylistic* virtuosity more than his philosophical insights.[20] A similar sensibility underlies his claim that what he found irresistible in the dictum of St Augustine that found its way into *Waiting for Godot* was the shape of the sentence, its symmetry before its sense:

I am interested in the shape of ideas even if I do not believe in them. There is a wonderful sentence in Augustine. I wish I could remember the Latin. It is even finer in Latin than in English. 'Do not despair; one of the thieves was saved. Do not presume; one of the thieves was damned.' That sentence has a wonderful shape. It is the shape that matters.[21]

As we shall see, this fondness for the shape of ideas finds a parallel in Beckett's increasing exploration through his career of highly wrought symmetries and patterns in his literary forms, both narrative and dramatic.[22] Foregrounding style and shape before sense or meaning is a tactic that Beckett will deploy in many different contexts and is a crucial facet of his aesthetic. Though this might seem to place him squarely in the modernist pantheon, there are some crucial differences that we shall examine later.

Given Beckett's growing suspicion of philosophical systems and his elaboration of the experience of doubt, confusion and bewilderment, it is ironic that his work has been continually read as exemplary of various philosophical fashions, from existentialism to structuralism to post-modernism. Anthony Cronin is surely right in thinking that, in general, 'too much has been made of Beckett's interest in philosophy and too little of his impatience with it'.[23] Hearkening to his epiphany and to the change in tone of his post-war work, Beckett remarked in an interview, '*Molloy* and the others came to me the day I became aware of my own folly. Only then did I begin to write the things I feel.'[24] One of the most widely under-considered aspects to Beckett is the significance of this 'folly', for it is at the crux of his artistic project. It sits ill-at-ease with much of the mythology surrounding Beckett as an all-knowing guru with a universal, pessimistic vision of the human plight. Beckett wrote his most accomplished work through abandoning the time-honoured quest in art to achieve illumination and clarity; instead, as he put it in *Krapp's Last Tape*, he sought to explore the dark he had always struggled to keep under. 'The more Joyce knew the more he could', Beckett remarked in his 1956 interview with Israel Shenker,

He's tending towards omniscience and omnipotence as an artist. I'm working with impotence, ignorance. There seems to be a kind of esthetic axiom that expression is achievement – must be an achievement. My little exploration is that whole zone of being that has always been set aside by artists as something unusable – as something by definition incompatible with art. I don't think impotence has been exploited in the past.[25]

Importantly though, this exploration is not undertaken from a position of authority. Beckett's work does not treat impotence as, simply, inert subject matter, dealt with in a conventionally naturalist or omnipotent manner. He is not dealing from an omniscient perspective with ignorant characters. Rather the ignorance and impotence suffuse textual meaning on every level. Neither author nor reader knows for sure the answers to the questions the suffering characters pose themselves, nor those implicitly posed by their plight. This being the case, the exploitation of impotence as artistic raw material has important implications for conventional power relations, in which power and impotence, master and slave, are simple opposites.

As with the dangers of scepticism, there is, to begin with, something of a contradiction in the idea of 'working with' impotence. If it is turned into material that can be worked with, then impotence ceases to be the opposite of power. Steven Connor puts it thus:

> Impotence is not a simple condition, for it exists in a complicated relationship to questions of power. Impotence is always failure under specific conditions. To 'work with' impotence is to enter into a reordering of the relationships of power and powerlessness, because it is an attempt to take possession of one's poverty, to master impotence by affirming it, to resist subjugation by embracing it.[26]

If, as the truism goes, knowledge is power, then the opposition between knowledge and ignorance is rewired similarly to that of power and powerlessness. To 'know' that one is ignorant is, in a sense, to undermine that ignorance just as the fool, who knows he is a fool, is on the first step to wisdom. If Beckett unravels the venerable attempts at metaphysical clarity in art into an exploration of perplexity and opacity, then he is also achieving a deeper clarity. Scepticism, the suspicion of certainty or attainable knowledge, is itself a *preliminary* to certain knowledge, as Descartes well knew.

However anti-rationalist, however distrustful of philosophy, Beckett is motivated by truth, by the need to be faithful to the chaos and confusion he perceived around him. He said in his 1961 interview with Tom Driver:

The confusion is not my invention. We cannot listen to a conversation for five minutes without being acutely aware of the confusion. It is all around us and our only chance now is to let it in. The only chance of renovation is to open our eyes and see the mess. It is not a mess you can make sense of.[27]

This idea of 'letting in' the 'confusion' gives the lie to the postmodern notion of Beckett's language as unqualifiedly performative: of the artist as Prospero, conjuring up endless stories within stories to show that reality is just an illusory will-o'-the-wisp, with no more ontological weight than all the other arbitrary and ephemeral fictions. The confusion for Beckett is there independently, a real referent – if a highly muddled one – independent of some postmodernist play of signifiers. It is not Beckett's invention. Rather he is impelled to bear testament to the 'mess' without the distortions of a beguilingly transformative aesthetic. He is motivated by a puritanical, Protestant imperative to be *true* to this confusion and, as we shall see, this has important effects on the stylistic and formal devices he uses in his drama and fiction. He strives to let the 'confusion' into the realm of expression without colouring it, or recasting it into spurious coherence. Unfortunately, even to recognize confusion, to give it any linguistic reality, is inevitably to distort it for this recognition implies a degree of control. Hence, as Beckett is painfully aware, 'to be an artist is to fail' (P, 125).

Of longer standing than the postmodern reading of Beckett's work as performative and ludic is the more traditional, humanist notion of him as presenting us with a timeless vision of humanity. The rootlessness and unspecificity of Beckett's geographical locales, like the blurred identity and uncertain subjectivity of his characters, has often been read as a mark of universality, the very lack of coherence and definition indicating some sort of archetypal ur-Site, populated by characters whose very indeterminacy suggests an allegorical embodiment of the universal 'human condition'. However, rather than an ascent to universalism, the pervasive uncertainty in Beckett could conversely be regarded as the failure to adequately grasp the determinate, which remains in Beckett's world as slippery and agonizingly ineffable as Watt's pot or the meanderings of the Unnamable. The muddle and disarray with which Beckett's work is concerned contributes to its peculiar feeling of immediacy and particularity. For if Beckett's dramatic settings are stripped and indeterminate, there is also a revelling in the specific, the bodily and the immediate. One thinks of Gogo's smelly feet or Krapp's banana or the detritus of Winnie's handbag. As

James Knowlson observes: 'He has often been treated as if he were a cold formalist dealing in abstractions. Yet there is an intense concern in his writing with the physical, the concrete, the here and now.'[28] Confidence in objective knowledge leads to generalizability, which in turn forms the bedrock for pronouncements of a universal, transhistorical nature. However there is nothing like a wave of vertigo to give one the feeling of the here and now, and the dizzy lostness of Beckett's people means that, like Lear on the heath, they can rarely ignore the pressing urgency of their immediate surroundings. This is especially true in the drama, where, unlike the prose, the characters' propensity for memories and story-telling is never allowed to take them away from the contrapuntal materiality of the stage. Perhaps, then, the lack of specificity of Beckett's sites simultaneously points in both directions – above and below the particular – establishing an archetypal setting and at the same time wryly undercutting it, or evacuating it of portentous meaning. In Act II of *Godot*, when Estragon describes Pozzo, splayed on the ground, as 'all humanity', there is more than a hint of parody (CDW, 78). The dichotomy is, perhaps, best summed up in the 1976 play *That Time* where the refrain 'not knowing who you were from Adam' sums up an identity that is both archetypal/original and utterly befuddled (CDW, 391).

Given the centrality of uncertainty and ambiguity to Beckett's artistic project, it is not surprising that his plays, notwithstanding a deluge of critical exegesis, defy attempts to decipher them allegorically, or to translate them into a philosophical system. It is not just that the drama is opaque, but also that its very *raison d'être* is opacity, indeterminacy and ambiguity. Beckett significantly remarked that 'The key word in my plays is "perhaps"'.[29] *Waiting for Godot*, however, is unusual in Beckett's dramatic canon in that certain key speeches, such as Vladimir's soliloquy on time and habit, seem to invite the sort of philosophical reading that Beckett was increasingly to disavow: 'Astride of a grave and a difficult birth. Down in the hole, lingeringly, the grave-digger puts on the forceps. We have time to grow old. The air is full of our cries. [*He listens.*] But habit is a great deadener' (CDW, 84). This sort of synoptic glimpse of the lifespan concentrated to a moment becomes increasingly rare in Beckett's work – later characters cannot even muster the knowledge of their immediate condition, let alone the human condition. Like his earlier, unperformed play, *Eleutheria* (written in 1947), the traces of Beckett's philosophical pessimism have not yet been absorbed into the thematic uncertainties, and stringent formal symmetries, of the later drama. This is, perhaps, one of the reasons for the play's apparent comprehensibility and, hence, great popularity. We can decipher the theme of *Waiting for Godot* in the terms adumbrated in *Proust*, where life is an endless struggle to offset the vagaries of time and the insatiability of desire by distracting ourselves through vain hope – waiting for Godot to arrive – or through trivial play – 'habit is a great deadener'.[30] Yet there is much more to *Godot* than this vision of the futility of life; one suspects that Beckett was frustrated that these passages have been continually used as interpretative hooks. He felt that 'the early success of *Waiting for Godot* was based on a fundamental misunderstanding, critics and public alike insisted on interpreting in allegorical or symbolic terms a play which was striving all the time to avoid definition'.[31] *Waiting for Godot* is all about this avoidance of definition. Like Vladimir and Estragon, the audience, too, wait for the arrival of a meaning that is continually deferred. Godot, as one critic puts it, has a *function*, rather than a *meaning*.[32] Theatrically, his function is to create suspense and dramatic cohesion amidst the inertia and boredom on stage. Thematically, he signifies a radical absence, a trope for the agnosticism that pervades the play; his non-arrival denies both protagonists and spectators the luxury of coherence and resolution. The action – or lack of it – underscores a powerful epistemological absence. Action presupposes a reasonably autonomous self and a world of intelligible causality and, since neither is available in Beckett's plays, there is little action on his stage. Estragon's famous description of the play in which he appears – 'nothing happens, nobody comes, nobody goes, it's awful!' (CDW, 41) – is wryly summed up by Vivian Mercier's famous remark, 'nothing happens, twice'.[33] In order to make theatre of this condition, Beckett must rewrite the rulebook, strive for a new grammar of the stage, more anti-dramatic than dramatic, which will resist exposition, climax and dénouement and incarnate boredom, inaction and opacity.

The shards of pessimistic soliloquy that make it to the surface in *Waiting for Godot* never get beyond the mordant parody of Hamm's struggle for grandiloquence in *Endgame*: 'Can there be misery [*he yawns*] loftier than mine? No doubt. Formerly. But now?' (CDW, 93). In the canon of tragedies that this play so often invokes, this misery was expressed – 'formerly' – in the lofty style that Hamm strives unsuccessfully to emulate. Hamm is a tragic hero depleted of lyricism, just as his name is an amputated version of the most famous tragic hero of all. Like the painkillers and everything else in this play, lyrical grandeur is fast disappearing. There is plenty of comic striving for the magisterial touch – particularly in Hamm's attempt to tell his chronicle to his

unwilling audience – but not much significance behind the portentousness:

> A little poetry. [*Pause.*] You prayed – [*Pause. He corrects himself.*] You
> CRIED for night; it comes – [*Pause. He corrects himself.*] It FALLS: now
> cry in darkness. [*He repeats, chanting.*] You cried for night; it falls:
> now cry in darkness. [*Pause.*] Nicely put, that. [*Pause.*] (CDW, 133)

Bombastic language is immediately deflated by the corporeal, the gross,
or the everyday: 'My anger subsides, I'd like to pee' (CDW, 103).

The characters in both plays tell stories about their past that seem
uncertain or wholly fictional. Memories seem no more reliable than
expectations; the past is just as inscrutable as the future. In the later
play, however, meaning seems even more inaccessible, the inaction
even less comprehensible. The characters occasionally comment wryly
on the drama: 'HAMM: We're not beginning to ... to ... mean something? CLOV: Mean something! You and I, mean something! [*Brief
laugh*] Ah that's a good one!' (CDW, 108). All we can be sure of in this
enigmatic play is that, in Clov's refrain, 'Something is taking its
course.' Beckett has moved further into the dramatic form, away from
the philosophical obsessions of his pre-war work, to the extent that T.
W. Adorno, in the most famous essay on this play, can praise it for
putting 'drama in opposition to ontology', for dramatizing an incoher-
ent situation, untranslatable into the circumscribed language of ratiocination and conceptuality: 'Understanding *Endgame* can only be
understanding why it cannot be understood, concretely reconstructing
the coherent meaning of its incoherence.'[34] As well as his fascination
with the dramatic power and precision of gesture and movement, one
of the reasons that Beckett turns to the stage is in order to use *silence* to
indicate this incoherence. The most expressive moments in these plays
often occur in the pauses and silences, indicating, at turns, repression,
fear, anticipation or horrified inarticulacy. Much of what Beckett has to
say in his drama lies in what is omitted, when his characters cannot
muster the words or the play-acting to forestall the encroaching
silence, or the 'dead voices' that haunt Vladimir and Estragon when
they stop speaking.

The Irish geography of Beckett's memory: the politics of form

Along with the pessimism of Beckett's early criticism, comes a proclivity for universal declarations about the 'timeless' human condition and

a disdain for the merely 'local' concerns of politics and historical events. If the mature Beckett dramatizes ignorance, incoherence and confusion, replacing the didactic pessimism of *Proust* with a far less haughty, more bewildered emphasis, then what effect does this shift have on the political and historical purchase of his art? In general the social context of Beckett's work has been underestimated. The tendency, especially in English and French criticism, has been to depict Beckett as an ahistorical pessimist.[35] In much criticism of his work the importance of history and politics, the contextual concerns of Beckett's cultural moment, are underplayed in the emphasis on absolute, transcendent articulations of the human plight or, more recently, in the emphasis on postmodern self-referentiality. History is seen simply as a pretext for these concerns. Like Murphy, anxious to retreat into the self-contained, authentic core of his own mind, Beckett's art is seen as loftily uninterested in the tawdry distractions of day-to-day life. And, or so the story goes, as history and politics are jettisoned in the interests of universal authenticity, geography and national locale are shed along with it – we are left with the characteristically rootless Beckettian landscape.

Beckett's early journalism and reviews have buttressed the tendency in criticism to regard him as 'somehow safely self-contained, free of any ideological constraints that would compel us to deal with him beyond the formal restrictions of the texts themselves'.[36] In these pieces, Beckett often dismisses the particular and the national as distractions from art's eternal mission. He scorned the 'antiquarianism' of the Irish literary revival, indicting a literature which occupied itself in the 'local' concerns of politics and history. He even rebukes his close friend Thomas McGreevy for over-emphasizing the national element in Jack Yeats's painting, arguing that the greatness of a painter is not to be sought in his treatment of 'the local accident, the local substance', but rather 'with the issueless predicament of existence' (D, 97). Hence, it is often assumed that the Irish inflection in Beckett's work – crammed full for all its deracinated status with names, topography and locutions from Beckett's birthplace[37] – is simply a residue of a provincial world that he has happily transcended; at best, it is a quaint background colouring to set off a vision of the human condition that is trans-historical, too big to be contained within the boundaries of one nation, of one historical period. Seamus Deane, for instance, claims that 'Beckett's repudiation of Ireland is of a piece with his repudiation of history'.[38]

Yet it is fallacious to assume that his writing occupies some sterile, evacuated imaginative site, in quarantine from its own historical context. Beckett's fiction and plays operate on a different plane to his early polemical pieces and often contradict them. If he indicts McGreevy for over-emphasizing the Irish elements in Jack Yeats's painting, we should not, therefore, embargo all readings of Beckett alert to his Irish provenance. That is not to say that there are no perils in an overly insistent and crudely handled appropriation of Beckett as a 'national' writer. Recent bibliographers wisely warn that the area presents 'very real dangers of a simplistic and reductionist approach to a complex question'.[39] Beckett is energized from many different traditions, Irish and European. Mindful of these dangers, we can nonetheless recognize that the Irish elements in Beckett are not, as they are often regarded, just a dispensable backdrop to a transcendent vision. Some recent works have focused on the prevalence of Irish geographical locales in much of Beckett's work, but what is, perhaps, more important than Beckett's memory of Irish geography is the Irish geography of Beckett's memory.[40] The overt topographical references hint, more fundamentally, at the encoding of certain paradigms and models of Irish cultural and historical experience in Beckett's literary method. For instance, the indeterminacy of the Beckettian landscape may point towards the colonial *erasure* of history and identity rather than the transcendence of it. As Declan Kiberd astutely remarks: 'Their surroundings seem decontextualised because they represent a geography which has been deprived of a history.'[41] It is true that Beckett's skeletal characters and desolate landscape are haunted by the ghosts of Auschwitz. Yet it is also the case that the fragmentary narratives, the splintered memories, and the refusal of a dominative narrative voice betoken the fractured consciousness of a country with a traumatic history of famine, displacement, persecution and lost language.[42] In Ireland, there is a tradition of literary fragmentation, as well as a painfully fragmented literary tradition. Declan Kiberd argues that Beckett could never have written a work like T. S. Eliot's *The Waste Land*, where

> each fragment seems radiant, urging the reader to infer the whole of which it was an integral part before the tradition exploded into pieces. But Irish tradition never knew such coherence, with the consequence that in Beckett's texts, the part achieves an integral rigour-without-radiance. As a result, the reader can never infer the whole of which it seldom, if ever,

would have constituted a part anyway ... Eliot might in his great poem have lamented the collapse of a tradition and, with it, of a stable subject, but for Beckett these things never existed to begin with.[43]

Beckett's work does not mourn a lost totality but, in the endless agonizing of his bewildered characters, in his scrupulous, hairsplitting breakdown of the processes of narration, and in his intense exploration of the nature of a theatrical space that is at once the culmination of the Western dramatic tradition and its radical debunking, it resists the possibility of totality altogether. Or, perhaps more accurately, it exposes totality as a factitious illusion.

Other traces of an Irish sensibility in Beckett's work can be perceived in the very phenomena of displacement and exile that are so often its dominant themes. Steven Connor regards the experience of alienation in Beckett's work as richly historical and contemporary, but also as distinctively national:

> In embracing the condition of the migrant or the exile, Beckett's work belongs, as it were, 'securely' to our era of displacement, willed and unwilled, and speaks to a growing sense that diaspora is our original condition; that all homelands are more or less violent hallucinations. And it is perhaps in this sense that Beckett is the most Irish of writers.[44]

So, Beckettian confusion may be as much a result of marginality as of modernism. Displacement and diaspora are deeply ingrained in Irish experience and Beckett's feelings of alienation, of rootlessness and lack of origin, were variously felt by other Irish writers from Swift to Flann O'Brien. However, as Vivian Mercier has argued, they are given a distinctive twist in the Protestant, Anglo-Irish class from which Beckett hails.[45] This caste, acutely aware of its interstitial, in-between position between Irishness and Englishness often teeters on the brink of identity crisis: 'The pressure on him to be wholly English or wholly Irish can erase segments of his individuality for good and all. "Who am I?" is the question that every Anglo-Irishman must answer, even if it takes him a lifetime, as it did Yeats.'[46] Anglo-Irish writers sought to compensate for the feeling of homelessness through impatriation or expatriation, through immersion in Irish culture, like Synge and Yeats; or, like Wilde and Shaw, through an ostentatious public life in London. If Yeats compensated for the lack of a coherent tradition by inventing his own, then Beckett registers the initial condition more directly. He explores the sense of limbo in itself. Beckett's Protestant Irish origin fed his skill in delineating this experience of alienation, of life in the void.

However, the aspect to Beckett that most chimes with a recurrent feature of Irish tragedy lies in the intriguing relation between form and content, style and substance in his work. Theorists have emphasized the history of stylistic unease in Irish letters. Colonial persecution, the decimation of famine, and the rapid loss of the indigenous language, all exacerbated Ireland's cultural dislocation and alienation. The sense of being on the periphery and the bleak social conditions that thrived in Ireland for so long prevented the sense of integration or reconciliation, the bourgeois confidence, which might have fuelled the classic realist novel, as it did in England.[47] Obsessiveness about style and form is ubiquitous in Irish letters. A more harmonious relation of form to content requires a stability and confidence that a fractured post-colonial consciousness cannot easily access. Neither the integrative, mythic modernism of T. S. Eliot nor the provincial realism of George Eliot can thrive in this fractured, amnesiac mindset. This dissonance between form and content is courageously encountered and exhaustively explored in Beckett's dwindled plays and novels.

Like other modernist texts, Beckett's work is peopled by perpetually befuddled, moribund characters, wantonly persecuted by inscrutable powers. Yet if its dominant atmosphere is one of dereliction and incoherence, it is written in a prose of balletic poise and control. Beckett crafts his kaleidoscope of greys with the surest of hands. However, unlike in naturalist or realist fiction where the narrative perspective is objective and omniscient, Beckett's manner of expression, though scrupulously and gratifyingly separate from his subject matter, is never dominative. 'There will be no form', he tells Tom Driver, and

> this form will be such a type that it admits the chaos and does not try to say that the chaos is really something else. *The form and the chaos remain separate. The latter is not reduced to the former.* That is why the form itself becomes a preoccupation, because it exists as a problem separate from the material it accommodates. To find a form that accommodates the mess that is the task of the artist now. [My italics][48]

Beckett's achievement is his discovery of a form which, though separate from his subject matter, is nonetheless yielding and compliant, managing to loyally express a welter of disfigurement without distortion (or, more accurately, without re-figurement). 'Achievement' and 'discovery' here must be heavily qualified for form can never really be separate from content, the mess can never be delivered in its original impurity. The act of representation itself will always impose spurious coherences. Hence, for Beckett 'to be an artist is to fail, as no other dare fail' (P, 125). Form and content, word and world, are inseparable, but Beckett probes that area where they diverge, stretching them apart to rend apertures through which each can be glimpsed as if momentarily free of the other. In the process, Beckett's work tears as many holes in the status of the self-contained artwork as it does in the conventional humanist subject.

So Beckett is inclined to sequester form from content. This sort of 'distance' between the means and the object of expression has recently been identified by Thomas Kilroy as an endemic feature of Anglo-Irish, Protestant drama:

> All creative distancing involves some movement towards abstraction and the perfection of the idea, the radical reshaping of human action for particular effects. (A reminder: one of the favourite aesthetic terms used by Beckett was the word 'shape'.) In this respect Beckett's plays could be read as a bringing to a conclusion this whole tradition of Anglo-Irish theatricality, a theatricality of disconnection, of lines which can never meet except in the perfect diagram of the stage action, a theatricality of imagined space between the mind of the playwright and the material on which he is working.[49]

In Beckett's case, there is sometimes a feeling that his forms, particularly of his later work, the style and symmetries of both of his drama and prose, could almost get on perfectly well if they were not shackled to the straitening business of expression. Expression seems a pretty futile affair anyway, doomed as it is to distortion and invention. We know that Beckett as a director always underplayed the meaning of his plays and concentrated, instead, on the shape and rhythm of the delivery, the fidelity of the production to rigorous and rigid stage directions.[50] There is in the drama, as in the prose, a balletic control in its mode of expression that contrasts with the agonized meanderings of the characters and their stories. Structurally, his work is highly patterned and often beautifully wrought. Certain passages have an air of controlled tranquillity, unique to Beckett. These moments are achieved by an effortless economy of language. Consider the following famous exchange from *Waiting for Godot*:

ESTRAGON: All the dead voices.
VLADIMIR: They make a noise like wings.
ESTRAGON: Like leaves.
VLADIMIR: Like sand.
ESTRAGON: Like leaves.
[*Silence.*]
VLADIMIR: They all speak together.
ESTRAGON: Each one to itself.
[*Silence*]
VLADIMIR: Rather they whisper.
ESTRAGON: They rustle.
VLADIMIR: They murmur.
ESTRAGON: They rustle.
[*Silence.*] (CDW, 58)

The wonderfully sprung rhythm of this passage and the evocative, soothing susurration strains against the macabre subject matter to eke out a certain compelling dissonance between the language and the characters' guilty torment. Vladimir and Estragon are too close: they listen to the dead voices while we listen to the poetry. Hence Vladimir's desperate 'Say something!' following the long silence at the end of the exchange (CDW, 59). Importantly, though, the appeal of this exchange is very different from that, say, of the conventional tragic soliloquy. It does not lyricize the suffering. It does not even express it directly, but rather catches those dead voices elliptically, in the excruciating pauses.

The novels also have this atmosphere of control and precision, explored in different ways as Beckett grew older. Middle-period novels such as the trilogy are peppered with commas, so that each sentence becomes an ever-longer series of qualifications. These commas, masterfully controlled as they are, often have a soothing effect and give the prose a compelling sense of rhythm and pace, yielding up its powerful evocations with an economy and grace beyond the ken of more expansive or coloured lyrical description. As his later drama becomes more and more stylized and ritualistic, as his prose becomes more compressed, repetitive and self-referential, there is a feeling that it is on the verge of detaching from its subject matter altogether, that the narrative has been demoted from text to pretext, simply an occasion for the shape of its expression. If we look at later novellas like *Imagination Dead Imagine* (1965) or *Worstward Ho* (1983), we witness more than ever what Beckett meant when he spoke about the 'serenity' in his form. Here the short, pared-down sentences, the reiterations of words and phrases, and their recasting in ever-new variations, give an air of ritual and predetermined pattern at odds with the eschatological and purgatorial content. It is as though he is trying to get on with as little content as is possible, trying to free his gorgeously wrought patterns and shapes from the onerous business of expression without, however, aestheticizing or distorting his object. The sense of ceremonial repetition is clearer still in the late 'dramaticules'. In the 1967 play *Come and Go*, for instance, the *leitmotif* of whispered revelation and shocked reaction occurs three times with carefully orchestrated movement and gesture, as the audience learn that all three of the heroines are unknowingly suffering from some unspecified disease.[51] Such choreographed rhythms together with a ritualistic air of pre-ordained structure, dominate all of Beckett's later drama, just as the terse verbal variations of his later prose are marked by scrupulous systems of accretion and diminution. Again, it is as if these minimalist works are mesmerized by their own method, finding solace in abandoning their debased subject matter for their own, internal symmetries.

If, as he claimed to Shenker, Beckett is not master of his material, he is certainly master of his form. The precision and symmetry of Beckett's craft contrasts with the squalidness of his subject matter. Literature has rarely produced a prose stylist of such linguistic poise, so economic and delicate with words, nor a dramatist so scrupulously concerned with shape, pattern, movement and gesture. If his material is chaotic, messy and disjointed – like the rambling, fragmented stories of his geriatric narrators – then their plight is rendered with painstaking, surgical exactitude. This may be one reason why he claimed in the Driver interview that in his work form and content remain separate. That, unlike Kafka, there is 'consternation' *behind* the form, not in it: 'Kafka's form is classic, it goes on like a steam roller – almost serene. It *seems* to be threatened all the time – but the consternation is in the form. In my work there is consternation behind the form, not in the form.'[52] As a young man, Beckett praised Joyce's *Work in Progress* for a subversive identification of form and content;[53] one of the many ways in which he will later react against the methods of Joyce is in his scrupulous exploration of that area where they are distinct.[54]

This separateness is crucial for the aesthetics of suffering, the tragic strain, in Beckett's work. It implies that the opposition between suffering and its artistic representation resists the Nietzschean model of tragedy, where the unbearable Dionysian swirl is redeemed by its expression in ordered Apollonian form. While the Dionysian sphere pertains to the untempered nature of reality, the Apollonian obtains to modes of its appearance, or to its artistic re-presentation. For Nietzsche, the Dionysiac is a primal swirl of chaos that can only be tolerated by the imposition of an external, and ultimately illusory, controlling Apollonian force:

> The more aware I become of those omnipotent art impulses in nature, and find in them an ardent longing for illusion, and for redemption by illusion, the more I feel compelled to make the metaphysical assumption that the truly existent, the Primal Oneness, eternally suffering and contradictory, also needs the delightful vision, the pleasurable illusion for its constant redemption.[55]

There is, then, a tug of war between the metaphysical pull towards chaos and the textual pull towards a transcending and containing order. For Nietzsche, the presentation of Greek tragedy on stage and in choral form miraculously redeems the Wisdom of Silenus into a pleasurable and sublime spectacle. Lyrical crystallization alchemically transforms suffering and chaos into aesthetic rapture.

Though there is a clearly articulated polarity between Beckett's hyper-choreographed forms and his chaotic content, the Nietzschean model is anathema to his highly puritanical and anti-Romantic sensibility. For him words are a 'stain on the silence', a lamentably necessary distortion rather than a redemptive delight – which is not to say that he does not delight in words; he does, but his pleasure seems more grounded in their musical symmetries and shapes, rather than in their lyrical, transformative power. The Nietzschean model is precisely that which he decries in the Driver interview, for it is a tragic model that does not admit the chaos, but rather tries 'to say that the chaos is really something else'. If form redeems content or the chaos, then it also dominates it and this is something that Beckett cannot tolerate, for to his sensibility it smacks of the bogus and distortive. One might also say that to his anti-totalitarian mind the holistic, integrative control of both conventional realism and modernism smacks of the coercive and the authoritarian. Hence he emphasizes the limitations of artistic power; his own creatures are artists in their way, story-tellers who seem little able to control their ragged and chaotic narratives. In his interview with Israel Shenker, he explicitly dissociates himself from the Nietzschean tragedian, with his power of Apollonian transformation: 'I think anyone nowadays who pays the slightest attention to his own experience finds it the experience of a non-knower, a non-can-er (somebody who cannot). The other type of artist – the Apollonian – is absolutely foreign to me.'[56] Notably, Beckett does not claim to be a Dionysian artist. Rather he strips the Nietzschean tragic dichotomy of all its portentously Romantic qualities. He does not confront some exquisitely erotic, de-individuating abyss, but rather an area of exploration which he can only deflatingly describe as a 'mess' or a 'confusion', as much mundane as it is miserable. Or miserable precisely because of its relentless mundanity. The abyss for Beckett, has more to do with boredom than with apocalypse.[57]

Yet there is always a haunting absence engendered by the effort at sequestering form from content, all the more pressing and unignorable because the attempt at occlusion is so striking. In this respect, Beckett's stylistic patterns have a similar function to the high-flown, poetic language of Synge, or to the racy urban eloquence of O'Casey, that draw attention to an unbearable social and economic stagnation even as they try to occlude or paint over it. In all three cases, the relationship between 'reality' and its artistic representation, between the Dionysian and the Apollonian, is grounded in dissonance. In the Niestzschean model, and the endless derivations it has spawned, the two collide only in order to collude; in most Irish tragedy, however, the conflict does not lead directly to poetic integration. The oft-cited hyper-lyricism of the Irish stage is as often as not designed to show the impotence of 'talk' as much as its efficacy. For all the imaginative eloquence of Synge's and O'Casey's characters, the material conditions in which they live are, and remain, appallingly bleak. Aesthetics and social reality are often depicted as tragically incommensurate: form simply sweetens its subject matter, it does not redeem it.

As we saw in relation to Synge and O'Casey, this distance between self-delighting language and recalcitrant material reality is particularly suited to drama, where the relentless materiality of the stage undercuts or gives the lie to the lyrical alternatives proffered. However imaginatively or rhythmically rich his speech, the stage never lets us forget that a hobo is a hobo. The dissonance is anticipated in some of his Irish predecessors, but in Beckett's case the incommensurability between form and content, between aesthetics and reality, is relentlessly telegraphed.

In Beckett's mature work, form's relation to content is never authoritarian or autocratic. Style does not just take over or swamp substance, as it perhaps does at certain moments in Joyce's *Ulysses*. It does not aspire to package or subsume its subject matter as an integrative whole. It is as if style is in flight from, rather than in control of, subject matter. It is a movement of withdrawal rather than victory. Beckett's literary form progressively seems to aspire towards the self-contained, hermetic existence of *Murphy*'s Mr Endon, envied by the hero because he is able to play a game of chess simply for the shape and design of the movements, without engaging with the activity of his opponent. There are other moments in Beckett's writing that can be read as proleptic metaphors for his future style – those moments when shape and pattern seem to provide solace or distraction from the protagonists' torment. One thinks of Molloy's satisfactions and frustrations in seeking a cyclical pattern for his sucking stones, or of Moran, mesmerized by the dance of his bees, or of Vladimir and Estragon's little canter with their hats. These episodes are not simply shape without substance, any more than the later Beckett is just a cold formalist. The very lack of 'meaning' to these games loudly proclaims the 'mess' against which they are shored up as protection. A clinical formalism can evoke a chaotic mess in so far as both are, in a sense, empty. Similarly, in Beckett's work, though the prose is dispassionate in itself, it draws attention to the pain and suffering of the characters through the omission of evaluative engagement. Beckett is often praised for his lidless stare at the tormented human condition – as one critic put it for gazing at the Medusa without turning to stone. This praise is well-deserved, with the caveat that his gaze is often refracted through a stylistic mirror that reflects the monstrous but is itself beautifully wrought. The reflection, however, remains unprettified.

So, one of the many paradoxes in Beckett is the pervasive, energetic ambivalence between his love and distrust of art. He savours the powerful precision of language and theatre, the manifold possibilities of shape and pattern, while at the same time he finds the aspect of pretence disquietingly bogus. Perhaps this ambivalence is of a piece with his characters' simultaneous yearning for silence and infatuation with speech and storytelling. It certainly would seem to underrun the converse aspect to the liberation of form from chaotic content – the determination to keep content untainted or undominated by formal devices. The challenge, we might remember, is to find a form that lets in the chaos and does not try to say that the chaos is something else. This challenge, though, is not in service of an 'art for art's sake' credo, an enjoyment of literary language freed from any referential or mimetic onus. It is, rather, to prevent the corruption that the signifier might impose upon its referent. Even in the thirties Beckett had recognized, *pace* his early position in 'Dante ... Bruno . Vico .. Joyce', that form and content needed to remain separate. It is evident in the hostility to calcified 'literary language' on display in his famous letter to Axel Kaun:

> more and more my own language appears to me like a veil that must be torn apart in order to get at the things (or the Nothingness) behind it ... Is there any reason why that terrible materiality of the word surface should not be capable of being dissolved, like for example the sound surface torn by enormous pauses, of Beethoven's seventh Symphony, so that through whole pages we can perceive nothing but a path of sounds suspended in giddy heights, linking unfathomable abysses of silence? (D, 171–2)[58]

So even here, ten years before Beckett has embarked on his most important work, we see the poles of word and world, sign and substance at loggerheads. He seeks to tear language apart so that an extralinguistic reality is glimpsed, using words simply in order to clinch 'the dissonance between the means and their use' (D, 172). Interestingly, at this stage Beckett wants to do violence unto language not to erode expression, but in order to achieve a deeper or more profound expression – not one that articulates overtly, but one that gestures through its omissions. As Terry Eagleton remarks: 'If Beckett is more modernist than postmodernist, it is because his world has shattered into fragments which leave rather at their centre not just a blank, but a hole whose shape is still hauntingly reminiscent.'[59] And Beckett is instinctively aware that this attitude is different to the integrative, mythic methods of Joyce. Joyce seeks to unlock reality within language, Beckett strives to find it in the fissures and gaps left by language: 'With such a programme, in my opinion, the latest work of Joyce has nothing whatever to do. There it seems to be rather an apotheosis of the word. Unless perhaps Ascension to Heaven and Descent to Hell are somehow one and the same' (D, 172). Beckett's impatience is with a language gone stale, lifeless and formulaic through overuse. Yet it comes from an urge to express something real, even if that something is utterly ineffable, or, simply, nothingness. He cannot be sure, and the foregrounding of this uncertainty is the most rigorous effort to unearth reality of all: 'the puristic horror of deceit which nonetheless knows itself to be unavoidably mystified.'[60]

When this urge is actually configured as an 'obligation', as it so often is in Beckett's work, this sensibility becomes ever more redolent of his Protestant family background. In the oft-quoted 1949 dialogues with Georges Duthuit, conducted when Beckett was in the process of writing the trilogy, he speaks of the need for the 'expression that there is nothing to express, nothing from which to express, no power to express, no desire to express, together with the obligation to express' (D, 139). This emphasis on 'obligation', as Anthony Cronin points out, is a significant shift from the earlier declarations of 'need' to express, or even a 'compulsion' to do so: 'it removes us from the sphere of psychology into that of morality, perhaps even into that of theology.'[61] The hostility he displays towards artifice and storytelling is the puritan distrust of the graven image, of the false ritualistic consolation.[62] Beckett rifles through the stores of language for the right words, minimizing representation in his search for an unmediated referent. Just as the puritans closed down the theatres, Beckett writes a sort of anti-drama that grows ever sparer and sparser in form, pared down to a minimum in an attempt to clinch its ineffable object. Of course, the object is persistently elusive. The signifier will always obtrude. However, even if destined to failure, Beckett's aesthetic is far more mimetic than redemptive. Language is not there to sweeten the object, but to avoid distorting it, even if that avoidance means shrinking back into its own shapes and symmetries. Beckett avoids 'distorting' the object by the extreme scrupulousness of his art. But this ironically throws that art into greater relief.

The representational hubris of much conventional literature is leached away to leave a dwindled hesitant voice, marked with humility and humanity. However, so much emphasis has been placed by Beckettians on 'the art of failure', that the very serious 'obligation' to express has perhaps been underestimated. After all, this failure can itself be expressive of something. In a very telling remark that touches on both, seemingly paradoxical, imperatives felt by Beckett, he claimed to Lawrence Harvey his ambition to let 'Being' into literature through a proper 'syntax of weakness'.[63] Though the syntax has been dismembered, Beckett's art, Orpheus-like, still sings. Here we have both the serious effort of referentiality and the recognition that this is a fraught, elliptical enterprise, evoked by linguistic acquiescence more than artistic authority. So the urgency of the 'real world' is felt in Beckett's work not through a dominative artistic voice, but by a remarkably original reorganization of the syntax of expression.

After Eden: loss, guilt and the 'Law'

Beckett's aesthetic development, as delineated thus far, can be further illuminated by the consideration of an exemplary theme: his mutating use of the Edenic motif, and its related systems of crime and punishment, loss and nostalgia. This is a crucial theme in Beckett's work, central to his notion of tragedy. From *Proust* to *Waiting for Godot* to the purgatorial later work, allusions to the Fall abound and a heavy, ineluctable sense of guilt and punishment is ubiquitous. As seen in relation to Synge, the conception of a lost Eden was highly current in the Irish revival, but Beckett restructures this time-honoured tragic paradigm in important ways. Through the refusal of totalization in his work and his exploration of an art of bewilderment and scepticism, he resists the temptation to configure the myth in terms of historical nostalgia. Nothing is reliable for Beckett, least of all memory of the past. Moreover, far from a true haven, Eden contains loss as an essential prospect. The Unnamable yearns for somewhere a bit more reliable: 'Quick, a place. With no way in, no way out, a safe place. Not like Eden' (T, 320). Unlike the Irish antiquarians, for whom he cherished a particular distaste,[64] and unlike the conservative, modernist nostalgia of Eliot, Beckett's prelapsarian world cannot be visualized, just as the Garden of Eden cannot be conceived in a fallen state.

As with Beckett's resistance to ratiocination, there is a political dimension to this uncertainty. Theodor Adorno (who planned to dedicate his posthumously published work *Aesthetic Theory* (1970) to Beckett) exhorts a wariness of Utopias, be they of the past or of the future. For Adorno, Utopian visions are inevitably conceived within the debased social conditions that must be removed before true emancipation can occur. To predict the nature of utopia before these conditions are removed is to view Eden through tainted post-lapsarian lenses. One must draw back from defining Utopia, be it of the past or of the future, just as in the Hebrew tradition even to utter the name of Yahweh is to blaspheme. Such caution in the face of political didacticism feeds Adorno's aesthetic theory, aimed at salvaging art from polemicism, at resisting the fraudulent coherence of the conceptual modes available within the degraded society: 'It is not the office of art to spotlight alternatives, but to resist by its form alone the course of the world, which permanently puts a pistol to men's heads.'[65] For Adorno, the stylized formal choreography that we have examined in Beckett's work offers the promise of political redemption that the content would seem to deny. Beckett himself seems to agree: 'Paradoxically, through form, by giving form to what is formless, the artist can find a partial way out. Perhaps it is only in this sense that there may be any underlying affirmation.'[66]

Beckett's reconfiguration of the Edenic model provides one frame for this sort of formal resistance. Through it, he expresses his sense that something is missing, that at a fundamental level there is something perverse and wrong with the world without falling prey to the allure of a false nostalgia. As we have seen, in his early work, such as *Proust*, Beckett has no trouble identifying the culprits – time and desire – in universal terms, yet in his mature work he becomes increasingly wary of philosophising on the malaise. Here, mystery, bewilderment and a sense of aporia overtake the modernist hauteur of his pre-war prose and journalism. Instead of Yeats's yearning for an eighteenth-century Irish Ascendancy heyday, Beckett's unreliable narrators repeatedly register the problems of memory, of resurrecting a lost past or tradition. When nostalgic moments occur, like Nell and Nagg reminiscing about their trip together on Lake Como, they are invariably laced with parody. Just as Estragon forgets what happens to him each day, and Malone seems to make up his own past with increasing disgust, so Beckett registers the recalcitrance and opacity of historical memory. However, if he resists the temptations of nostalgia, neither does he give in to the opposite allures of amnesia. Plagued with fragments of the past which they cannot amalgamate into a consoling coherence, Beckett's people are never granted the solace of an easy oblivion. The dead voices haunt Estragon and Vladimir, and a terrible sense of guilt and obligation haunt all Beckett's characters. They can only treat the past like obstinate and unwieldy extensions of themselves, which can neither be successfully repressed nor properly incorporated.

If the idea of a loss is central to the Eden myth, so also is the concept of original sin – that aboriginal offence that leads to the Fall. As we shall see, the same uncertainty and causal confusion that effects Beckett's treatment of loss also disorientates his mature treatment of guilt, where crime and punishment are typically muddled together. However, the young Beckett centres the concept of Guilt in a definition of tragedy that is avowedly 'universalist'. In *Proust*, Beckett gives his only definition of tragedy, wholly identified at this stage with Original Sin:

There is no right and wrong in Proust nor in his world. (Except possibly in those passages dealing with the war, when for a space he ceases to be an artist and raises his voice with the plebs, mob, rabble, canaille). Tragedy is not concerned with human justice. Tragedy is the statement of an expiation, but not the expiation of a codified breach of local arrangement, organized by the knaves for the fools. The tragic figure represents the expiation of the original sin, of the original and eternal sin ... of having been born.

> Pues el delito mayor
> Del hombre es haber nacido. (P, 49)

This definition is pilfered almost word for word, down to the quotation from Calderón's *La Vida es Sueno* – 'For man's greatest offence/Is that he has been born' – from Schopenhauer's *The World as Will and Representation*.[67] *Proust* is riddled with such borrowings, and the indictments of time, desire and habit in that work may well derive from Schopenhauerian pessimism.[68] Though obviously derived from the Christian myth, this pessimistic model of Original Sin – whereby birth itself is the transgression that leads to the sufferings of life – refuses the Christian notion of redemption, where the loss of Eden is ultimately a Fortunate Fall. In the pessimistic philosophy of Schopenhauer and the early Beckett, the mythic aboriginal crime is used as the basis for a universal pessimism, not offset by any religious happy ending. However, as definitions of literary tragedy go, this one is highly contentious. To be sure, discussion of tragedy often attracts this sort of cosmic, universalizing idiom, but the heavy investment in the idea of original sin, however much it fits Schopenhauer's pessimism, scarcely accommodates the work of Shakespeare or Chekhov. Significantly, however, the tie-in with original sin proved compelling for the young Beckett, who curiously regarded it as central to Proust's great novel – not often considered a tragedy. He is attracted to this conception of an aboriginal 'crime' because it allows him to ascribe the cause of all human suffering to a general and transhistorical origin. Hence his brisk dismissal of the merely particular, 'the codified breach of local arrangement, organized by the knaves for the fools'. More anomalously, this dismissal veers towards a pseudo-Nietzschean disdain for the 'plebs, mob, rabble, canaille', misanthropic sentiments a long way from the post-war Beckett, so often praised for his humanity, courage and compassion.

If this definition of artistic tragedy stands on shaky ground, then the idea that life itself is eternally tragic due to original sin is no more sustainable.[69] As Beckett will later realize, universal pessimism depends on a panoptic perspective that can only be bogus, or, more likely, covertly dependent on the real historical suffering that Beckett here seeks to downgrade to the 'local' and incidental. Against Beckett's description of 'real' tragedy as 'original and eternal', one might contend that the airbrushing of specific historical suffering out of the definition is based in a denial of particularity that is ultimately reductive and dangerous. Regardless of how right or wrong Beckett's particular complaint about Proust's novel is, if the history of day-to-day human suffering is barred entry to this 'timeless' tragic vision, one wonders from where the concept really derives. A philosophy of tragedy cannot have some sort of an a priori foundation; it must derive from a perception or an experience of suffering within a social context, just as a generic definition of dramatic tragedy must, at some level, be founded on actual plays. In that sense, it is history and social experience which are prior to the tragic 'essence', not the other way round. Any system of universal pessimism must reach for actual historical suffering to ground itself. As Schopenhauer himself queries, 'For whence did Dante get the material for his hell, if not from this actual world of ours?'[70] The idea that the endless litany of historical suffering is simply the symptom of a universal condition must itself be derived from experience. Inevitably based on the evidence of perception, conclusions on the nature of suffering must derive from induction, not deduction. Since it is inductively arrived at, it must, consciously or unconsciously, be based on an amalgam of particular instances, occurring within real social life. In their hasty assumption of a universal perspective from which to condemn existence, Beckett and Schopenhauer shuffle off this origin of their pessimism in history. At some point in the process of abstraction, the sequence is inverted: historical suffering is viewed as a symptom of universal malaise, whereas one could just as easily say that doctrines of universal pessimism are a symptom of historical suffering. History must be prior: the experience of suffering can be theorized, but not abstracted.

The fact that pessimism must be rooted in history rather that outside it, that pain must be physical, before it is ever metaphysical, is borne out by another, perhaps more obvious criterion. Judgements of value and valuelessness must explicitly or implicitly be comparative. There must be a context, a relative mode, in which they are made. In other words to say something is 'bad' doesn't make sense without some inkling of an alternative. By extension, suffering cannot be comprehended without a conception of its absence, of how it could be otherwise. How, then, can one say that life in itself is universally tragic or terrible? From what Olympian height can such a value judgement be made? It may be the realization of these difficulties that prompted Beckett's later resistance to his association with the 'Theatre of the Absurd':

> I have never accepted the notion of a theatre of the absurd, a concept that implies a judgement of value. It's not even possible to talk about truth. That's part of the anguish. One can not even speak of the truth that is part of the distress. [71]

So in his post-war phase Beckett comes to realize that universal pessimism involves logical contradictions. He shifts far from the position he embraced in the thirties to the extent that he can claim: 'If pessimism is a judgement to the effect that ill outweighs good, then I can't be taxed with some, having no desire or competence to judge. I happen simply to have come across more of the one than the other.'[72] Again, that is why Beckett is most social and historical when he is most bewildered and philosophically agnostic. When suffering cannot be ascribed to universal or providential forces, the shapes and patterns of politically derived suffering – the persecution and interrogations that recur in his later drama, for instance – become all the more visible. When the epistemology of transcendence and ahistoricism crumbles, a more immanent sensibility, alert to the pressures of the particular, emerges. Adorno declared in his famous essay on *Endgame*: 'Absurdity for Beckett is no longer diluted to an abstract Idea of existence, to be illustrated in a Situation. The poetic process abandons itself to absurdity without a guiding intention.'[73] In order to assert that life as a whole is terrible or absurd, alternatives must be evoked. We have no alternatives. Therefore to condemn existence in absolute, cosmic terms is to position oneself in a position of transhistorical observation that can only be bogus. There is no context, no comparative facility, in which the value judgement can be made.

As we might predict, then, the stance of the later Beckett contrasts strikingly with the universalist declarations on the nature of the tragedy we find in *Proust*. Having given his definition in his monograph, Beckett does not explain what he means by the 'expiation' of original sin in tragedy. Schopenhauer, on the other hand, is clear about tragic expiation, claiming that its value lies in turning away from life, and the insatiable Will. Since, in tragedy, existence is unveiled in all its unalleviable misery, since all, including individual identity, is revealed as delusion, the spectator is lured towards the highest form of life, that of the ascetic: 'Thus we see in tragedy the noblest of men, after long conflict and suffering, finally renounce for ever all the pleasures of life and the aims they pursued so keenly, or cheerfully and willingly give up life itself.'[74] For Schopenhauer, tragic catharsis points toward stoic resignation as a proper response to the spectacle of life in all its profane vanities and endless sufferings. Tragedy is an ascetic as well as an aesthetic moment and in this bifurcation lies its triumph, for art and stoicism are the twin panaceas, according to Schopenhauer, through which the misery of existence can be obviated. Influenced by the Vedas, the Upanishads and other Eastern philosophy, Schopenhauer espouses a contemplative renunciation and dedicates the fourth book of *The World as Will and Representation* to an elaboration of the virtues of quietism. Tragedy is valued precisely because it reveals the vanity of earthly desire and, hence, implicitly encourages the spirit of renunciation and resignation.

It seems that initially Beckett has a similar notion of quietism in mind. He speaks, in *Proust*, of 'the wisdom of all the Sages from Brahma to Leopardi, the wisdom that consists not in the satisfaction but in the ablation of all desire' (P, 18) and declares that 'wisdom consists in obliterating the faculty of suffering rather than in a vain attempt to reduce the stimuli that exasperate that faculty' (P, 63). Many of Beckett's characters, particularly in the earliest phase of his writing, seem to set out for ascetic, quietistic withdrawal from the harried world of relationships and work. Murphy is motivated by such an impulse, as is Victor Krap, from Beckett's first full-length play *Eleutheria*. Even Molloy yearns to become an 'incurious seeker' (T, 59). Yet there is in these instances a rueful loss of Schopenhauer's faith in the possibility of ablating the faculty of desire. In *Murphy* the quietude and isolation for which the eponymous hero craves are denied him, when it is learned that the complete apathy he seeks is reserved for the insane. He is unable to emulate the total withdrawal of a Mr. Endon. Arsene in *Watt* expresses the dilemma thus:

> It is useless not to seek, not to want, for when you cease to seek you start to find, and when you cease to want, then life begins to ram her fish and chips down your gullet until you puke, and then the puke down your gullet until you puke the puke, and then the puked puke down your gullet until you begin to like it.[75]

The hard message that both Murphy and Arsene learn is the familiar Buddhist aporia that the yearning for an ablation of desire is a desire itself, and hence self-defeating, or cruelly self-sustaining.

The ascetic principle is but one of Schopenhauer's tenets that Beckett initially embraces but later rejects, while still maintaining certain elements and structures. To return to the Eden theme, as we have seen Beckett initially takes his definition of tragedy directly from Schopenhauer, tying tragedy directly to the sin of 'having been born'. And, as might be expected, throughout Beckett's work there are continual allusions to guilt and to original sin. *Waiting for Godot*, for instance, is rich in Edenic iconography.[76] Estragon claims his name is Adam, Pozzo answers to both Cain and Abel, and, of course, one of the many symbolic allusions of the lone tree is to the tree of knowledge:

VLADIMIR: Suppose we repented.
ESTRAGON: Repented what?
VLADIMIR: Oh… [*He reflects.*] We wouldn't have to go into the details.
ESTRAGON: Our being born? (CDW, 13)

However, Estragon's suggestion is inadequate – the guilt here is no longer just that of original sin. Or, if it is, this is no longer the satisfactory answer it was in *Proust*. There, the definition was grand and definite; now, expressed as a query rather than an assertion, it is less certain coming from these confused, dishevelled characters. Like the echoes of canonical tragedy in *Endgame*, the Edenic allusions in *Godot* seem fragmented, uncertain and exhausted. The guilt in Beckett's early work – Belacqua's horror at eating the lobster, Murphy's negligence of Celia – seems clearly originated, as in a more universalist way does the guilt of birth in *Proust*. Now guilt seems to have become detached from any intelligible origin. Punishment and damnation are dished out in a seemingly arbitrary, or at best inscrutable manner. In *Godot* one of the thieves was saved, the other damned. For no reason, Godot beats one of the boys, but not his brother. Pozzo might just as well have been in Lucky's shoes and vice versa 'If chance had not willed otherwise' (CDW, 32). Providence, as Lucky recondidtely observes, punishes some for 'reasons unknown' (CDW, 42). The obsession in *Godot* with redemption and damnation stems from the haunting presence of sin and culpability that cannot be located. Those dead voices that torment Estragon and Vladimir are mysterious, we do not hear them. Earlier it was argued that Beckett's Edenic structure, unlike that of the Irish Revivalists, eschewed the siren call of nostalgia for a lost past. There is no shortage of loss in Beckett – as in *Endgame*, the minimal action often follows a path of depletion. Yet, notwithstanding this loss, there is little hearkening back to a pre-lapsarian past. It almost seems, paradoxically, as if the loss was there from the beginning. How can this be? How can there be a pervasive sense of loss without an acute awareness of what it is that has been lost? We do not know the Godot who is missing in Beckett's world, no alternatives are offered to the debased, tormented existence depicted. Yet, as Adorno remarked: 'Even in the most sublimated work of art there is a hidden "it should be otherwise".'[77]

The counterpoint to Edenic loss – guilt – is also originless in Beckett's world. All of Beckett's characters are seared by guilt, yet the crime that engendered this guilt proves elusive. It is as if in Beckett's world, like Kafka's *The Trial*, crime and punishment have become intermeshed. Life is both crime and punishment. The culpability is ubiquitous, but the crime is persistently elusive. Like Joseph K, the typical Beckettian character can find no meaning for his or her 'trial' (with its appropriate double-meaning of both inquisition and random torment). In a sense, the 'Fall' in Beckett is a fall into language. Language is both crime – the 'stain on the silence' – and, for Beckett's reluctant narrators, the punishment. Again, it is a question of elusive origin, of uncertain authority. The lack of an identifiable crime (or an identifiable 'sin') is of a piece with the reordering of sequence and causality in Beckett's world. If we compare a tragic play sometimes regarded as proleptically Beckettian, Yeats's *Purgatory* (1939), with Beckett's drama, this point is forcefully made. Here, the guilt is massively centred: the inescapable cycle emanates centrifugally from a clear transgression against Yeatsian eugenics – the coupling of a Big House heiress to a stablehand. To the added pain of the characters, the similarly inescapable cycle of *Godot* does not have such a clear origin or cause. A play which does ostensibly seem based on an identifiable transgression, the adultery in *Play*, is an utter parody of bourgeois values and, as the title indicates, of conventional dramatic action. The characters try to understand the reason why they are tormented by the interrogating light in whose glare they are forced to speak, dragged into consciousness, memory, and language. This is especially true of W1, the betrayed wife: 'Is it that I do not tell the truth, is that it, that some day somehow I may tell the truth at last and then no more light at last, for the truth?' (CDW, 313). Yet the effort to make sense of the punishment does not bear fruit. If it were sure that this purgatory was an atonement of some sort, that would make some consoling sense, but even this seems unlikely:

'Penitence, yes, at a pinch, atonement, one was resigned, but no, that does not seem to be the point either' (CDW, 316). The prevalence in Anglo-Irish drama of a definite crime committed before the action is continued in Beckett's plays, but with a radical causal shift and formal disorientation. The atonement is pressing, but the crime is elusive.

As Beckett's career advances, then, the guilt experienced by his characters becomes an indefinite dispositional guilt – as opposed to moral guilt – floating arbitrarily without origin or end.[78] It could be argued that the removal of the 'origin' of original sin, within some tight mythic frame liberates a radical potential. When cause and effect are not sequestered into an abstract, unchanging relationship, then guilt and punishment, if painfully rootless, are ill-equipped to repress their political unconscious. This is another way in which the 'syntax of weakness' can make Beckett's work all the more attuned to the urgently contemporary. An uncertain aetiology may make the relation of guilt to punishment less definite, but it also renders it less self-contained, and the patterns and shapes of the social context of the text can seep through. Hence so much of the suffering in Beckett is haunted by echoes of authoritarian or fascist persecution, for all its deracinated, unspecific nature. Whether or not Pozzo and Hamm are Ascendancy landowners lording it over the exploited peasantry, the relations between master and slave here are configured in despotic terms that have as much to do with a historical as with a universal condition. They can gesture towards Irish landlordism – and there are references in both *Godot* and *Endgame* to suggest this is the case – or towards fascist tyranny. Stripped of overt reference they become paradigms, just as Godot alludes to the principle of desire and disappointment, rather than any specific allegorical referent. 'Let us be content with paradigms', as Moran says, when he has tired of listing his various, specific torments (T, 159). This method, then, is not an evasion or transcendence of history, but rather lends an amorphous quality to Beckett's work that is indefinite and evocative, rather than abstract and universal.

The shadows of authoritarianism get darker in Beckett's later work, paradoxically regarded by critics as the most distant from material reality. The inquisition and surveillance that the later characters undergo, the power, victimage, manipulation and paranoia, have many strikingly contemporary echoes in a century of totalitarian regimes. Witness the relentless interlocuting light in *Play*, forcing the characters to speak; in *Cascando* and *Words and Music* the characters are overseen by quasi-despotic interrogators. Plays from the eighties, such as *Catastrophe*

(1982) and *What Where* (1983) are intensely concerned with persecution and torture, a content that is played off against the theatrical form, so that in 'a masterstroke of compression, Beckett at once foregrounded and fused the tyrannies of theater and state'.[79] Interrogations in glaring light, oppressive power relations, edicts passed down from higher authority and the constant, inescapable signs of surveillance, all characterize Beckett's later drama and prose. On one level, the muddle and confusion of the later characters makes their plight terribly uncertain, but on another makes it pressingly immanent. This 'trial' that they experience is for a mysterious crime, but it is conducted in a very familiar manner.

The trilogy, with its interlocutions, edicts and punishments passed down from an inscrutable higher authority, teems with the paraphernalia of persecution. Crammed with authoritarian relationships, it is even more concerned with ubiquitous, originless guilt than the drama, possibly because there is a direct confrontation with an inscrutable and discredited 'Law'. When Molloy goes to the town in search of his mother he has no idea why he is arrested for leaning on his bicycle in the middle of the street. The 'Law' is singular, monological, abstract and nameless: 'But there are not two laws, that was the next thing I thought I understood, not two laws, one for the healthy, another for the sick, but one only to which all must bow, rich and poor, young and old, happy and sad' (T, 21). Molloy's comic incomprehension of the vocabulary and the mechanics of the Law lead to his arrest. Typical of the Beckettian character, Molloy is a tramp, a misfit, an oddball – not a non-conformist by volition, not a 'dropout', but one who is unable to learn the conventions of social behaviour. He is poignantly and comically keen to be included. He is confused by the mysterious mechanics of political power and hierarchy and, stumblingly, tries to make sense of it. He was arrested, he decides, because he was stationed in a deplorable manner, his

> feet obscenely resting on the earth, my arms on the handlebars and on my arms my head, rocking and abandoned. It is indeed a deplorable sight, a deplorable example, for the people, who so need to be encouraged, in their bitter toil, and to have before their eyes manifestations of strength only, of courage and of joy, without which they might collapse, at the end of the day, and roll on the ground. I have only to be told what good behaviour is and I am well-behaved, within the limits of my physical possibilities. (T, 24–5)

His naive eagerness to be a good citizen parodically reveals the dubious standards upon which the law is based. The 'Law' functions to expunge dissent; misfits and non-conformists transgress by posing the possibility of an alternative way of viewing the world. Molloy's innocuous activity – leaning on his bicycle in a restful posture – is enough to pose a bad example. The society in which Molloy is an outsider – as we will discover when the Morans, father and son, make their appearance – is motivated by the worst sort of bourgeois complacency. But its Kiplingesque ethos of fortitude, resilience and good spirits is wryly mocked by the very existence of moribunds like Molloy. So acute is Molloy's confusion and suffering that he is eager to be accepted and to conform. He cannot. When he tries to take on the values of the authorities as he encounters them, we find him endorsing a crude parody of the status quo. Hence it is undermined not by political sophistication but by social innocence. Molloy speaks longingly of the day when he will 'know that I know nothing' (T, 25).

The episode is important also insofar as it anticipates the more abstracted power figures and hierarchical relations that dominate the rest of the trilogy. Moran declares that the cause for which he worked 'was in its essence anonymous, and would subsist, haunting the minds of men, while its miserable artisans should be no more' (T, 105). However, the names of his superiors, Youdi and Gaber, have a deliberate echo of God (Dieu/Yahweh) and his archangel messenger (Gabriel). If they are configured as members of the secret service, Gabriel and Youdi also seem to have celestial affiliations. Similarly, the interlocutors and commanders that beset Malone in the frantic ravings of his final moments, the strange 'master' in *The Unnamable*, all have divine echoes and have been interpreted in religious terms.[80] Explaining the nature of 'his delegates', the Unnamable tells us:

> They also gave me the low-down on God. They told me I depended on him, in the last analysis. They had it on the reliable authority of his agents at Bally I forget what, this being the place, according to them, where the inestimable gift of life had been rammed down my gullet. (T, 273)

Here, clearly, God is a sort of secret police commander whose 'agents' – like Moran – keep files and present 'reports' on subversive activity. So Beckett effects an innovative turnabout of the conventional legitimation of political power structures. In response to the long-held association of artificial human authority with divine order – the monarch as God's representative on earth and so forth – Beckett adopts the opposite manoeuvre, depicting God's relationship with his subjects in terms of societal power relations. So his characterizations simultaneously borrow the hierarchical grid – societal power justifying itself in divine terms – and at the same time invert it, casting God or divine power in the role of a fascist dictator, with all the paraphernalia of surveillance, 'delegates', interrogation and torture.

In the context of the 'Law', then, Beckett presents the authoritarian hierarchy upside down, projecting God into material reality in a parody of the elevation of material power to divine status. This inversion is of a piece with his confusion of the linear relation between sin and guilt, crime and punishment. We are often uncertain as to which comes first: life is often configured as a crime, the sin of birth, but it is also, for Beckett's characters, a punishment. The two overlap. In an important scene in *Malone Dies*, Macmann, lies cruciform on the ground:

> The idea of punishment came to his mind ... And without knowing exactly what his sin was he felt full well that living was not a sufficient atonement for it or that this atonement was in itself a sin, calling for more atonement, and so on, as if there could be anything but life for the living. And no doubt he would have wondered if it was really necessary to be guilty in order to be punished but for the memory, more and more galling, of his having consented to live in his mother, than to leave her [*sic*]. And this again he could not see as his true sin, but as yet another atonement which had miscarried and, far from cleansing him of his sin, plunged him in it deeper than before. And truth to tell *the ideas of guilt and punishment were confused together in his mind,* as those of cause and effect so often are in the minds of those who continue to think. (T, 220) [Emphasis mine]

Birth and life are both original sin and original punishment entwined inextricably together in a horrific coil. The more he is punished by life the more he sins and hence the more deserving of punishment. The Unnamable ponders his situation in the same terms, aware of the desperate, inscrutable identification of crime and punishment: 'Perhaps one day I'll know, say, what I'm guilty of. ... But this is my punishment, my crime is my punishment, that's what they judge me for, I expiate vilely, like a pig, dumb, uncomprehending, possessed of no utterance but theirs' (T, 339). Far from the solemn catharsis of traditional tragedy – or the Schopenhauerian expiation advocated in *Proust* – the expiation in this post-tragic world is squalid and vile, utterly bereft of the aesthetic consolations of poetic utterance or of the epistemological ennoblement of new insight or *anagnorisis*. Rather, in this confused and confusing world, the causal patterns, and the narrative sequence, have been ruptured. Punishment breeds punishment, suffering breeds suffering. More overtly even than in the drama, the cause/effect relationship of birth as the aboriginal crime and life as the corresponding tragic punishment, which we saw adumbrated in *Proust*, has yielded to a guilt overlaid with fundamental perplexity, now bereft even of the comforts of a coherent or understandable cause or origin.

In his essay 'Fate and Character' Walter Benjamin argues that, because it is only activated by guilt and misfortune, not by innocence and happiness, Fate belongs in the realm of the Law, not in the realm of religion, where it is usually placed. Benjamin relates the confusion of crime and punishment, in the context of historically distinguishing 'justice' from the 'law', to the emergence of tragedy. Tellingly, tragedy is the path through which the all-important distinction between law and justice falls into relief. Law, after all, often cloaks itself in the guise of a justice to which it has no relation. The relevant passage is worth quoting at some length:

> Mistakenly, through confusing itself with the realm of justice, the order of law, which is only a residue of the demonic stage of existence when legal statutes determined not only mens' relationships but also their relation to the gods, has preserved itself long past the time of the victory over the demons. It was not in law but in tragedy that the head of genius lifted itself for the first time from the mist of guilt, for in tragedy demonic fate is breached. But not by having the endless pagan chain of guilt and atonement superseded by the purity of man who has expiated and is with pure god. Rather, in tragedy pagan man becomes aware that he is better than his god, but the realization robs him of speech, remains unspoken. Without declaring itself, it seeks secretly to gather its forces. *Guilt and atonement it does not measure justly in the balance, but mixes indiscriminately.* There is no question of the 'moral world order' being restored; instead, the moral hero, still dumb, not yet of age – as such he is called a hero – wishes to raise himself by shaking that tormented world. The paradox of the birth of genius in moral speechlessness, moral infantility, is the sublimity of tragedy. It is probably the basis of all sublimity, in which genius, rather than God, appears. Fate shows itself, therefore, in *the view of life, as condemned, as having, at bottom, first been condemned then become guilty*.[81] [Emphasis mine]

Benjamin's masterful articulation of the subliminal political significance of ancient tragedy resonates strongly with Beckett's work. The Beckett of *Proust*, who defines tragedy as an expiation, moves in his later prose to the more subtle position, articulated by Benjamin here, that tragedy is not simply a form of purification or expiation within the existing systems of crime and punishment. Rather, for Benjamin, tragedy actually sheers off the realm of the Law altogether by radically rewriting its foundational vocabulary of guilt and innocence. Benjamin, like George Steiner, does not view tragedy as leading to the restitution of moral order, but nonetheless holds onto the idea that human beings are moral, too moral indeed for the degraded authority to which they are subject: they realize that they are better than their gods.

An important implication of Benjamin's attitude is the role tragedy plays at the level of *form*; aimed at the heart of the cause and effect relationship, it effects a radical epistemological disruption. Beckett's stylistic innovations – and stylistic evacuations – operate on this front also. The formal hesitancy that we have examined in Beckett's work, its assault on its own processes of articulation and its restless dissatisfaction with artifice, profoundly thwarts the seamless, undisturbed categories engrained in causally coherent narrative, such as naturalist fiction, that underpin a neat reciprocity between law and punishment. It is through formal reconfiguration that the radical element at the heart of the Eden myth is liberated from the overt conservatism of the closed, determinate narrative – deriving, perhaps, from Benjamin's 'demonic fate' – with its ideology of an inherently debased humanity. Moreover, the emphasis placed on 'speechlessness' in Benjamin's idea of tragedy is strikingly proleptic of Beckett's perpetual flirtation with silence and nothingness. Ultimately, Beckett's protagonist realizes that the ways of God, the persecutor, are without cause or reason, and he or she confronts the degradation of this situation with a horrified inarticulacy. Yet the realization that, in Benjamin's words, 'he is better than his God' comes as a stricken recognition. When Molloy recounts the 'pains in the balls' he has studied, he tells us that his favourite subject was anthropology on account of 'its inexhaustible faculty of negation, its relentless definition of man, as though he were no better than God, in terms of what he is not. But my ideas on this subject were always horribly confused, for my knowledge of men was scant and the meaning of life beyond me' (T, 38). To be able to study the human race in scientific terms, in the context of definition and control, would be a welcome relief; the realization that this is impossible, that people cannot be contained within the systems of ratiocination, that they are subjects not objects, throws Molloy into ignorance and silence.

Related to the operation of law and surveillance in Beckett's mature work is the pervasive sense of obligation which governs the action of these characters. The characters in the trilogy have an increasingly diffuse identity – like the mutations of the narrator of the *Unnamable* – but all must obey the edicts and imperatives handed down by their 'prompters': those persecuting voices that plague the Beckettian protagonist. Whereas Belacqua and Murphy were insistent in their indolence, scrupulous in their rejection of their responsibilities, the later characters have carefully delineated duties to carry out. Molloy's quest for his mother and subsequent chronicle of his quest, Moran's search for Molloy, or the fragmented story-telling of Malone and the Unnamable – often clearly derive from obligation. They are at one level an effort to expiate the omnipresent guilt but, in a mysterious way, end up adding to it. Again, the Unnamable speaks of 'the unintelligible terms of an incomprehensible damnation' and claims 'I was given a pensum, at birth perhaps, or for no particular reasons, because they dislike me, and I've forgotten what it is. But was I ever told?' (T, 282, 284). The sense of imperative, as opposed to volition, gets steadily stronger in the course of the trilogy. Molloy is not free to stay in the forest at the end of his narrative: 'I would have had the feeling, if I stayed in the forest, of going against an imperative, at least I had that impression' (T, 79). Very often these imperatives contribute to the religious iconography that pervades the trilogy. To ignore them, is not only a secular crime, but a religious sin: 'perhaps I could have stayed there, without remorse, without the painful impression of committing a fault, almost a sin. For I have greatly sinned, at all times, greatly sinned against my prompters' (T, 79–80). These psychological or quasi-religious prompters are as inscrutable as the police he met earlier in his quest. The imperatives which Moran follows move internally in the same way. As his journey progresses, and Moran becomes more and more like Molloy, the outward authoritarianism of the secret service is replaced by prompters similar to those that goad Molloy: 'the voice I listen to needs no Gaber to make it heard. For it is within me and exhorts me to continue' (T, 121).

The characters of the trilogy challenge orthodox epistemology in their *manner of* thinking, not just through its matter or the literal objects of their thoughts (rarely are they profound). In other words the challenge to the governing values and assumptions of society takes place at the level of form, not content. This challenge, as we saw in the case of Molloy's run-in with the Law, happens from a base of ignorance. In this subversion they replicate Beckett himself, who disavowed polemicism for radical scepticism, for a stance of unknowing. It is far more subversive to critique the forms of thought upon which a society is based, rather than to indict its politics within the limited discourse that those politics have produced. One of the ways Beckett does this is through his presentation of humane bewilderment. Most things, Molloy tells us, he doesn't understand immediately,

> Not that I was hard of hearing, for I had quite a sensitive ear, What was it then? A defect of the understanding perhaps, which only began to vibrate on repeated solicitations, or which did vibrate if you like but at a lower frequency, or a higher, than that of ratiocination, if such a thing is conceivable, and such a thing is conceivable since I conceive it ... And without going so far as to say that I saw the world upside down (that would have been too easy) it is certain I saw it in a way inordinately formal, though I was far from being an aesthete or an artist (T, 47).

By placing 'ratiocination' as only one set of frequencies amongst others, Molloy hints at the possibility of other ways of knowing – or unknowing – the world. Unknowing is important. In casting off so much of the recognizable material world in his prose, Beckett also casts off, or throws into relief, many of the ideological frames upon which social life is based. We saw this in the context of the law and power relations. Beckett's art involves discovering new possibilities in the creative order, inverting its values and challenging its assumptions. What is suggested by Beckett's work, then, is that there are alternative ways of reading the world other than the well-worn grooves followed by Western civilization and its attendant hierarchies. Moving ever inward and downward in his relentless battle with language, his impatience with its frozen inaccuracies, Beckett earns Adorno's praise:

> Kafka's prose and Beckett's plays, or the truly monstrous novel *The Unnameable* [sic], have an effect by comparison with which officially committed works look like pantomimes. Kafka and Beckett arouse the fear of which existentialism merely talks about. By dismantling appearance, they explode from within the art which committed proclamation subjugates from without, and hence only in appearance. The inescapability of their work compels the attitude which committed works merely demand ... the element of ratification which lurks in resigned admission of the dominance of evil is burned away.[82]

So if, as in Beckett's case, the dialectic of guilt and punishment refuses any clear origin or idyllic prelapsarian innocence, it can nonetheless have politically subversive implications. To be sure, we cannot envisage a prelapsarian condition, but there is an acute sense of absence in Beckett's dilapidated world, offset by his honed and harmonious literary methods – to invoke Adorno's words again, 'it should be otherwise'. However if life in the fallen state is a pale shadow of what it might have been, then there is a sense in which one is not fully or properly alive. Beckett gives an image of the world as a degraded place – cruel, unfair, unjust – a poor reflection of what it *should* be.

Another way of expressing that one is not fully alive – that existence has been compromised or debased – is to say that one was never fully or properly born. Beckett seems to have been fascinated by the idea of such a suspended condition. Ostensibly, the fascination derives from his attendance on 2 October 1935 at a lecture given by C. G. Jung, where the psychologist spoke of a girl he treated 'who had never really been born'.[83] There are several references to this limbo-state in Beckett's work, yet the most direct allusion occurs in *All That Fall*, where Maddy Rooney speaks poignantly of the girl mentioned by 'one of these new mind doctors' who 'had never really been born' (CDW, 196).[84] In *Watt*, there is an identical aphorism dislocated in the addenda: 'never been properly born'.[85] Usually, it is assumed that this lecture had an influence on Beckett in purely psychological terms, that it struck him – he was undergoing psychoanalysis himself at the time – solely in terms of its relevance to his own condition. However given his obsession with the 'sin of birth', there is reason to believe that the image of partial birth captured his imagination for philosophical or even theological reasons as well as for literal, biological self-diagnosis. In other words birth is regarded as a failed consummation not just because of a personal trauma, but because it is, in general, only a phantasm of what it should be in a 'prelapsarian' state. In his fifties, Beckett spoke urgently to Lawrence Harvey of 'Being' as an intuited 'presence, embryonic, undeveloped, of a self that might have been but never got born, an *être manqué*'.[86] At the age of sixty-two, he spoke to Charles Juliet of the obligation he felt to bring back to life in his art an '*être assassiné*', killed before he was born, yet whom he had always felt buried inside him.[87] Such references indicate that Beckett regarded the Jung lecture in terms broader than the merely personal. Furthermore, this idea of an *être manqué* suggests that birth is a catastrophe for Beckett not just in absolute terms – the start of the supposedly absurd catastrophe that is life – but because it is the *inadequate* start to an *inad-*

equate existence. There is something deviant and perverse about existence in the world as it stands. Of course, perversity and deviance
suggest a norm, an alternative to existence in the present. Beckett
speaks in *Proust* of the 'only Paradise that is not the dream of a
madman, the paradise that has been lost' (P, 74). We cannot conceive
of our prelapsarian state; in the misery of Beckett's characters,
however, it is always a haunting presence through the massive privation left by its absence.

The notion that Beckett is craving for a prelapsarian – or post-post-
lapsarian – life might seem opposed to the position of Christopher
Ricks, who argues in his influential *Beckett's Dying Words* that Beckett is
overwhelmingly motivated by the siren calls of oblivion, that he
belongs to a tradition of writing which, rather than affirming life, profoundly spurns it, that his work is fundamentally fueled by the psychological motivations of *thanatos* rather than *eros*:

> For Beckett, tradition and the individual talent converge upon an
> escape yet more total and more final than that escape from personal-
> ity and emotions which Eliot envisaged ... For, last trumping even
> the escape from personality and emotions, and constituting the only
> entire escape from them, must be the escape from consciousness, and
> in particular the guaranteed form of this, the escape into death.[88]

Though there are moments in Beckett's *oeuvre* when a yearning for
silence yields to an almost Keatsian longing for oblivion, the
Unnamable emphatically disagrees with Ricks. He does not want to
leave the world, but conversely craves for a *fuller* sense of being:

> And I for my part have no longer the least desire to leave this world,
> in which they keep trying to foist me, without some kind of assur-
> ance that I was really there, such as a kick in the arse, for example,
> or a kiss, the nature of the attention is of little importance, provided
> I cannot be suspected of being the author. (T, 315)

It is the desire to have been really there that, *pace* Ricks, motivates the
Beckettian character. In this sense, then, he can be regarded as motivated
by *eros*, rather than *thanatos*, by a life urge rather than a death urge.

Yet, there is also a sense in which the ostensibly opposite poles of
the dialectic between *eros* and *thanatos* ultimately meet at the same
point. ('Mahood I couldn't die. Worm will I ever get born? It's the

same problem' (T, 323).) Continually in Beckett, birth and death are conflated. The gravedigger putting on his forceps in *Godot* is the most famous instance. Malone, as his expiration draws nearer, also regards himself in these terms: 'Yes, an old foetus, that what I am now, hoar and impotent, mother is done for, I've rotted her, she'll drop me with the help of gangrene, perhaps papa is at the party too, I'll land head-foremost mewling into the charnel house' (T, 206). As he approaches death the ceiling rises and falls, like a uterus. The scene is set for a labour: 'All is ready. Except me. I am being given, if I may venture the expression, birth to into death [*sic*], such is my impression' (T, 260). So death itself is configured as a birth. Perhaps, given that being alive is 'never being properly born', death, as the consummation devoutly to be wished, is also in a sense the completion of a birth.

So the urge for life in a prelapsarian state, freed from the 'imprisonment' of time and space, may ultimately be the same as yearning for the release of death and oblivion, such as Ricks discerns in Beckett. The difference may be only a question of emphasis. Nonetheless, it is an important distinction, if only because in political terms it is important to recognize that pessimism can be born not only in quietism and rejection of the world, but also in rejection of the world as it presently stands. Beckett cannot really be taxed with the nihilism or sheer despair with which he is often associated. This is not through interpretative sleight of hand to recast him as some sort of optimist or meliorist. Yet if there were no hope the struggle would not be so acute: 'If there were only the mess,' Beckett is reputed to have said, 'all would be clear.'[89] The temptations of absurdism are scrupulously resisted in the mature Beckett. Absurdism would reduce confusion to a negative certainty – a certainty of the purely arbitrary nature of suffering that could be answered by hands thrown in the air. Yet he realizes that there is light as well as darkness, that birth and death intermingle.

Underpinning Beckett's vision is a high seriousness, a sense of obligation and imperative. His characters do not occupy a causeless universe but rather one that, like the social lives of many in the historical actuality from which he writes, seems mysteriously governed. There is a sin that needs to be expiated but it is ineffable, endlessly elusive. Original sin is more than a parodied trope here. It pervades Beckett's universe, derived as it is from the traumas of the cultural experience – Irish and European – that he has undergone. Beckett refuses the two easy poles, one espousing a divinely orchestrated world, the other godless chaos, choosing the tortuous, confused quest in between.

Afterword

The Introduction to this book sought to demonstrate that, because of its central importance to philosophical and cultural discourse, theories and definitions of tragedy are about more than just tragedy. Dealing as they do with extreme situations, with grave suffering, loss, death and guilt, these theories and definitions illuminate central beliefs and ideologies of a culture. Tragedy has long since burst its banks within literary studies and occurs in philosophy, psychoanalysis, politics, sociology, anthropology and theology. These disciplines move towards tragedy just as it moves towards them, adding ever-new layers of meaning and association. If dramatic tragedy has been found useful for understanding psychoanalytical precepts, so psychoanalytic tragedy has been imported into our understanding of tragedy. Tragedy is an endlessly fecund term, and its theories have an intimate association with the structures of thought and context of meaning through which a society mediates or represents profound suffering and loss. This cultural weight accounts for some of the difficulty in definition. 'Tragedy' and the 'tragic' carry too diverse a semantic baggage, they reach too wide a context, to be precisely categorized.

The synergy between tragic theory and other fields of enquiry operates *within* literary studies also. Just as discussion of tragedy moves out to wider areas of literary investigation, so too do pivotal literary critical and cultural concerns – even those ostensibly unconnected with tragic theory – chime with tragedy's central preoccupations. When a writer is engaged in artistic representation, particularly the representation of grave suffering and loss, the discourse of tragedy is not far away. Hence central issues in the three dramatists – evasion in Synge, meliorism in O'Casey and confusion in Beckett – can profitably be compared to debates and issues in tragic theory. These authors manifest similar and dissimilar attitudes to suffering and its dramatic representation. They have a different relation to the central conundrum in tragic discourse: the question of value.

The Introduction argued that tragedy not only concerns the loss of valued objects, it is also a metavalue: synonymous with masterpiece as a literary term, curiously shrouded in esteem in its everyday use. As seen, much commentary on tragedy stresses its expressive profundity. Whether it is approached as a source of insight into universal elements of human nature or read in a historically specific context, its province is regarded as *fundamental* conflict: the conflict of human will with fate or the interpersonal conflict generated by contradictions in the social structure. But if tragedy is taxed with a strong ontological onus, then this can collide with other compensatory values. For instance, it is difficult for tragedy to simultaneously meet the imperatives of veracity and those of poetic justice. A more pertinent collision in this book is that between tragic truth and tragic beauty. If tragedy is expected to be true to its object, then how can the transformative aspect of aesthetics and representation be negotiated? This oppositional relation of form to content, of language to reality, connects with a long tradition of tragic theory. Nietzsche's notion that abysmal reality is redeemed by its ordered, lyrical representation, that Dionysian chaos is made bearable through the illusions of Apollonian form, is perhaps the most famous manifestation of the dialectic. However, in all three of the writers here examined, the relationship between language and reality, Apollo and Dionysus, is strikingly unreconciled. Far from an erotic communion of beautiful language and ugly reality, in Irish drama the talk seems to counterpoint rather than redeem the material and emotional penury on stage. However exquisitely wrought, the gallous story never manages to transform the dirty deed. This distance between language and reality might seem to renege on the requirements of representation: since the language dwells in the imaginative never-never land of Synge's heroes and O'Casey's braggarts or in the balletic, yet pointless wordplay and stageplay of Beckett, it might seem to avoid addressing the squalid material realities of the life it depicts. Yet the omissions often speak louder than the language, whose very eloquence distances it from the pressing drudgery of day-to-day life. This uneasy dialectic, this mutual rebuke between content and form, may well be the characteristic Irish strategy in which form highlights content not through direct representation, but through strategies of counterpoint, omission and contrast: lyricism overlaying sterility and decay. One thinks, in this context, of Beckett's memorable definition of literary style as a bow tie over a throat cancer. The contesting tragic values – a redemptive versus a confrontational aesthetic – gain a mutual independence on the Irish stage. This might be the Irish answer to the dilemma of the mirror and the lamp, the contesting imperatives of representation and redemption. And this may also be one reason why the stage has seen some of the most notable literary achievements in Ireland this century. The impulse towards lyricism – the Synge-song, the witty urban eloquence of O'Casey, the cadenced symmetries of Beckett – are redressed by the sheer, material given-ness of the stage setting.

Productions of their plays need to be mindful of this crucial anomaly. Too many stagings of Synge and O'Casey work have tended to reproduce cosy naturalism. From one perspective, the well-swept hearth and bustling domestic space seems the natural forum for vivid storytelling and colourful fantasy. It may even accord with a genial stereotype of garrulous Irishness. But the fantasy and lyricism in Synge and O'Casey comes in reaction to a desolate social reality. As in the case of Beckett, language here is a form of pathology. Far from simply the organic outgrowth of a cosseted and charming social life, lyricism is often a delusory, and cruelly inadequate response to a life of squalid claustrophobia, the imaginative equivalent of the escapist alcoholism that so often accompanies it. We see the opposition endure in contemporary dramatists like Sebastian Barry and Marina Carr, noted for the lyricism of their language and the concomitant desolation of their subject matter. Despite the beguiling imaginative visions, the comic interplay and racy wordplay, Irish drama, at its most honest, is true to the fissure between language and reality, poetry and violence, the gallous story and the dirty deed. Typically what we experience in Irish theatre is a broken promise: the transformative aesthetic, in which poetry turns all things to loveliness, is denied us. Like a legacy which is not paid, or a Godot that does not arrive.

Notes

Chapter 1   Introduction: The Loss of Tragic Value and the Value of Tragic Loss

1. To cite just one instance: on the 1989 Penguin reprint of R. F. Foster's *Modern Ireland 1600—1972* is the *New York Times Review of Books* verdict that it was a 'dazzling description of the nation's tragedy.' The use of the word in this context is pervasive.
2. Denis Donoghue, 'Romantic Ireland', *We Irish: Essays on Literature and Society* (Berkeley and Los Angeles: University of California Press, 1986), p. 24.
3. Brendan Bradshaw famously calls for a historiography that accommodates the 'catastrophic' dimension to Irish history. See his 'Nationalism and Historical Scholarship in Modern Ireland', *Irish Historical Studies*, vol. 26, no. 104 (November, 1989), pp. 329–51.
4. Stephen Booth, *King Lear, Macbeth, Indefinition, and Tragedy* (New Haven and London: Yale University Press, 1983), p. 81.
5. For a study that seeks to evaluate the tragic status of all these dramatists, see R. B. Heilman, *Tragedy and Melodrama: Versions of Experience* (Seattle: University of Washington Press, 1968).
6. It was commonplace in the twentieth century to declare the impossibility of tragedy in the modern climate. The most famous examples include J. W. Krutch, 'The Tragic Fallacy', *The Modern Temper: A Study and a Confession* (London: Jonathan Cape, 1930), pp. 115–43; George Steiner, *The Death of Tragedy* (London: Faber & Faber, 1961). Lionel Abel's *Metatheatre* (New York: Hill & Wang, 1963) distinguishes between tragedy – a rarer genre than supposed, including the Greeks and Racine – and metatheatre, a modern tradition of subjective drama, inaugurated by Hamlet. See also, Susan Sontag, 'The Death of Tragedy', *Against Interpretation and Other Essays* (1966; New York: Doubleday, 1990), pp. 132–9.
7. Krutch, *The Modern Temper*, p. 119.
8. For a recent engagement with this venerable question, see A. D. Nuttall, *Why Does Tragedy Give Pleasure?* (Oxford: Clarendon Press, 1996).
9. John Milton, 'Of that Sort of Dramatic Poem which is call'd Tragedy', *The Complete Poetical Works*, ed. H. C. Beeching (London: Humphry Milford, 1913), p. 505.
10. Joseph Addison, 'English Tragedy' (1711), *Critical Essays from The Spectator*, ed. Donald F. Bond (Oxford: Clarendon Press, 1970), p. 210.
11. Clifford Leech, *Tragedy* (London: Methuen, 1969), p. 32.
12. Steven Connor, *Theory and Cultural Value* (Oxford: Blackwell, 1992), p. 11.
13. For the debate on genre in modern literary theory, see Jacques Derrida, 'La Loi du genre/The Law of Genre' in *Glyph 7* (Spring, 1980), pp. 176–201, trans. Avital Ronell, pp. 202–32; Alastair Fowler, *Kinds of Literature: An Introduction to the Theory of Genres and Modes* (Cambridge, MA: Harvard University Press, 1982); Paul Hernadi, *Beyond Genre: New Directions in*

Literary Classification (Ithaca, NY: Cornell University Press, 1972), and Marjorie Perloff (ed.), *Postmodern Genres* (Norman: University of Oklahoma Press, 1988) esp. Ralph Cohen, 'Do Postmodern Genres Exist?', pp. 11–27.

14. For feminist commentary distrustful of a masculine ethos of tragedy which always portrays women as 'victims', see Linda Bamber, *Comic Women, Tragic Men: A Study of Gender and Genre in Shakespeare* (Stanford, California: Stanford University Press, 1982), and Eva Figes, *Tragedy and Social Evolution* (London: John Calder, 1976), esp. chapter 4, 'Women', pp. 93–136.

15. For instance, Augusto Boal sought to counter the conservative, Aristotelian notion of catharsis as 'purgation' with the idea that the emotional release of energy in tragedy could be put to radical ends. *The Theatre of the Oppressed*, trans. Charles A. and Maria-Odilla Leal McBride (London: Pluto Press, 1979), especially 'Aristotle's Coercive System of Tragedy', pp. 1–32.

16. See especially the chapter 'Tragedy and Revolution' in Raymond Williams, *Modern Tragedy* (1966; London: Hogarth Press,1992), pp. 61–84.

17. Bertold Brecht is an inevitable precursor to all materialist or historicist accounts of drama. See 'A Short Organum for the Theatre' in *Brecht on Theatre: The Development of an Aesthetic*, ed. and trans. John Willett (New York: Hill & Wang, 1966), pp. 179–205. We have seen that Raymond Williams's *Modern Tragedy* embodies this method, but for other historicist approaches, see John Orr, *Tragic Drama and Modern Society: Studies in the Social and Literary Theory of Drama from 1870 to the Present* (London: Macmillan – now Palgrave, 1981) and Figes, *Tragedy and Social Evolution*. Lucienn Goldmann's *The Hidden God: A Study of Tragic Vision in the Pensées of Pascal and the Tragedies of Racine*, trans. Philip Thody (London: Routledge & Kegan Paul, 1976) is also a foundational work in the area.

18. Aristotle, *Poetics*, trans. Malcolm Heath (London: Penguin, 1996), p. 10.

19. Though Eva Figes has made a dexterous connection between this etymological root and the thematic functioning of the tragic hero as a sort of 'scapegoat', acting as a projection for the fears and psychological impurities of the audience. See *Tragedy and Social Evolution*, pp. 11–13. A more ingenious connection still comes from the commentator who saw in a goat's body, with furry front and bald behind, a metaphor for tragic action as starting in success and ending in failure.

20. Arthur Miller, 'Introduction' to *Collected Plays* (London: Cresset Press), pp. 31–2.

21. This point is made by John Drakakis and Naomi Conn Liebler in the Introduction to *Tragedy* [Longman Critical Readers] (London and New York: Longman, 1998), p. 3.

22. For instance, Simon O. Lesser, *Fiction and the Unconscious* (Boston: Beacon Press, 1957), Roy Morrell, 'The Psychology of Tragic Pleasure' in Essays in Criticism, no. 6 (January 1956), pp. 22–37, Bennett Simon, *Tragic Drama and the Family: Psychoanalytic Studies from Aeschylus to Beckett* (New Haven and London: Yale University Press, 1988), and Richard Kuhns, *Tragedy: Contradiction and Repression* (Chicago and London: Chicago University Press, 1991).

23. See for instance Michelle Gellrich, *Tragedy and Theory: The Problem of Conflict since Aristotle* (Princeton: Princeton University Press, 1988), pp. 8–22; Booth,

King Lear, Macbeth, Indefinition and Tragedy, pp. 82–90; Murray Krieger, *The Tragic Vision: Variations on a Theme in Literary Interpretation* (New York: Holt, Rinehart & Winston, 1960), pp. 3–5; H. A. Mason, *The Tragic Plane* (Oxford: Clarendon Press, 1985), pp. 3, 100 and passim.

24. Gellrich, *Tragedy and Tragic Theory*, p. 10.
25. For an elaboration of the differences between the three playwrights and, in particular, the radical humanist and anthropomorphic turn in Euripides, see H. D. F. Kitto, *Greek Tragedy: A Literary Study* (1939; 3rd edn London: Methuen, 1961).
26. While Johnson and Schlegel often had fulsome praise for Shakespeare's achievement, they did not suppose he wrote tragedies, as his plays differed so vastly from the Greek prototype. But the definition, as the regard in which these plays were held increased, broadened to include them. For a delineation of this process, see Clayton Koelb, '"Tragedy" as an Evaluative Term', *Comparative Literature Studies* vol. XI, no. 1 (March 1974), pp. 69–84.
27. John Dennis, *The Advancement and Reformation of Modern Poetry* (London: Rich. Parker, 1701), sig. A6v.
28. T. R. Henn, *The Harvest of Tragedy* (London: Methuen, 1956), p. 282.
29. Mason, *The Tragic Plane*, p. 1.
30. Geoffrey Chaucer, *The Riverside Chaucer*, ed. Larry D. Benson 3rd edn (Boston: Houghton Mifflin, 1987), p. 241.
31. Miguel de Unamuno, *The Tragic Sense of Life in Men and Peoples*, trans. J. E. Crawford Flitch, intro. Salvador de Madriaga (London: Macmillan, 1921), p. 17. The notion of life as inherently tragic is often associated with Schopenhauer. Yet he usually restricts his usage of the term to the dramatic or literary meaning, though he frequently compares dramatic tragedy to real life. Occasionally, however, the weight of his pessimism bursts the distinction and, in an anticipation of Unamuno, he moves beyond metaphor to describe life itself as a tragedy: 'The life of every individual, viewed as a whole and in general, and when only its most significant features are emphasized is really a tragedy ... The never-fulfilled wishes, the frustrated efforts, the hopes mercilessly blighted by fate, the unfortunate mistakes of the whole life, with increasing suffering and death at the end, always give us a tragedy.' Arthur Schopenhauer, *The World as Will and Representation* (1818, 1844, 1859), trans. E. F. J. Payne, 2 vols (New York: Dover, 1966), I: 322.
32. Ludwig Wittgenstein, *Philosophical Investigations*, ed. G. E. M. Anscombe and R. Rhees, trans. G. E. M. Anscombe (Oxford: Blackwell, 1953).
33. Hegel famously read *Antigone* as concerned with the clash of valid but partial ethical imperatives: those of family (represented by Antigone) and those of state (represented by Creon). This conflict ultimately contributes to the ongoing revelation of world-spirit or *Geist*. See G. W. F. Hegel, *Aesthetics: Lectures on Fine Art*, trans. T. M. Knox, 2 vols (Oxford: Clarendon, 1975), II: 1212–16. Many would now question Hegel's reading of this play, as well as his general ideas on tragedy. However, if his notion of tragic resolution and progress has fallen into disrepute, his emphasis on conflict and dialecticism has endured. A. C. Bradley's *Shakespearean Tragedy* (1904; London: Macmillan – now Palgrave, 1957) is possibly the most famous neo-Hegelian interpretation of tragedy.

34. Steiner, The Death of Tragedy. More recently, Steiner has extended his conception of tragedy as utter bleakness and the absence of redemption or hope. See his 'Absolute Tragedy', *No Passion Spent: Essays 1978–1996* (London and Boston: Faber & Faber, 1996), pp. 129–141.
35. W. B. Yeats, *Autobiographies* (London: Macmillan, 1955), p. 189. H. A. Mason's more recent remarks echo this Yeatsian sentiment: 'Tragedy speaks to us all in so far as we are human, and the fuller the better.' *The Tragic Plane*, p. 2.
36. Booth, *King Lear, Macbeth, Indefinition and Tragedy*, p. 84.
37. Oscar Mandel, *A Definition of Tragedy* (New York: New York University Press, 1961), pp. 63, 63–4. For a similar aversion to definition based in response and emotion, see also Geoffrey Brereton, *Principles of Tragedy* (London: Routledge & Kegan Paul, 1968). For Brereton, such an emphasis 'destroys the possibility of establishing any absolute critical standards whatever', leading to 'an ultimate subservience to spectator reaction.' p. 31.
38. Figes, *Tragedy and Social Evolution*, p. 145.
39. Williams, *Modern Tragedy*, p. 29.
40. Ibid., p. 45.
41. Ibid., p. 14.
42. James Joyce, *A Portrait of the Artist as a Young Man* (1916; Harmondsworth: Penguin, 1960), p. 204.
43. Richard H. Palmer, *Tragedy and Tragic Theory: An Analytical Guide* (Westport, CT and London: Greenwood Press, 1992), p. 1.
44. Williams, *Modern Tragedy*, pp. 49.
45. Brereton, *Principles of Tragedy*, p. 18.
46. Williams, *Modern Tragedy*, p. 48.
47. The early Georg Lukács emphasizes the ontological purchase of tragedy: 'Tragedy can extend in only one direction: upwards. It begins at the moment when enigmatic forces have distilled the essence from a man, have forced him to become essential: and the progress of tragedy consists in his essential, true nature becoming more and more manifest.' 'The Metaphysics of Tragedy', *Soul and Form*, trans. Anna Bostock (London: Merlin Press, 1971), p. 156. Normand Berlin, by contrast, claims that 'tragic dramatists touch ... dark feelings and thoughts, and their appeal to mystery vibrates responsive chords within us that are too deep for intellect to reach, let alone explain.' *The Secret Cause: A Discussion of Tragedy* (Amherst: University of Massachusetts Press, 1981), p. 175.
48. Murray Krieger, for instance, claims that the 'tragic spirit' contrasts with 'the ethical with which it is at war and which, in defense of society, must seek to punish it'. *The Tragic Vision*, pp. 74–5.
49. 'Tragedy is the description of the terrible side of life. The unbearable pain, the wretchedness and misery of mankind, the triumph of wickedness, the scornful mastery of chance, and the irretrievable fall of the just and the innocent are all here presented to us; and here is to be found a significant hint as to the nature of the world and existence.' Schopenhauer, *The World as Will and Representation*, I: 252–3.
50. Nietzsche, *The Birth of Tragedy*, trans. Shaun Whiteside, ed. Michael Tanner (1872; London: Penguin, 1993), p. 25.
51. Ibid., p. 22.

52. Krieger, *The Tragic Vision*; Timothy J. Reiss, *Tragedy and Truth: Studies in the Development of a Renaissance and Neoclassical Discourse* (New Haven and London: Yale University Press, 1980); Angelos Tirzakis, *Homage to the Tragic Muse*, trans. Athan Anagnostropoulos (Boston: Houghton Mifflin, 1978).
53. Booth, *King Lear, Macbeth, Indefinition, and Tragedy*, p. 84.
54. Reiss, *Tragedy and Truth*, p. 11.
55. Ibid., p. 283.
56. Karl Jaspers, *Tragedy is Not Enough*, trans. Harald A. T. Reiche et. al. (1947; London: Victor Gollancz, 1952), pp. 99–100.
57. Tom F. Driver, 'Beckett by the Madeleine' [interview], *Columbia University Forum*, vol. 4, no. 3 (Summer 1961), p. 23.
58. C. E. Trevelyan, *The Irish Crisis* (London: Longman, Brown, Green and Longman, 1848), p. 1.
59. Oliver MacDonagh, *States of Mind: A Study of Anglo-Irish Conflict 1780–1980* (London: George, Allen & Unwin, 1985), p. 13.
60. For the major contribution to debates on the Rising, see Theo Dorgan and Máirín Ní Dhonncadha (eds), *Revising the Rising* (Derry: Field Day, 1992).
61. Quoted in R. F. Foster, *Modern Ireland, 1600–1972* (London: Allen Lane, 1988), pp. 482–3.
62. Quoted in Declan Kiberd, *Inventing Ireland*, p. 216.
63. Ibid., p. 200.
64. W. B. Yeats, *Collected Poems* (London: Macmillan, 1933), p. 204.
65. W. J. Mc Cormack, *From Burke to Beckett: Ascendancy, Tradition and Betrayal in Literary History* (Cork: Cork University Press, 1994), p. 10.
66. See, for example, W. J. Mc Cormack, *From Burke to Beckett: Ascendancy, Tradition and Betrayal in Literary History* (Cork: Cork University Press, 1994), and Terry Eagleton, 'Ascendancy and Hegemony', *Heathcliff and the Great Hunger: Studies in Irish Culture* (London and New York: Verso), pp. 27–103.
67. Walter Benjamin, 'Theses on the Philosophy of History', *Illuminations*, trans. Harry Zohn, ed. and intro. Hannah Arendt (London: Jonathan Cape, 1970), p. 258.
68. J. M. Synge, 'Preface' to *Poems* (CW1, xxxvi).
69. Daniel Corkery, *Synge and Anglo-Irish Literature: A Study* (Dublin and Cork: Cork University Press, 1931), p. 95.
70. No one was more responsible for engendering the cult of Synge as a Romantic tragic figure than W. B. Yeats. See, 'J. M. Synge and the Ireland of his Time', *Essays and Introductions* (London: Macmillan, 1961), pp. 311–42. For a study of the incorporation of Synge into Yeats's heroic iconography, see R. F. Foster, 'Good Behaviour: Yeats, Synge and Anglo-Irish Etiquette', *Paddy and Mr Punch* (London: Allen Lane, 1993), pp. 195–211.
71. Yeats, 'J. M. Synge and the Ireland of his Time', p. 319.
72. See Seamus Deane, 'Synge and Heroism', *Celtic Revivals* (London: Faber & Faber, 1985), pp. 51–62.
73. Paul Ricoeur, *The Symbolism of Evil* (Boston: Beacon Press, 1967), p. 4.
74. For the classic treatment of O'Casey's 'anti-heroic' ethos, see David Krause, *Sean O'Casey: The Man and his Work* (London: MacGibbon & Kee, 1960).
75. G. J. Watson, *Irish Identity and the Literary Revival* (1979; Washington, DC: Catholic University of America Press, 2nd edn, 1994), p. 266.

76. Steiner, *Death of Tragedy*, p. 16.
77. Simon, *Tragic Drama and the Family*, p. 221. Significantly, Simon has no compunction about classifying Beckett as a tragedian and even hails *Endgame* as an 'archetypal modern tragedy'. p. 11.
78. Interview with Gabriel D'Aubarède in Lawrence Graver and Raymond Federman (eds), *Samuel Beckett: The Critical Heritage* (London; Routledge, 1979), p. 217.
79. As John Orr puts it, the addition of a comic element is an 'indispensable framework for the tragedy of dissolved identity, the tragedy of the diminished hero who no longer knows who he is, who lives out his life, at times consciously, in a masquerade'. *Tragicomedy and Contemporary Culture: Play and Performance from Beckett to Sheppard* (London: Macmillan – now Palgrave, 1991), p. 15.
80. This sense that comedy can intensify the tragic moment, making it less grand and hence more bleak, was recognized, in existential terms, by Schopenhauer: 'Thus, as if fate wished to add mockery to the mystery of our existence, our life must contain all the woes of tragedy, and yet we cannot even assert the dignity of tragic characters but, in the broad detail of life, are inevitably the foolish characters of a comedy.' *The World as Will and Representation*, I: 322.

Chapter 2   A Gallous Story or a Dirty Deed?

1. Richard Ellmann, *James Joyce* (1959; Oxford: Oxford University Press, 1983), p. 124.
2. Ibid.
3. James Joyce, *Letters*, eds Stuart Gilbert and Richard Ellmann, 3 vols (New York: Viking Press, 1966), II: 35.
4. Ellmann, *James Joyce*, p. 129. For an analysis of Joyce's classical aesthetics, see S.L. Goldberg, *The Classical Temper* (London: Chatto & Windus, 1961), pp. 41–65.
5. See Ellmann, *James Joyce*, p. 125.
6. James Joyce, *A Portrait of the Artist as a Young Man* (1916; Harmondsworth: Penguin, 1960), p. 204.
7. For such an interpretation, see R. P. Draper, 'Introduction' in R. P. Draper (ed.), *Tragedy: Developments in Criticism* (London: Macmillan – now Palgrave, 1980), p. 11.
8. Ellmann, *James Joyce*, p. 267.
9. Defenders of the play still strive to make it fit more neatly into Aristotle's criteria for tragedy. Leslie D. Foster argues against the critics that have erroneously 'beatified' Maurya. In refusing to give her blessing to Bartley she is in fact guilty of tragic error. 'Without tragic error', Foster claims, 'the play lacks a turning point, lacks conflict and actions and emphasises passive suffering'. See Leslie D. Foster 'Maurya: Tragic Error and Limited Transcendence in *Riders to the Sea*', *Éire-Ireland: A Journal of Irish Studies*, vol. XVI, no. 3 (Fall 1981), p. 98. More recently, Daniel Day also disputes the prevailing image of Maurya as a static and hence anti-tragic character, arguing with extensive reference to the *Poetics* that the play incarnates a

'uniquely modern catharsis'. Daniel Davy, 'Tragic Self-Referral in *Riders to the Sea*' in *Éire-Ireland*, vol. XXIX, no. 2 (Summer 1994), pp. 77–91.

10. David R. Clarke, 'Synge's 'Perpetual Last Day': Remarks on *Riders to the Sea*' in Suheil B. Bushrui (ed.), *Sunshine and the Moon's Delight: A Centenary Tribute to John Millington Synge, 1971–1909* (London: Colin Smythe, 1972), p. 50; Ernest Boyd, *Ireland's Literary Renaissance* (Dublin: Maunsel, 1916), p. 322. A. C. Partridge found an 'undoubted likeness to the *Hippolytus* of Euripides'. *Language and Society in Anglo-Irish Literature* (Dublin: Gill and Macmillan – now Palgrave, 1984), p. 218.

11. Arthur Griffith, 'Review of *Riders to the Sea*' in *The United Irishman*, 5 March, 1904. Quoted in Nesta Jones, *File on Synge* (London: Methuen, 1994), p. 21.

12. For instance, in his full-length exploration on the nature of tragedy, Robert Heilman contends that *Riders to the Sea* – classified as inferior 'melodrama' – is simply about natural disasters, to be opposed to the authentically tragic arena of inner conflict. Robert Bechtold Heilman, *Tragedy and Melodrama: Versions of Experience* (Seattle and London: University of Washington Press, 1968), pp. 38–9.

13. Georg Lukács, 'The Metaphysics of Tragedy', *Soul and Form*, trans. Anna Bostock (London: Merlin Press), p. 153.

14. Daniel Corkery, *Synge and Anglo-Irish Literature: A Study* (Dublin and Cork: Cork University Press; London and New York: London, Green, 1931), p. 95.

15. Ibid., p. 71.

16. Ibid., p. 74.

17. Mindful of the principles adumbrated in Synge's prefaces, Corkery sums up his aesthetic thus: 'his idea of literature was: an imaginative treatment of the profound and common interests of life so that exaltation might result.' Ibid., p. 67.

18. Ibid, p. 71.

19. Ibid.

20. Seamus Deane, *Strange Country: Modernity and Nationhood in Irish Writing since 1790* (Oxford: Clarendon Press, 1997), p. 143. See, also, Seamus Deane, 'Synge and Heroism', *Celtic Revivals: Essays in Modern Irish Literature 1880–1980* (London and Boston: Faber & Faber, 1985), pp. 51–62.

21. W. B. Yeats, 'J. M. Synge and the Ireland of his Time', *Essays and Introductions* (London: Macmillan, 1961), p. 319. Yeats repeats this assessement in 'The Irish Dramatic Movement' calling Synge 'the only man I have ever known incapable of a political thought or of a humanitarian purpose', *Autobiographies* (London: Macmillan, 1955), p. 567. John Masefield claimed that Synge 'was the only Irishman I have ever met who cared nothing for either the political or the religious issue'. *John M. Synge: A Few Personal Recollections* (Dundrum, Dublin: Cuala Press, 1915), p. 11. Lady Gregory said that Synge 'seemed to look on politics and reforms with a sort of tolerant indifference', *Our Irish Theatre* (Gerrards Cross: Colin Smythe, 1972), p. 123.

22. Seamus Deane, *Strange Country*, p. 143.

23. This point is made by G. J. Watson, who claims that if people criticize Synge's language for being inauthentic, then he must 'bear some of the responsibility for the confusion'. *Irish Identity and the Literary Revival* (1979; Washington, DC: Catholic University of America Press, 2nd edn, 1994), p. 50.

24. 'In writing the *Playboy of the Western World*, as in my other plays, I have used one or two words only that I have not heard among the country people of Ireland, or spoken in my own nursery before I could read the newspapers.' (CWIV, 53).
25. See E. A. Kopper, '*Riders to the Sea*' in E. A. Kopper (ed.), *A J. M. Synge Literary Companion* (New York: Greenwood Press, 1988), pp. 40–1.
26. For a reading of Synge as a modernist writer, see Richard Fallis, 'Art as Collaboration: Literary Influences on J. M. Synge' in Kopper (ed.), *A J. M. Synge Literary Companion*, pp. 145–60.
27. Thomas Kilroy has recently emphasized the prevalence of this sort of 'distancing' in Anglo-Irish drama. See 'The Anglo-Irish Theatrical Imagination' in *Bullán: An Irish Studies Journal*, vol. 3, no. 2 (Winter 1997/Spring 1998), pp. 5–12.
28. Christopher Innes, *Modern British Drama 1890–1990* (Cambridge: Cambridge University Press, 1992), p. 225.
29. Robin Skelton, *The Writings of J. M. Synge* (London: Thames & Hudson, 1971), pp. 100–1.
30. Declan Kiberd, 'J. M. Synge – Remembering the Future', *Inventing Ireland* (London: Jonathan Cape, 1995), pp. 166–88.
31. Christopher Murray, 'Synge: ironic revolutionary', *Twentieth-Century Irish Drama: Mirror up to Nation* (Manchester and New York: Manchester University Press, 1997), p. 64.
32. Ibid., p. 80.
33. W. B. Yeats, 'The Tower', *Collected Poems* (London: Macmillan, 1933), p. 223.
34. Innes, *Modern British Drama*, p. 226.
35. Murray, *Twentieth-Century Irish Drama*, p. 79.
36. See E. H. Mikhail, *J. M. Synge: Interviews and Recollections*, fwd. Robin Skelton (London: Macmillan – now Palgrave, 1977). Denis Donoghue, in a strikingly antipathetic review of his letters, declares that Synge's 'constitution was determined to be gloomy'. See 'Synge in his Letters', *We Irish: Essays on Irish Literature and Society* (Berkeley: University of California Press, 1986), p. 210.
37. Yeats had a lasting initial impression of his first meeting with Synge in Paris: 'I did not divine his genius, but I felt he needed something to take him out of his morbidity and melancholy.' See W. B. Yeats, 'The Tragic Generation', *Autobiographies*, p. 343.
38. W. B. Yeats, *Essays and Introductions*, p. 322. Yeats's famous remark – 'We begin to live when we have conceived life as tragedy' – orbits around a related notion of tragedy as insight. *Autobiographies*, p. 189.
39. Synge 'had to undergo an aesthetic transformation, analogous to religious conversion, before he became the audacious, joyous, ironical man we know'. W. B Yeats, *A Vision* (London: Macmillan, 1962), p. 167.
40. Synge told Padraic Colum that the impetus for the composition of *Riders to the Sea* was his foreboding of death and his depression over the process of his own ageing. Mikhail (ed.), *J. M. Synge: Interviews and Recollections*, p. 66.
41. See George Steiner, *The Death of Tragedy* (London: Faber & Faber, 1961) and Lucien Goldmann, *The Hidden God: A Study of Tragic Vision in the 'Pensées' of Pascal and Racine*, trans. Philip Thody (London: Routledge & Kegan Paul, 1976).

42. The origin of this sentiment, the simple eloquence of which exerted a strong fascination on Synge, lies in a letter from Martin MacDonagh ('Michael' in *The Aran Islands*) on the death in childbirth of his brother's wife: 'But at the same time we have to be satisfied because a person cannot live always.' Quoted in David H. Greene and Edward M. Stephens, *J. M. Synge 1871–1909* (New York: Macmillan, 1959), p. 112.

43. 'We must unite asceticism, stoicism, ecstasy; two of these have come together but not all three.' W. B. Yeats, 'Preface' to the *Poems* of J. M. Synge (CWI, xxxiv).

44. At the start of Act III, Lavarcham anticipates this dual symbol of the grave when she responds to Cunchobor's question if she has travelled all the way from Alban with Deirdre and Naoise: 'I have then, though I've no call now to be wandering that length to a wedding or a burial, or the two together. ' (CWIV, 241). She thinks the funeral will be Naoise's and the wedding between Deirdre and Conchubor. Ironically both funeral and wedding are Deirdre's and Naoise's.

45. W. J. Mc Cormack, *Fool of the Family: A Life of J. M. Synge* (London: Weidenfeld & Nicolson, 2000).

46. Weldon Thornton claims that 'while he could not accept his family's dogmas, he was in temperament and attitude quite close to them, and in his own thinking transmuted rather than rejected their religion'. *J. M. Synge and the Western Mind* (Gerrards Cross: Colin Smythe, 1979), p. 34.

47. There is some division amongst critics about the impact of Darwin on Synge's sensibility. While, for Weldon Thornton, the impact was 'fundamental and paradigmatic', *J. M. Synge and the Western Mind*, p. 41, Anthony Roche thinks that 'The Darwin passage has if anything been over-emphasized'. 'J. M. Synge: Christianity versus Paganism', in Kopper (ed.), *A J. M. Synge Literary Companion*, p. 112. W. J. Mc Cormack concludes that Synge retrospectively projected the trauma into adolescence: 'It is probable that Synge's crisis with Darwinism did not occur in childhood but in his mid-twenties.' *Fool of the Family*, p. 43.

48. Grattan Freyer, 'The Little World of J. M. Synge' in *Politics and Letters*, vol. 1, no. 4 (1948), pp. 50–2.

49. 'With each visit to the islands Synge sheds the subjectivity that marks very strongly the early experiences, in favour of a more scrupulous objectivity.' Eugene Benson, *J. M. Synge* (London and Basingstoke: Macmillan – now Palgrave, 1982), p. 26. Another critic discerns in the visits a progression equivalent to the aesthetic triumvirate of Stephen Dedalus in *A Portrait of the Artist as a Young Man*: lyrical, epic, dramatic. See Arnold Goldman, *Synge's the Aran Islands: A World of Grey* (Gerrards Cross: Colin Smythe, 1991), p. 25.

50. 'John Millington Synge alone of the Revivalist dramatists developed a full understanding of the implications of scientific comparativism. Synge studied in France under the leading "celtologists" of his age, and brought to the Aran Islands, and subsequently to the plays he wrote for the Irish theatre, a knowledge of the nature of the primitive psyche antithetical to the romantic vision which was his (and his contemporaries) first impulse …' Sinéad Garrigan Mattar, *Primitivism and the Writers of the Irish Dramatic Movement to 1910* (D. Phil. thesis, University of Oxford, 1997), p. 11.

51. For an overview of the various ambivalences and ambiguities of Synge's search for identity, see Watson, *Irish Identity and the Literary Revival*, pp. 35–86.
52. Yeats, *Essays and Introductions*, p. 241.
53. Comparing the funeral scene to the eviction scene, Arnold Goldman stresses the 'interdependence of the natural and social contexts'. *Synge's The Aran Islands: A World of Grey*, p. 11.
54. He claims that 'Synge was as deeply moved by it [the eviction scene] as he was when he realized one day that he had been talking with men who were living in the shadow of death'. Corkery, *Synge and Anglo-Irish Literature*, p. 146.
55. Mary C. King, *The Drama of J. M. Synge* (London: Fourth Estate, 1985), p. 28.
56. Murray Krieger, *The Tragic Vision: Variations on a Theme in Literary Interpretation* (New York: Holt, Rinehart & Winston, 1960), pp. 10–11.
57. See Nicholas Grene, *Synge: A Critical Study of the Plays* (London: Macmillan – now Palgrave, 1975), p. 32.
58. Yeats, *Essays and Introductions*, pp. 326–7.
59. Deane, *Celtic Revivals*, p. 55.
60. Alan Price recognizes this melancholic underside to the comic aspects of *The Well of the Saints*: 'unblurred by morbidity, [the play] reflects with some compassion, a melancholy view of the human condition'. *Synge and Anglo-Irish Drama* (London: Methuen, 1961), p. 130.
61. Yeats, 'Preface' to *The Well of the Saints* (III, 67).
62. Elsewhere Yeats identifies a 'harder' opposition at work. Synge's 'delight in setting the hard virtues by the soft, the bitter by the sweet, salt by mercury, the stone by the elixir gave him a hunger for ugly surprising things, for all that defies hope'. 'Preface' to *Poems* (CWI, xxxiv).
63. Quoted in King, *The Drama of J. M. Synge*, p. 4.
64. Mary Fitzgerald Hoyt writes, 'Even the Tramp, who sympathizes with Nora and moves her with his "fine bit of talk" is a poor match for her, for despite his romantic (and Romantic) description of the itinerant life, she soberly recognises the harsh realities lurking behind his fine words.' 'Death and the Colleen: The *Shadow of the Glen*' in Alexander G. Gonzalez (ed.), *Assessing the Achievement of J. M. Synge* (Westport, CT and London: Greenwood Press, 1996), p. 54.
65. See King, *The Drama of J. M. Synge*, p. 10. Extensive references to Nietzsche occur in the Synge notebooks for the year 1894–5, ibid., p. 105.
66. Lady Gregory described the play as 'a dramatization of his [Synge's] own life under a thin disguise of fiction, but so direct that it was devoted more to stating, illustrating, and discussing the problems of his particular experience than to interpreting universal emotions'. Recounted in Andrew Carpenter (ed.), *My Uncle John: Edward Stephens's Life of J. M. Synge* (Oxford: Oxford University Press, 1974), p. 147.
67. J. M. Synge, *When the Moon has Set* in *Long Room* [*Bulletin of the Friends of the Library*, Trinity College Dublin], nos 24–5 (Spring-Autumn 1982), p. 17. I have found it preferable in the case of *When the Moon has Set* to use the above version, which is the full two-act play rejected for the Abbey by Yeats and Lady Gregory. The version published in the Oxford University Press *Complete Works* is a conflation of two separate and later one-act drafts.
68. The relevant (and oft-quoted) passage runs:
    Everyone is used in Ireland to the tragedy that is bound up with the lives of farmers and fishing people; but in this garden one seemed to feel the tragedy

of the landlord class also, and of the innumerable old families that are quickly dwindling away. These owners of the land are not much pitied at the present day, or much deserving of pity ... The desolation of this life is often of a peculiarly local kind, and if a playwright chose to go through the Irish country houses he would find material, it is likely, for many gloomy plays that would turn on the dying away of these old families ... (CWII, 231).

69. Reading this play in the Anglo-Irish Gothic tradition, W. J. Mc Cormack finds an intriguing ancestral resonance. A large portion of the Synge estate originated with the playwright's great-great-grandfather, John Hatch of Lissenhall, near Swords, Co. Dublin, who died near the end of the eighteenth century. He had come by the lands through a dubious bequest by his cousin, a Mr Samuel McCracken of Roundwood, Co. Wicklow. McCracken had committed suicide following a sordid affair with a maidservant in his house. Her new husband had threatened to prosecute him at the assizes. The will was contested unsuccessfully by a nephew, William Stewart, the beneficiary of a second, unwitnessed will. See W. J. Mc Cormack (ed.), 'Introduction' to 'Irish Gothic and After 1820–1945' in *The Field Day Anthology of Irish Writing*, gen. ed. Seamus Deane, 3 vols. (Derry: Field Day Publication, 1991), II: 846–49.

70. Mary C. King describes her as a 'Catholic peasant woman'. In later versions, including that reproduced in the *Collected Works*, the class dimension is suppressed. Instead, the relationship simply prefigures the main plot between Columb and Sister Eileen (and between Synge and Cherrie Matheson): Mary Costello had refused to marry Columb's Uncle because of his atheism. Appearing as an old madwoman – in the two-act version she has been long dead – she beseeches Sister Eileen to be true to her natural impulses and marry Columb.

71. King regards the action as an attempt to 'expurgate the Ascendancy sense of guilt through the transference of guilt to Stephen Costello'. 'Introduction', *When the Moon has Set*, p. 12.

72. Ibid., p. 13.

73. Synge, *When the Moon has Set*, p. 21.

74. Synge's photographs from Aran show pigs living domestically among the people. See J. M. Synge, *My Wallet of Photographs*, arranged and intro. by Lilo Stephens (Dublin: Dolmen, 1971). Engels memorably noted the tendency of the Irish in England to live with their pigs: 'The Irishman allows the pig to share his own living quarters. This new, abnormal method of rearing livestock in the large towns is entirely of the Irish origin ... The Irish man lives and sleeps with the pig, the children play with the pig, ride on its back, and roll about in the filth with it.' Friedrich Engels, *Conditions of the Working Class in England* (London and New York: Macmillan, 1958), p. 106.

75. For depictions of the Irish in nineteenth-century caricature, see L. P. Curtis, *Apes and Angels: The Irishman in Victorian Caricature* (Washington: Smithsonian Institute, 1971). See also R. F. Foster, 'Paddy and Mr Punch', *Paddy and Mr Punch* (London: Allen Lane, 1993), pp. 171–94. 'The favourite cliché of the Irish pig as "The Gintleman that Pays the Rent" was converted into a murderous wild boar, armed with a blunderbuss: "the gentleman that *won't* pay the rent"', p. 186.

76. King, *The Drama of J. M. Synge*, p. 38.

77. Sigmund Freud, 'Totem and Taboo' (1913), *The Origins of Religion*, The Penguin Freud Library, vol. 13, ed. Albert Dickson, trans. James Strachey (London: Penguin, 1990), pp. 243–340.

78. Sigmund Freud, 'Civilization and its Discontents' (1930), *Civilization, Society and Religion*, The Pelican Freud Library, vol. 12, ed. Albert Dickson, trans. James Strachey (London: Penguin, 1985), p. 326.

79. Walter Benjamin, 'Theses on the Philosophy of History', *Illuminations*, trans. Harry Zohn, ed. and intro. Hannah Arendt (London: Jonathan Cape, 1970), p. 258.

80. See, for instance, W. J. Mc Cormack (ed.), 'Introduction' to 'Irish Gothic and After 1820–1945' in *The Field Day Anthology of Irish Writing*, II: 846–9 and *From Burke to Beckett: Ascendancy, Tradition and Betrayal in Literary History* (Cork: Cork University Press, 1994), and Terry Eagleton, 'Ascendancy and Hegemony', *Heathcliff and the Great Hunger: Studies in Irish Culture* (London and New York: Verso), pp. 27–103.

81. As seen in the Introduction, notable examples include G. B. Shaw's *Mrs. Warren's Profession*, Oscar Wilde's *An Ideal Husband*, J. M. Synge's *The Playboy of the Western World*, and W. B. Yeats's *Purgatory*.

82. W. B. Yeats, *Essays and Introductions*, p. 321.

83. Greene and Stephens, *J. M. Synge 1871–1909*, pp. 22–3. In 1887 Edward brutally evicted a tenant named Hugh Carey and his two dependent elderly sisters from his aunt's estate in Glanmore, Co. Wicklow. As Synge's biographers record, 'The cruelty and efficiency with which he went about his duties made it an event Synge never forgot.' Ibid., p. 23.

84. Daniel J. Casey claims that Synge was always 'embarrassed by the notoriety of the Synges and the Traills [his mother came from a notorious family of evangelical zealots] in recent Irish history'. 'John M. Synge: A Life Apart' in Kopper (ed.), *A J. M. Synge Literary Companion*, p. 5.

85. Eagleton, *Heathcliff and the Great Hunger*, p. 43.

86. 'A radical is a person who wants change root and branch, and I'm proud to be a radical.' Quoted in Ann Saddlemyer (ed.), *The Collected Letters of J. M. Synge*, vol. I 1871–1907 (Oxford: Clarendon Press, 1983), p. xiii.

87. The work of Declan Kiberd has usefully delineated this dialectic, particularly in relation to *The Playboy of the Western World*. See *Synge and the Irish Language* (1979; Dublin: Gill and Macmillan, 2nd edn, 1993) and *Inventing Ireland*, pp. 166–90.

88. George Moore, letter to the *Irish Times*, 13 February 1905, p. 6.

89. Kiberd, 'Preface to Second Edition', *Synge and the Irish Language*, p. xiii.

90. C. L. Innes, 'Naked Truth, Fine Clothes and Fine Phrases in Synge's *The Playboy of the Western World*' in Joseph Ronsley (ed.), *Myths and Reality in Irish Literature* (Waterloo, Ontario: Wilfrid Laurie University Press, 1977), p. 74.

91. For an analysis of the use of clothes imagery in *Playboy*, see ibid., pp. 63–75.

92. Ibid., p. 74.

93. Deane, *Celtic Revivals*, p. 55.

94. T. R. Henn, *The Harvest of Tragedy* (London: Methuen, 1956), p. 202.

95. Yeats, *Collected Poems*, p. 121.

96. Grene, *Synge: A Critical Study of the Plays*, p. 51.

97. Benjamin, *Illuminations*, p. 263.

98. W. B. Yeats, 'Preface' to *The Well of the Saints* (CWIII, 67).

99. The inconsistencies and problems in the play have been well rehearsed. Seán Ó Tuama is typical in concluding that, despite some magnificent passages, 'the language is completely inadequate tonally to create the milieu in which the kings and princes can operate'. *Repossessions: Selected Essays on the Irish Literary Heritage* (Cork: Cork University Press, 1995) , p. 229.

Chapter 3   Delusion and Disillusionment

1. *Irish Times*, 30 March 1960. Quoted in Garry O'Connor, *Sean O'Casey: A Life* (London: Hodder & Stoughton, 1988), p. 366.
2. Quoted in ibid.
3. Samuel Beckett, *Disjecta: Miscellaneous Writings and a Dramatic Fragment*, ed. Ruby Cohn (London: John Calder, 1983), p. 82.
4. Ibid.
5. 'Sean O'Casey, *Blasts and Benedictions: Articles and Stories*', selected and intro. by Ronald Ayling (London: Macmillan, 1967), p. 51.
6. Quoted in a letter from Tom Curtis to Eileen O'Casey reproduced in Eileen O'Casey, *Sean*, ed. and intro. J. C. Trewin (Dublin: Gill and Macmillan, 1971), p. 247.
7. One biographer is highly sceptical of O'Casey's retrospective images of his childhood: 'O'Casey was increasingly to adopt, and develop for the sake of his image, a violently anti-authoritarian stand. Where witnesses at the time … saw a gentle, pacific boy, O'Casey when he recalled his early days portrays himself as a lawless upstart, especially ill-disposed towards those men who did not give him unqualified praise or attention.' Garry O'Connor, *Sean O'Casey: A Life* (London: Hodder & Stoughton, 1988), p. 23.
8. Robert G. Lowery, 'Sean O'Casey: Art and Politics' in David Krause and Robert G. Lowery (eds), *Sean O'Casey: Centenary Essays* (Gerrards Cross: Colin Smythe, 1980), p. 153.
9. J. W. Krutch, '*Modernism' in Modern Drama: A Definition and an Estimate* (Ithaca: Cornell University Press, 1953), p. 99.
10. George Steiner, *The Death of Tragedy*, (London, Faber & Faber, 1961), p. 128.
11. Gabriel Fallon, *Sean O'Casey: The Man I Knew* (London: Routledge & Kegan Paul, 1965), p. 24.
12. Christopher Murray, *Twentieth-Century Irish Drama: Mirror up to Nation* (Manchester and New York: Manchester University Press, 1997), p. 101.
13. See Bernice Schrank, *Sean O'Casey: A Research and Production Sourcebook* (Westport, CT and London: Greenwood Press, 1996), pp. 232–44, 246–58, 263–75.
14. A notable instance of the impact of the Troubles on productions of O'Casey's plays was the introduction, which became the norm, of Ulster accents for the Dublin Protestant characters. The Golden Jubilee Production of *The Plough* in 1976 introduced an Ulster accent for Bessie Burgess. Ibid. p., 53.
15. Murray, *Twentieth-Century Irish Drama*, p. 94. For an anti-nationalist celebration of O'Casey, see Peter Costello, *The Heart Grown Brutal: The Irish Revolution in Literature from Parnell to the Death of Yeats 1891–1939* (Dublin: Gill and Macmillan, 1977), pp. 106–11. For some major contributions to the revisionist/nationalist debate in Irish historiography, see Ciaran Brady

(ed.), *Interpreting Irish History: The Debate on Historical Revisionism* (Dublin: Irish Academic Press, 1994).

16. Major sceptical analyses of the politics of O'Casey's plays include Raymond Williams, *Drama from Ibsen to Brecht* (1952; London: Hogarth Press, 1993), pp. 147–53; Seamus Deane, *Celtic Revivals: Essays in Modern Irish Literature 1880–1980* (London and Boston, Faber & Faber, 1985), pp. 108–23; 'Irish Politics and O'Casey's Theatre', in Thomas Kilroy (ed.), *Sean O'Casey: A Collection of Critical Essays* (Englewood Cliffs, NJ: Prentice Hall, 1975), pp. 149–58; G. J. Watson, *Irish Identity and the Literary Revival: Synge, Yeats, Joyce and O'Casey* (1979; Washington, DC: Catholic University of America Press, 2nd edn 1994), pp. 245–87; D. E. S. Maxwell, *Modern Irish Drama 1891–1980* (Cambridge: Cambridge University Press, 1984), pp. 96–113; Declan Kiberd, *Inventing Ireland* (London: Jonathan Cape, 1995), pp. 218–38. The fullest studies to rescue O'Casey from his hagiographers are C. Desmond Greaves, *Sean O'Casey: Politics and Art* (London: Lawrence & Wishart, 1979) and James Simmons, *Sean O'Casey* (London: Macmillan – now Palgrave, 1983).

17. Watson, *Irish Identity and the Literary Revival*, p. 265.

18. Seamus Deane makes the complaint succinct: 'All of O'Casey's gunmen are shadows, and consequently his aggression towards politics is a form of shadow boxing.' *Celtic Revivals*, p. 109.

19. Interestingly, we can see the opposition in nascent form in *The Story of the Irish Citizen Army*. At this stage, however, O'Casey bemoans how the workers' duty to their families undermines the commitment they can give to the 1913 Lockout, regarding these pressures for material survival as the reason for the failure of the labour movement and the related success of the Irish Volunteers. In 1919, O'Casey laments that the family and the real-life pressures of material survival disrupt political action. By the time of the trilogy, the sequence is inverted. Sean O'Casey, *The Story of the Irish Citizen Army* (1919; Dublin: Talbot Press, 1971), p. 8.

20. D. E. S. Maxwell emphasizes the thematic similarity between Dickens and O'Casey in *Modern Irish Drama 1891–1980*, p. 103 as does Thomas Kilroy, 'Introduction', *Sean O'Casey: A Collection of Critical Essays*, p. 8.

21. O'Casey's putative suspicion of 'isms' – an odd stance, really, for a committed supporter of the Soviet Union – is extolled by his liberal humanist advocates as his great virtue. Rebutting what he sees as the reductive readings of O'Casey's Marxist critics, David Krause identifies O'Casey's 'individualistic and autonomous drama ... it echoes yet liberates itself from all 'isms', especially expressionism and Marxism'. 'The Risen O'Casey: Some Marxist and Irish Ironies' in Robert G. Lowery (ed.), *O'Casey Annual No. 3* (London and Basingstoke: Macmillan – now Palgrave, 1984), p. 142. The following study challenges this reading of O'Casey.

22. Williams, *Drama from Ibsen to Brecht*, p. 147. Francis Mulhern extends Williams's reading, claiming that O'Casey's position 'was in fact the ideological effect of the naturalistic theatrical modes which at that time, he had not yet discarded'. See 'Ideology and Literary Form: A Comment' *New Left Review* 91 (1975), p. 85. See also Terry Eagleton's response to Mulhern in *New Left Review* 92 (1975), pp. 107–8.

23. For instances of such attempts, see Lowery, 'Sean O'Casey: Politics and Art', pp. 121–64 and Jack Mitchell's caustic review of Desmond Greaves's

Notes 189

Sean O'Casey: Politics and Art in Robert G. Lowery (ed.), *O'Casey Annual No. 1* (London and Basingstoke: Macmillan – now Palgrave, 1982), pp. 195–211.

24. Maik Hamburger, 'Anti-illusionism and the Use of Song in the Early Plays of Sean O'Casey' in Robert G. Lowery (ed.), *O'Casey Annual No. 2* (London and Basingstoke: Macmillan – now Palgrave, 1983), p. 3. Christoper Innes claims that 'at the Abbey – where the Dublin trilogy was regularly performed – the prosaic, self-enclosed realism of the productions limited their effect'. *Modern British Drama 1890–1990* (Cambridge: Cambridge University Press, 1992), p. 88.

25. Some critics have recognized the importance of the anti-realist elements in the trilogy. See Bernice Schrank, 'The Naturalism in O'Casey's Early Plays' in *Sean O'Casey Review*, no. 4 (1977), pp. 41–8, and Christoper Innes, 'The Essential Continuity of Sean O'Casey', in *Modern Drama*, no. 33 (1990), pp. 419–33. There are some promising signs in recent productions in Ireland that more cognizance is being paid to this neglected potential. Garry Hynes's 1991 production of *The Plough and the Stars* opted for a Brechtian emphasis. The players had white faces and exaggerated make-up, while the tempo was slow and incantatory, highlighting anguish and pathos, rather than the usual boisterousness.

26. Greaves, *Sean O'Casey: Politics and Art*, p. 107.

27. See for example, Watson, *Irish Identity and the Literary Revival*, p. 249 and Katharine Worth, 'O'Casey, Synge and Yeats', in *Irish University Review* (Spring 1980), pp. 103–17. Worth sees *Gunman* as 'a more sombre play'. O'Casey's people are more deluded than Synge's because the 'fantasy of being a gunman never collapses', p. 107.

28. With apologies to David Krause for indulging in the 'malicious Irish game of identifying O'Casey with his satirized characters'. 'The Risen O'Casey: Some Marxist and Irish Ironies', p. 154. Christopher Innes claims that 'the poet–protagonist is in many ways a self projection'. *Modern British Drama*, p. 77.

29. There is some disagreement amongst scholars about the precise time when O'Casey turned from nationalism. Desmond Greaves claims that he supported the Rising until 1919. *Sean O'Casey: Art and Politics*, p. 10. But see Mitchell's caustic review of Greaves in *O'Casey Annual No. 1*, p. 200. Certainly his departure from the Citizen Army, over a dispute with Countess Markievicz, was recent enough to have caused, at least, feelings of doubt and uneasiness at his own non-involvement in the Rising.

30. O'Connor, *Sean O'Casey*, p. 94.

31. For an elaboration of this play as a national allegory, see Innes, *Modern British Drama*, pp. 82–4.

32. Watson, *Irish Identity and the Literary Revival*, p. 268.

33. There are elements in the play, then, which complicate Christopher Innes's distinction between O'Casey and Beckett: 'it is the characters' failure of moral perception, not the existential nature of the world (as in Beckett) that is responsible for the chaos.' *Modern British Drama*, p. 79.

34. See 'The Cap in the Counting House' (A1, 339–48).

35. O'Casey originally intended that Johnny's sorry story should be the main focus of the tragedy. See Fallon, *Sean O'Casey: The Man I Knew*, p. 17.

36. Watson, *Irish Identity and the Literary Revival*, p. 263.

37. David Krause, *Sean O'Casey: The Man and his Work* (London: MacGibbon & Kee, 1960).
38. Deane, *Celtic Revivals* p. 111.
39. Krause, *Sean O'Casey: The Man and his Work*, p. 53.
40. Krutch, *'Modernism' in Modern Drama*, p. 99.
41. Fallon, *Sean O'Casey: The Man I Knew*, p. 22. Christopher Murray claims that the scene 'shoulders aside catharsis in favour of irony'. *Twentieth-Century Irish Drama*, p. 104. J. W. Krutch claims that it would be 'difficult to find anywhere else in dramatic literature so extraordinary a combination of farce with loathing and a black despair'. *'Modernism' in Modern Drama*, p. 99.
42. Quoted in Watson, *Irish Identity and the Literary Revival*, p. 283.
43. O'Connor, *Sean O'Casey: A Life*, p. 94.
44. Quoted in Greaves, *Sean O'Casey: Politics and Art*, p. 86.
45. Ibid., p. 120.
46. Nicholas Grene, 'The Class of the Clitheroes: O'Casey's Revisions to *The Plough and the Stars* Promptbook' in *Bullán: An Irish Studies Journal*, vol. IV, no. 2 (Winter 1999/Spring 2000), pp. 57–66. This explains some of the verbal infelicities that have been noted in the Romantic exchanges between Jack and Nora: O'Casey was not wholly successful in bringing the linguistic register down a social peg. Grene concludes that 'the result of the partial revision is to leave Nora in particular a sort of palimpsest character, now one thing now another', p. 62.
47. Costello, *The Heart Grown Brutal*, p. 110.
48. W. B. Yeats (ed.), *The Oxford Book of Modern Verse* (Oxford: Clarendon, 1936), p. xxxv. For a thorough treatment of Yeats and the First World War, see Fran Brearton, *The Great War in Irish Poetry* (Oxford: Oxford University Press, 2000), pp. 43–82.
49. 'We feel in England that we have treated you rather unfairly. It seems history is to blame.' James Joyce, *Ulysses* (1922; London: Penguin, 1992), p. 24.
50. See Mary Fitzgerald, 'How the Abbey Said No: Readers' Reports and the Rejection of *The Silver Tassie*' in Lowery (ed.), *The O'Casey Annual No. 1*, pp. 73–87.
51. Sean O'Casey, *Letters, Vol. I, 1910–41*, ed. David Krause (London: Macmillan, 1975), p. 238.
52. Yeats had earlier remarked to Lady Gregory, 'Casey was bad in writing of the vices of the rich which he knows nothing about, but he thoroughly understands the vices of the poor.' Quoted in *Lady Gregory's Journals*, vol. 1: 1916–1925, ed. Daniel J. Murphy (Gerrards Cross: Colin Smythe, 1978), p. 511.
53. O'Casey, *Letters*, *I*, p. 268.
54. W. B. Yeats, 'The Tragic Theatre', *Essays and Introductions* (London: Macmillan, 1961), p. 241.
55. Ibid, p. 245.
56. O'Casey, *Letters*, *I*, p. 272.
57. See Simon Williams, 'The Unity of *The Silver Tassie*' in *Sean O'Casey Review*, no. 4 (Spring 1978), pp. 91–112 and Marguerite Harkness, '*The Silver Tassie*: No Light in Darkness' in *Sean O'Casey Review*, no. 4 (Spring 1978), pp. 131–7.
58. Similarly Harry's refrain in the final act – 'For mine is a life on the ebb,/ Yours a full life on the flow!' (ST, 118) – portends the morbid logic of Pozzo

in *Waiting for Godot*: 'The tears of the world are a constant quantity. For each one who begins to weep, somewhere else another stops. The same is true of the laugh' (CDW, 33).

59. Brian Friel, *Translations, Selected Plays* (London and Boston: Faber & Faber, 1984), p. 446.

Chapter 4   Beyond Tragedy

1. Vivian Mercier, *Beckett/Beckett* (Oxford: Oxford University Press, 1977), p. 13.
2. Though valiant attempts have been made to turn Beckett into a tragedian in the Aristotelian sense. See, for instance, Normand Berlin, 'The Tragic Pleasure of *Waiting for Godot*' in Enoch Brater (ed.), *Beckett at 80/Beckett in Context* (New York and Oxford: Oxford University Press, 1986), pp. 46–63.
3. Martin Esslin, 'Beckett and his Interpreters', *Essays on Brecht, Beckett and the Media* (London: Eyre Methuen, 1980), p. 91.
4. John Fletcher and John Spurling, *Beckett: The Playwright* (New York: Hill & Wang, 1972), pp. 78–9.
5. For a famous comparison between *Endgame* and *King Lear*, see Jan Kott, *Shakespeare Our Contemporary* (New York: Doubleday, 1964). See also, Normand Berlin, 'Boundary Situation: *King Lear* and *Waiting for Godot*', *The Secret Cause: A Discussion of Tragedy* (Amherst: University of Massachusetts Press, 1981), pp. 113–28.
6. The distinction between the syntactic and the semantic is made by Frederic Jameson in *The Political Unconscious: Narrative as a Socially Symbolic Act* (London: Methuen, 1981), pp. 107–8.
7. Anthony Cronin regards this remark as 'of immense importance – not only to the understanding of *Godot* but to the rest of his work as well'. See his *Samuel Beckett: The Last Modernist* (London: HarperCollins 1996), p. 422.
8. Quoted in Cronin, *The Last Modernist*, p. 556.
9. Samuel Beckett, *Watt* (London: John Calder, 1976), p. 47.
10. John Orr, *Tragicomedy and Contemporary Culture: Play and Performance from Beckett to Sheppard* (London: Macmillan – now Palgrave, 1991), p. 15.
11. Arthur Schopenhauer, *The World as Will and Representation*, trans. E. F. J. Payne, 2 vols (New York: Dover, 1966), I: 322.
12. Eugène Ionesco, 'Experience of the Theatre', *Notes and Counternotes*, trans. Donald Watson (London: John Calder, 1964), p. 26.
13. Israel Shenker, 'Interview with Samuel Beckett', *New York Times*, 5 May 1956, p. 3.
14. Interview with Gabriel D'Aubarède, quoted in Lawrence Graver and Raymond Federman (eds), *Samuel Beckett: The Critical Heritage* (London: Routledge, 1979), p. 217.
15. 'Krapp's vision was on the pier in Dún Laoghaire; mine was in my mother's room. Make that clear once and for all,' Beckett exhorted Knowlson. Quoted in James Knowlson, *Damned to Fame: The Life of Samuel Beckett* (London: Bloomsbury, 1996), p. 352.
16. Samuel Beckett, *Disjecta: Miscellaneous Writings and a Dramatic Fragment*, ed. Ruby Cohn (London: John Calder, 1983).

17. Quoted in Deirdre Bair, *Samuel Beckett: A Biography* (London: Jonathan Cape, 1978), p. 115.
18. Interview with Gabriel D'Auberède. Graver and Federman (eds), *The Critical Heritage*, p. 217.
19. 'Beckett must have written the essay on Proust after having just put down Schopenhauer's *Die Welt als Wille und Vorstellung*, for the essay is littered with the will-weary philosopher's terms, distinctions, and values', claims David Hesla, *The Shape of Chaos: An Interpretation of the Art of Samuel Beckett* (Minneapolis: University of Minneapolis Press, 1971), p. 51.
20. Reading Schopenhauer in preparation for his monograph on Proust, Beckett described the philosopher's work to Thomas McGreevy as an 'intellectual justification for unhappiness – the greatest that has ever been attempted'. Quoted in Cronin, *The Last Modernist*, p. 118. Later in life, he emphasizes how fine his *writing* is. See John Pilling, *Samuel Beckett* (London: Routledge & Kegan Paul, 1976), p. 7.
21. Quoted by Harold Hobsen, 'Samuel Beckett: Dramatist of the Year', *International Theatre Annual I* (London, 1956), p. 153. In an appropriate irony, Beckettians have trawled the Augustine corpus and have been unable to find this quotation, of which Beckett is so fond.
22. For a consideration of this aesthetic approach to philosophical dictums, see J. E. Dearlove, *Accommodating the Chaos: Samuel Beckett's Non-Relational Art* (Durham, NC: Duke University Press, 1982), especially ch. 1, 'The Shape of Ideas', pp. 3–14.
23. Cronin, *The Last Modernist*, p. 231.
24. Interview with Gabriel D'Aubarède in Graver and Federman (eds), *Samuel Beckett: The Critical Heritage*, p. 217.
25. Israel Shenker, 'Interview with Samuel Beckett', p. 3.
26. Stephen Connor, *Samuel Beckett: Repetition, Theory and Text* (Oxford and New York: Basil Blackwell, 1988), p. 170.
27. Tom F. Driver, 'Beckett by the Madeleine' [interview], *Columbia University Forum*, vol. 4, no. 3 (Summer 1961), p. 22.
28. Knowlson, *Damned to Fame*, p. xxi.
29. Quoted in Alec Reid, *All I Can Manage, More Than I Could: An Approach to the Plays of Samuel Beckett* (Dublin: Dolmen Press, 1968), p. 11.
30. Passages from *Proust* such as the following seem to have seeped into the thematic colouring of *Godot*:

> Habit then is the generic term for the countless treaties concluded between the countless subjects that constitute the individual and their countless correlative objects. The periods of transitions that separate consecutive adaptations (because by no expedient of macabre transubstantiation can the grave sheets serve as swaddling-clothes) represent the perilous zones in the life of the individual, dangerous, precarious, painful, mysterious and fertile, when for a moment the boredom of living is replaced by the suffering of being. (P, 19)

31. Quoted in Graver and Federman (eds), *Samuel Beckett: The Critical Heritage*, p. 10. When Alan Schneider asked Beckett the question, 'who or what does Godot mean?', he replied, 'If I knew, I would have said so in the play.' See

'Waiting for Beckett' in *Beckett at Sixty: A Festschrift* (London: Calder & Boyars, 1967), p. 38.

32. Michael Worton, '*Waiting for Godot* and *Endgame*: Theatre as Text' in John Pilling (ed.), *The Cambridge Companion to Beckett* (Cambridge: Cambridge University Press, 1994), p. 71.

33. Vivian Mercier, 'The Uneventful Event', *Irish Times* (18 February, 1956), p. 9.

34. Theodor W. Adorno, 'Towards an Understanding of *Endgame*', trans. Samuel M. Weber [originally 'Versuch, das Endspiel zu verstehen' (1961)] in Bell Gale Chevigny (ed.), *Twentieth-Century Interpretations of 'Endgame'* (Englewood Cliffs, NJ: Prentice Hall, 1969), p. 84.

35. Criticism in Germany, as with Adorno's work, has tended to be less apolitical than elswhere. However there have recently been some attempts in the English-speaking world to redress the ahistorical image of Beckett. Steven Connor, *Samuel Beckett: Repetition, Theory and Text* (Oxford: Basil Blackwell, 1988) analyses how formal repetition in Beckett challenges cultural hegemony. More recently H. Porter Abbot has investigated utopian and dystopian themes in Beckett's work. See 'Political Beckett', *Beckett Writing Beckett: The Author in the Autograph* (Ithaca and London: Cornell University Press, 1996), pp. 127–48. For Beckett's relevance to Irish politics, with an emphasis on post-colonial identity, see David Lloyd, 'Writing in the Shit', *Anomalous States: Irish Writing and the Post-Colonial Movement* (Dublin: Lilliput Press, 1993), pp. 41–58 and Declan Kiberd, 'Beckett's Texts of Laughter and Forgetting', *Inventing Ireland* (London: Jonathan Cape, 1995), pp. 530–50.

36. P. J. Murphy et al., *Critique of Beckett Criticism: A Guide to Research in English, French, and German* (Columbia, SC: Camden House, 1994), p. 1.

37. When his official biographer cited examples from his work of the prevalent Irish imagery of his childhood, 'Beckett nodded in agreement: "They're obsessional," he said, and went on to add several others,' Knowlson, *Damned to Fame*, p. xxi.

38. Seamus Deane, 'Joyce and Beckett', *Celtic Revivals: Essays in Modern Irish Literature 1880–1980* (London and Boston: Faber & Faber, 1985), p. 130.

39. Murphy et al., *Critique of Beckett Criticism*, p. 62.

40. For studies of these regional and topographical echoes, see Eoin O'Brien, *The Beckett Country: Samuel Beckett's Ireland* (Dublin: Black Cat Press, 1986), John P. Harrington, *The Irish Beckett* (Syracuse: Syracuse University Press, 1991) and Mary Junker, *Samuel Beckett: The Irish Dimension* (Dublin: Wolfhound, 1996).

41. Kiberd, *Inventing Ireland*, p. 539.

42. W. J. Mc Cormack feels that the dislocations and instability of the political situation in Ireland during Beckett's formative years are discernible in the shape and texture of his later work: 'The altering relations between territory and power, between division and authority, the violent ambiguity of Black-and-Tan terrorism, the emergence of a uniformed southern army where previously had been an unknown number of 'mufti' volunteers, border warfare and fratricidal civil conflict – these tangible features of Beckett's late childhood and adolescence are not wholly remote from the intimate dislocations of his writing.' *From Burke to Beckett: Ascendancy, Tradition and Betrayal in Literary History* (Cork: Cork University Press, 1994), p. 380.

43. Kiberd, *Inventing Ireland*, p. 537.
44. Steven Connor, 'Over Samuel Beckett's Dead Body' in S. E. Wilmer (ed.), *Beckett in Dublin* (Dublin: Lilliput Press, 1992), p. 104.
45. Vivian Mercier, 'Ireland/The World', *Beckett/Beckett* (Oxford: Oxford University Press, 1977), pp. 20–45.
46. Ibid., p. , 26.
47. For an analysis of the nineteenth-century Irish novel in the context of this difficulty, see Terry Eagleton, 'The Anglo-Irish Novel', *Heathcliff and the Great Hunger*, pp. 145–225.
48. Driver, 'Beckett by the Madeleine' p. 23.
49. Thomas Kilroy, 'The Anglo-Irish Theatrical Imagination', *Bullán: An Irish Studies Journal*, vol. 3, no. 2 (Winter/Spring 1998), p. 9.
50. See Dougald McMillan and Martha Fehsenfeld, *Beckett in the Theater*, 2 vols, vol I: *The Author as Practical Playwright and Director* (London and New York: John Calder, 1988) for an account of Beckett's directorial practice. Published memoirs and biographies also record Beckett's reluctance as a director to explain the meaning of his plays. For a recent description of working with Beckett by his favourite female interpreter, see Billie Whitelaw, *Billie Whitelaw – Who He* (London: Hodder & Stoughton, 1995).
51. Beckett succeeds here in creating, as one critic says, 'a triple dramatic irony worthy of Greek tragedy, whereby each character knows the fate of the other two, but not her own'. Keir Elam, 'Dead Heads: damnation-narration in the 'dramaticules'' in Pilling (ed.), *The Cambridge Companion to Beckett*, p. 147.
52. Shenker, 'Interview with Samuel Beckett', p. 3.
53. 'Here form *is* content, content *is* form. You complain that this stuff is not written in English. It is not written at all. It is not to be read – or rather it is not only to be read. It is to be looked at and listened to. His writing is not *about* something; *it is that something itself.*' Samuel Beckett, 'Dante ... Bruno . Vico .. Joyce' (D, 27).
54. Given this manifest separateness, it is difficult to understand how Frank Kermode, in an early piece, can level against Beckett's prose the same criticism that Yvor Winters heaped on Joyce: 'The procedure leads to indiscriminateness at every turn ... He is like Whitman trying to express a loose America by writing loose poetry. This fallacy, the fallacy of expressive or imitative form, recurs constantly in modern literature.' Beckett is, in fact, following the polar opposite path to this caricature of the Joycean enterprise. Frank Kermode in *Encounter* (July 1960), pp. 73–6, reproduced in Graver and Federman (eds), *The Critical Heritage*, pp. 198–205, p. 204.
55. Friedrich Nietzsche *The Birth of Tragedy* (1872), trans. Shaun Whiteside, ed. Michael Tanner (Harmondsworth: Penguin, 1993), p. 25.
56. Israel Shenker, 'Moody Man of Letters', p. 3.
57. For an interesting analysis of the contesting forces of boredom and apocalypse across modern Irish writing, see Seamus Deane, *Strange Country: Modernity and Nationhood in Irish Writing Since 1790* (Oxford: Clarendon Press, 1997), pp. 145–97. The opposition might be fruitfully compared with Beckett's opposition in *Proust* between the 'boredom of existence' and the 'suffering of being' (P, 28).
58. The veil imagery here, to which Beckett often returns, is heavily redolent of Schopenhauer's Oriental borrowings, particularly 'the veil of Maya' or the

Vedas, the locus of the delusory *principium individuationis*. In Schopenhauer's model of tragedy this delusory veil is stripped away. Schopenhauer, *The World as Will and Representation*, I: 253.

59. Terry Eagleton, 'Beckett's Paradoxes', *Crazy Jane and the Bishop and Other Essays in Irish Culture* (Cork: Cork University Press, 1998), p. 299.
60. Ibid., p. 306.
61. Cronin, *The Last Modernist*, p. 398.
62. See Declan Kiberd, 'Samuel Beckett and the Protestant Ethic' in Augustine Martin (ed.), *The Genius of Irish Prose* (Dublin and Cork: Mercier Press, 1985), pp. 121–30.
63. Lawrence Harvey, *Samuel Beckett: Poet and Critic*, (Princeton: Princeton University Press, 1970), p. 249.
64. His notorious description of Irish patriotism in *First Love* leaves his position in little doubt: 'Wherever nauseated time has dropped a nice fat turd you will find out patriots, sniffing it up on all fours, their faces on fire. Elysium of the roofless.' Samuel Beckett, *First Love* (London: Calder & Boyars, 1970), pp. 30–1.
65. Theodor W. Adorno, 'Commitment' (1965), Francis McDonagh trans. in Frederic Jameson (ed.), *Aesthetics and Politics* (London and New York: Verso, 1977), p. 180.
66. Charles Juliet, 'Meeting Beckett', trans. and ed. by Suzanne Chamier, *TriQuarterly 77* (Winter, 1989–90), p. 17. An extract from *Rencontre avec Samuel Beckett* (Saint-Clément-la-Rivière: Éditions Fata Morgana, 1986).
67. Schopenhauer, *The World as Will and Representation*, 1: 254. Schopenhauer repeats the Calderón quotation later in his work, II: 603.
68. In full-length studies of Beckett's philosophical influences, Schopenhauer's influence is mentioned only in passing and in conjunction with various other thinkers. See Hesla, *Samuel Beckett: The Shape of Chaos*, pp. 51–5; Pilling, *Samuel Beckett*, pp. 110–32; Stephen Rosen, *Samuel Beckett and the Pessimistic Tradition* (New Brunswick, NJ: Rutgers University Press, 1976), pp. 137–52. Relevant articles include J. D. O'Hara, 'Where There's a Will There's a Way Out: Beckett and Schopenhauer', *College Literature*, vol. 8, no. 3 (1981). pp. 249–70 and Lori Hall Burghardt, 'Talking Heads: Samuel Beckett's *Play* as a Metaphor for the Schopenhauerian Will', *The Comparatist*, vol. 6 (May 1988), pp. 32–9.
   Philosophers have also underestimated Beckett's role as a successor to Schopenhauer. Bryan Magee's *The Philosophy of Schopenhauer* (Oxford: Clarendon Press; New York: Oxford University Press, 1983) sets aside a chapter to analyse 'Schopenhauer's Influence on Creative Writers' (ch. 7, pp. 379–91). Beckett is not mentioned.
69. In a letter to Tom McGreevy of 1931, Beckett recounts a visit to Jack B. Yeats where the painter declared that 'you could work back from cruelty to original sin'. Beckett's judgement was an emphatic, 'No doubt'. Knowlson, *Damned to Fame*, p. 164.
70. Schopenhauer, *The World as Will and Representation*, I: 325.
71. Juliet, 'Meeting Beckett', p. 17.
72. Letter to Tom Bishop of New York University, 1978. Quoted in McMillan and Fehsenfeld, *Beckett in the Theater*, p. 13.
73. Adorno, 'Towards an Understanding of *Endgame*', p. 88.

74. Schopenhauer, *The World as Will and Representation*, I: 253.
75. Samuel Beckett, *Watt* (London: John Calder, 1976), p. 43.
76. A reading of *Waiting for Godot* that emphasizes its 'Fall' aspect is Bert O. States, *The Shape of Paradox: An Essay on Waiting for Godot* (Berkeley and Los Angeles: University of California Press, 1978). Interestingly, States praises Beckett for his scepticism: 'What made Beckett the ideal modern to write a play about "the Fall", as opposed, say, to Claudel, on one hand, or Ionesco, on the other, is that his peculiar skepticism of all firm positions rescued him (in this play at least) from both the artistic sin of faith and the shallowness of an easy despair'. Ibid, p. 2.
77. Adorno, 'Commitment', p. 194.
78. For an explanation of the distinction between dispositional and moral guilt, see John Carroll, *Guilt: The Grey Eminence Behind Character, History and Culture* (London: Routledge & Kegan Paul, 1985), p. 7.
79. H. Porter Abbott, *Beckett Writing Beckett*, p. 125.
80. For a reading of the trilogy alert to these religious overtones, see Hélène Baldwin, *Samuel Beckett's Real Silence* (University Park: PennState University Press, 1981). See also Josephine Jacobsen and William Mueller, *The Testament of Samuel Beckett* (New York: Hill & Wang, 1964).
81. Walter Benjamin, 'Fate and Character', *Reflections: Essays, Aphorisms, Autobiographical Writings*, trans. Edmund Jephcott, ed. and intro. Peter Demetz (New York: Schocken Books: New York, 1978), p. 307–8.
82. Adorno, 'Commitment', p. 191.
83. Knowlson, *Damned to Fame*, p. 176.
84. Knowlson reveals that this image of not being properly born also provides the basis for the woman in *Footfalls*: 'May in *Footfalls* is Beckett's own poignant recreation of the girl who had never really been born, isolated and permanently absent, distant and totally encapsulated within herself.' Ibid., p. 616.
85. Beckett, *Watt*, p. 248.
86. Lawrence E. Harvey, *Samuel Beckett: Poet and Critic*, pp. 247, 249.
87. Charles Juliet, 'Meeting Beckett', p. 19.
88. Christopher Ricks, *Beckett's Dying Words* (Oxford: Clarendon Press, 1993), p. 2.
89. Quoted Driver, 'Beckett by the Madeleine', p. 24.

Index